Patterns of Industrial Bureaucracy

PATTERNS

OF

INDUSTRIAL

BUREAUCRACY

By Alvin W. Gouldner

THE FREE PRESS

New York   London   Toronto   Sydney   Tokyo   Singapore

The author gratefully wishes to acknowledge the assistance of George Amos, Joseph Davis, Gunnar Hanson, Raymond Hartell, Phyllis Herrick, Lois Wladis Hoffman, Paul Mahany, Jo Ann Setel, Maurice R. Stein, Cornelius Vodicka, and Marcia Wooster.

The Free Press
A Division of Simon & Schuster Inc.
1230 Avenue of the Americas
New York, N.Y. 10020

First Free Press Paperback Edition 1964

Printed in the United States of America

printing number

   17 18 19 20 21 22 23 24 25

Contents

PREFACE

industrial sociology; it is a partial report, to be followed by another,* of an investigation of a single factory seen in the light of Max Weber's theory of bureaucracy. If, on the one side, this theory of bureaucracy can illuminate industrial research, data bearing on factory processes can, on the other side, help us to evaluate the theory, to modify and redirect it.

There are, of course, many standpoints in terms of which the raw data of factory life can be ordered and made meaningful; a theory of bureaucracy is only one of them. In a way, our work is an effort to document the assumption that it *is* fruitful to see a factory as a bureaucracy. This can be done only, however, if we do not allow ourselves to be frightened off by the emotional cargo that the term "bureaucracy" usually hauls along with it.

A comment about the term "punishment-centered bureaucracy" is particularly in order. It would be quite wrong to allow the associations conjured up by this phrase to be attached to the *whole* factory, or to the whole Company, that was studied. For this, like other concepts which have been stressed, refers only to a part which has been abstracted from the whole because it is *not* peculiar to this Company; the value of such a term derives precisely from its potential usefulness in analyzing many organizations.

Emerging as it does from the work of my teachers and my students, this is an "individual" product only in the conven-

---

* *Wildcat Strike,* Antioch Press, Yellow Springs, Ohio, to be published Spring, 1954.

tional sense. I have long since given up efforts to detect where I have pilfered ideas, hypotheses, or phrases from my teacher, Robert K. Merton, and I am grateful that he has always kept the doors to his rich wisdom unlocked. From the inception of this research to its present form, Mr. Merton generously provided an exacting critique of every facet of the work, editorial as well as scientific. The debt that I owe also to Paul Lazarsfeld, Robert Lynd, Robert MacIver, and Charles Page becomes ever more apparent to me with the passage of years.

The debt to my own students is no less real and honestly come by. Their role is, I hope, more suitably acknowledged in the methodological appendix which, as a matter of fact, was written with one of them, Maurice R. Stein. Mr. Stein served well beyond the "call of duty," lending brilliant assistance in the direction of the field work and the analysis of the data. Among many other responsibilities, Phyllis Herrick helped to keep our sprawling data in manageable form and dissolved administrative disorders with a thaumaturgist's touch. Raymond Hartell, Marcia Wooster, and Jack Lefcowitz contributed valuable manuscripts on special problems involved in the research. Particular thanks are due to Lois Wladis Hoffman for preparing a study of "succession" tensions which made me more aware of the shortcomings of my own work in this area. Should the style of this work attain any clarity, it owes much to the unflinching and skilled intervention of Helen Sattler Gouldner.

Our research could never have been undertaken in the first place without the unstinting cooperation of the Company's labor relations director; there was hardly a phase of the work to which he did not volunteer substantial and insightful guidance. Needless to add, the collective cooperation of other Company executives, and of the men at the plant, both workers and supervisors, was indispensable. We were truly sorry when the study was completed, for we had come to like and respect them as "men."

My former colleagues in sociology at the University of Buffalo, Nathaniel Cantor, Milton Albrecht, Llewellyn Z. Gross, the late Jerry Wolpert, Victor Barnouw, Norman Miller, psychologists Frances and Nathan Shenfeld, economists Joseph Shister and Jack Kaufman, and Jack Hyman of the School of Law, have allowed me to tax their patience with continual talk of gypsum manufacturing and helped substantially with expert advice in their respective specialties. Apologies are due particularly to my office mate, Norman Miller, whom I badgered un mercifully with each new problem and idea; it was an irresistible temptation to draw continually upon his infallible sociological "instinct."

The burdensome work of typing successive drafts of this manuscript was graciously and intelligently performed, at various times, by Carol Fitzgerald, Carol Wedum, and Helen Simone.

The many skills and varied specialties of all these people were technically helpful, but were all the more important because of the friendship in which they were offered. If, with all this talent so generously available, our study still has errors of fact and judgment, it is obvious that this is entirely the fault of the writer and of no one else.

A. W. G.

PART ONE

". . . advances in the sphere of the social sciences
are substantively tied up with the shift in practical
problems and take the guise of a critique of concept-
construction."

MAX WEBER, *The Methodology of the
Social Sciences*

AN APPROACH TO BUREAUCRACY

study of bureaucracy has alternated between tight analyses of specific civil services and panoramic historical surveys of diverse administrative systems. The first of these approaches is exemplified by the notable contributions of a Marshall Dimock, Fritz M. Marx, Carl Friedrich, Walter Sharp, or J. Donald Kingsley. The second finds unparalleled expression in the genius of Max Weber.

Both these approaches, however, have placed reliance largely on documentary sources. To a smaller degree they derive, also, from their authors' firsthand, but often impressionistic, observations. Only recently, however, has the study of bureaucratic organization induced sociologists to make direct and systematic observation in the field.[1] These last studies, with which the present effort is aligned, are identifiable by at least two shared characteristics. First, they have sought to bypass the difficulties inherent in documentary data by recording some of the more concrete behavior patterns discernible only to the disciplined observer on the scene. Secondly, they have found their main business to be in the analysis of a specific bureaucracy as a complex social system, concerned less with the individual differences of the actors than with the situationally shaped roles they perform.

Indeed, the social scene described has sometimes been so completely stripped of people that the impression is unintentionally rendered that there are disembodied forces afoot, able to realize their ambitions apart from human action. This has colored some analyses of bureaucracy with funereal overtones, lending dramatic persuasiveness to the pessimistic portrayal of administrative systems.

Since this study analyzes a modern factory administration, rather than examining bureaucracy in the more familiar civil service setting, it will draw upon a different scholarly tradition. Growing up about the concrete study of industrial processes, this tradition has of necessity concerned itself with social conflict, with action and resistance, and with the vagaries by which the governed yield or refuse consent to their governors. It invites special attention to those situations in which the advance of bureaucratization was effectively resisted. Rather than assuming that bureaucracy possesses Gibraltar-like stability, this perspective directs inquiry into the tensions and problems evoked by bureaucratization which, by undermining consent, make it no less vulnerable than other organizational patterns.

---

1. See, Philip Selznick, *TVA and the Grass Roots,* University of California Press, Berkeley and Los Angeles, 1949, and Peter Blau's forthcoming, *The Dynamics of Bureaucratic Structure: A Study of Inter-Personal Relations in Two Government Agencies.*

The empirical materials in this study comprise a case history of the bureaucratization of a gypsum factory. The events occurring there were not entirely unique, but provided occasions to cast light upon the social processes leading to different degrees of bureaucracy. This factory is composed of two easily distinguished production units, with two correspondingly different patterns of social organization. The first, sub-surface mining operations, is characterized by comparatively informal social relations and traditional work practices; this provides a crude but useful contrast with the surface factory units which are more formally organized and "rationally" administered. Since both these segments are part of the same plant, company, and community, a comparison of their distinctive work environments, belief systems, and interaction patterns seemed a promising way of developing hypotheses to account for their differing degrees of bureaucracy.

The objective of this case study, then, is to identify some of the variables relating to bureaucratization, hypothetically accounting for its growth or contraction. No effort has been made to specify metrically or quantify these variables or their interrelations. Measurement, it would seem, first requires some degree of clarity about what is to be measured. George Homans has cogently expanded upon these methodological assumptions:

"Sociology may miss a great deal if it tries to be too quantitative too soon. Data are not nobler because they are quantitative . . . Lord Nelson, greatest of all admirals, after explaining to his ship captains the plan of attack he intended to use at the battle of Trafalgar, went on to say, 'No Captain can do very wrong who places his ship alongside that of an enemy.' In the same way, no one who studies a group will go far wrong if he gets close to it, and by whatever methods are available, observes all that he can.[2] . . . The statistician might find fault with the passages for not letting him know the relation between the 'sample' and the 'universe', that is, the

---

2. George Homans, *The Human Group,* Harcourt, Brace and Company, New York, 1950, p. 22.

relation between the number of groups directly observed and the larger number for whose behavior the average is supposed to hold good. He might find some fault with the passages for giving us no idea of the number of groups—there must be a few—whose behavior deviates in some degree from the average . . . His criticisms are good, and they can be answered only by raising new questions: How much more effort, in men, time, and money, would be needed to get the kind of data he wants? Given a limited supply of all three, how far would getting his kind of data interfere with getting a wider, though admittedly less reliable, coverage of group behavior? These are questions not of scientific morality but of strategy . . ." [3]

While there have been many studies of bureaucracy, and an increasing number of industrial investigations, there have been few which have sought systematically to follow the clues set forth by a complex theory of bureaucracy. This study was, however, from its very beginnings guided and informed by a specific theory of bureaucracy—namely, Max Weber's.[4] Certainly it does not mean that this is to be an exegesis of Weber's work, for frequently the assumptions and conclusions of our research are at variance with his; it does mean that Weber's work was a starting point suggestive of critical problems and fruitful lines of study.

Instead of undertaking what has already been well done, a compact summary of Weber's conception of bureaucracy may be borrowed from Robert K. Merton: [5]

---

3. Ibid., p. 33.
4. See, C. W. Mills and H. Gerth (eds.) *From Max Weber*, Oxford University Press, 1946, New York, and A. M. Henderson and Talcott Parsons (eds.), *Max Weber: The Theory of Social and Economic Organization*, Oxford University Press, 1947, New York. The former volume very clearly indicates the political and ideological implications of Weber's theory of bureaucracy, while the latter gives the full theoretical context of the theory, placing it in the setting of Weber's more generalized theory of authority, of which bureaucracy was only one part.
5. Robert K. Merton, *Social Structure and Social Theory*, "Bureaucratic Structure and Personality," pp. 151-152, The Free Press, 1949, Glencoe, Ill.

"As Weber indicates, bureaucracy involves a clear-cut division of integrated activities which are regarded as duties inherent in the office. A system of differentiated controls and sanctions is stated in the regulations. The assignment of roles occurs on the basis of technical qualifications which are ascertained through formalized, impersonal procedures (e. g., examinations). Within the structure of hierarchically arranged authority, the activities of 'trained and salaried experts' are governed by general, abstract, clearly defined rules which preclude the necessity for the issuance of specific instructions in each specific case. The generality of the rules requires the constant use of categorization, whereby individual problems and cases are classified on the basis of designated criteria and are treated accordingly. The pure type of bureaucratic official is appointed, either by a superior or through the exercise of impersonal competition; he is not elected. A measure of flexibility in the bureaucracy is attained by electing higher functionaries who presumably express the will of the electorate (e. g., a body of citizens or a board of directors)."

Obviously, Weber's views diverge sharply from the popular stereotypes which see bureaucracy as synonymous with governmental inefficiency. To Weber, bureaucracy was one of the characteristic and ubiquitous forms of administration in modern society, not confined to government by any means. Moreover, he held it to be one of the most efficient forms of organization which had historically developed, superseding the undependable amateur with the qualified specialist.

Tensions in Weber's Theory

Inevitably, there were certain obscurities in Weber's work which, if clarified, may enable it to be put to better use. Several of these can be noted in Weber's discussion of the factors which make a bureaucracy "effective." He wrote:

"The effectiveness of legal (in the present context, "bureaucratic"— A. W. G.) authority rests on the acceptance of the validity of the following . . . 1. That any given legal norm may be established by agreement or imposition, on the grounds of expediency or rational values, or both, with a claim to obedience at least on the part of the members of the corporate group." [6]

Here a critical problem is disposed of in a surprisingly cavalier manner, for Weber fails to weigh the possibility that a bureaucracy's effectiveness, or other of its characteristics, might vary with the manner in which rules are initiated, whether by imposition or agreement. Tacitly, he seems to have assumed that the cultural setting of a specific bureaucracy would be neutral toward different methods of initiating bureaucratic rules. Since, however, our culture is not neutral but prefers agreed-upon, rather than imposed rules, these two cannot be fused together without blurring the dynamics of bureaucratic organization. It is partly for this reason that the present study will not talk about factory rules in general, but instead will consider different concrete rules, those dealing with absenteeism, safety, smoking, promotions and transfers, and will attempt to discriminate differences in pattern associated with different methods of installing the rules.

Weber was silent on several other questions: First, to *whom* did the rules have to be useful, if bureaucratic authority was to be effective? Secondly, in terms of *whose* goals were the rules a rational device? Whose end did they have to realize if the bureaucracy was to operate effectively? Weber tended to assume that the ends of different strata within a bureaucracy were identical, or at least highly similar, and hence was not compelled to distinguish them from each other. This appears to have derived partly from his use of the seemingly solidary government bureaucracy as an implicit model. Had he focused on the factory bureaucracy with its more evident tensions between supervisor and supervised, as this study shall, he would have been immediately aware that a given rule could be rational or expedient

---

6. Henderson and Parsons, Ibid., p. 329.

for achieving the ends of one stratum, say management, but might be neither rational nor expedient for workers.[7]

A "bureaucracy" can be said to have "ends" only in a metaphorical sense. To be precise, however, it is necessary to specify the ends of different people, or the typical ends of different strata within the organization. Such a refocusing suggests these ends may vary, are not necessarily identical or salient for all personnel, and, may in fact, be contradictory, a conclusion which will in no way startle students of industry, however much some students of administration have systematically neglected it.

Weber's abortive distinction between imposed and agreed-upon rules is indicative of two broader strands which are woven together in his theory. There is, first, his emphasis on bureaucracy as administration by the "expert" or the technically trained. Weber conceived of our epoch as one in which the dilettante was fast disappearing, and held modern modes of administration to be characterized by the prominence attached to specialized skills. In this vein he asserted:

"The choice is only between bureaucracy and dilettantism in the field of administration. The primary source of bureaucratic administration lies in the role of technical knowledge . . . [8] The question is always who controls the existing machinery and such control is possible only in a very limited degree to persons who are not technical specialists . . . [9] Bureaucratic administration means fundamentally the exercise of control on the basis of knowledge. This is the feature of it which makes it specifically rational . . . [10] Bureaucracy is superior in knowledge, including both technical knowledge and knowledge of the concrete fact within its own sphere of interest." [11]

---

7. This is considered more generally in our discussion of Wilbert E. Moore's, "Industrial Sociology: Status and Prospects," *American Sociological Review*, Vol. XIII, No. 4, Aug., 1948, pp. 396-400.

8. Henderson and Parsons, Ibid., p. 337.

9. Ibid., p. 337.

10. Ibid., p. 339.

11. Ibid., p. 339.

There was, however, another ingredient in Weber's conception of bureaucracy; this had to do with the role of *discipline*, an element that parallels his emphasis on "imposition" as a source of bureaucratic rules. According to Weber, bureaucracy is the "most rational offspring" of discipline.[12]

"The content of discipline," wrote Weber, "is nothing but the consistently rationalized, methodically trained and exact execution of the received order, in which all personal criticism is unconditionally suspended and the actor is unswervingly and exclusively set for carrying out the command." [13]

Talcott Parsons, one of the most perceptive commentators on Weber's theory, has stressed that, "*Above all* bureaucracy involves discipline . . . It is the fitting of individual actions into a complicated pattern in such a way that the character of each and its relation to the rest can be accurately controlled . . ." [14] Thus bureaucracy involves an emphasis on obedience; and by "obedience" Weber meant that the content of a command becomes "the basis of action for its own sake.[15]

Weber, then, thought of bureaucracy as a Janus-faced organization, looking two ways at once. On the one side, it was administration based on expertise; while on the other, it was administration based on discipline. In the first emphasis, obedience is invoked as a means to an end; an indivdual obeys because the rule or order is felt to be the best known method of realizing some goal.

In his second conception, Weber held that bureaucracy was a mode of administration in which obedience was an end in itself. The individual obeys the order, setting aside judgments either of its rationality or morality, primarily because of the

12. Mills and Gerth, Ibid., p. 254.
13. Mills and Gerth, Ibid., p. 254.
14. Talcott Parsons, *The Structure of Social Action*, McGraw-Hill Book Co., 1937, New York, p. 507.
15. Henderson and Parsons, Ibid., p. 327.

position occupied by the person commanding. The content of
the order is not examinable. In this vein, the Nazi guards in
concentration camps justified their unspeakable atrocities because, as they said, "We were given orders." In the first pattern,
then, the individual obeys, in part, because of his feelings about
the rule or order; in the second, he obeys *regardless* of his feelings.

Talcott Parsons has pointed up this equivocal character of
Weber's theory of bureaucracy in an astute but all too brief
footnote. He suggests that Weber had confused two distinct
types of authority: (a) authority which rest on "incumbency
of a legally defined office," and (b) that which is based on "technical competence." [16] Parsons uses the medical relationship as
the archtype of authority which is based on technical competence. He states that the doctor's "authority rests fundamentally on the belief on the part of the patient that the physician
has and will employ *for his benefit* a technical competence
adequate to help him in his illness." [17] (Our emphasis—A. W. G.)
The critical phrase here is, "for his (i.e., the patient's) benefit."
In other words, sheer technical competence by itself may not
elicit the patient's consent to the doctor's prescriptions.

The patient may reject the doctor's authority if he feels his
own needs are being violated in their relationship. He may,
for example, feel that the doctor is financially exploiting him.
Again, the inmates of Nazi concentration camps did not accept
the authority of the doctors who were "experimenting" on
them, even though they may have had no doubts concerning
the doctors' medical skills. Along similar lines, Parsons states
that this form of authority, that based on technical competence,
"depends entirely on securing . . . voluntary consent . . .[18]

---

16. Henderson and Parsons, Ibid., p. 59.
17. Ibid.
18. Ibid.

It seems clear, therefore, that Weber's conception of bureaucracy as the "rule of the expert," as in Parson's telescoped analysis of this pattern, is a form of authority not legitimated solely by the presence or use of technical skills. Apparently, it takes something more than this to elicit voluntary consent.

The conclusion to which this excursion has led is this: Weber seems to have been describing implicitly not one but two types of bureaucracy. One of these may be termed the "representative" form of bureaucracy, based on rules established by agreement, rules which are technically justified and administered by specially qualified personnel, and to which consent is given voluntarily. In examining factory patterns which exemplify this type, closer attention deserves to be paid to the role of "consent" and to the diversity of sources from which it springs. A second pattern which may be called the "punishment-centered" bureaucracy, is based on the imposition of rules, and on obedience for its own sake. Here, too, the pattern must be examined in its relation to the flow or withdrawal of consent. At an appropriate point it will be necessary to see whether this crude distinction can illuminate our empirical materials and, conversely, whether the data can help to refine and develop these conceptual starting-points.

The Functions of Bureaucratic Organization: Manifest and Latent

In handling empirical materials, Weber's theory of bureaucracy was a fruitful point of departure but did not, by itself, provide sufficiently general analytical tools; for these we had to turn to the directives contained in "structural-functionalism." A most useful statement of this approach, for the needs of empirical research, is that formulated in Robert Merton's *Social Theory and Social Structure*.[19]

From a functionalist's standpoint, the most basic question

19. Merton, Ibid., esp. Ch. I.

to be raised about bureaucratic organization is, how does it persist? In particular, the functionalist is concerned with the self-maintaining activities of an organization: What does it do that enables it to survive? Weber's answer to this question, though terse and undeveloped, does, nonetheless, seem clear enough:

"Experience tends universally to show," he writes, "that the purely bureaucratic type of administration . . . is, from a technical point of view, capable of attaining the highest degree of efficiency and is in this sense the most rational known means of carrying out imperative control over human beings." [20]

Bureaucracy is superior, explains Weber, to other historically known forms of administration, because of its stability, reliability, the calculability of results which it permits, and the large scope of its operations.[21]

In the functionalist's terms, Weber's analysis deals primarily with the "manifest" [22] functions of bureaucratic administration; that is, he explains its survival in much the same way that a bureaucrat would justify his use of bureaucratic devices, to wit, that they are efficient techniques for realizing some goal. This is the publicly accepted rationale for employing bureaucratic methods. A fuller explanation of bureaucratic survival, however, must take into account not only its publicly familiar

---

20. Henderson and Parsons, Ibid., p. 337.
21. Ibid.
22. The terms "manifest" and "latent" will be used in the following manner in this study: "Manifest" will refer to those consequences of a social pattern, e.g., bureaucracy, which are culturally prescribed for it; the term "latent" will likewise refer to a pattern's actual consequences but, in this case, these are not culturally prescribed or preferred. This working distinction has been used in place of meanings for these concepts established by Robert Merton. For Merton, a latent function is one whose adjustive consequences are not intended or recognized by the actors involved. In actual empirical research, however, it is often difficult to determine whether the actor recognizes or intends certain consequences; this seems particularly true in conflict situations where the actors may deliberately dissemble.

and prescribed consequences, but also those that are unintended and not conventionally discussed.

There is every ground for expecting that bureaucracies generate an intricately ramified network of consequences, many of which are below the waterline of public visibility. Though not easily accessible to view, these consequences can, nevertheless, contribute considerably to bureaucratic survival and development. It would be entirely premature, then, to assume that bureaucracies maintain themselves solely because of their efficiency.

In any event, emphasis will be placed upon the role of factors, other than those required for technical efficiency, that increase the degree of bureaucratization. An attempt will be made also to ascertain the significance of forces less seemingly inexorable than "increased" size, and to indicate the manner in which these more controllable contingencies contribute to bureaucratization.

There are still other aspects of Weber's discussion of the role of efficiency to which assent could not be given. For the most part, Weber tended to focus on the contribution which bureaucratic methods made to the organization as a *whole*. For example, he indicated that bureaucratic rules enhanced "predictability" of performance in an organization, by constraining disruptive personal friendships or enmities.

But do bureaucratic rules provide equally efficient vehicles for realizing the ends of *all* strata within an organization? Do factory rules, for example, enable workers to predict things which are of most concern to them? [23] It would seem that, under

---

23. For example: The workers' "channels of advancement are not clear, the how and when of getting ahead are not defined. When they ask their boss how they can get ahead, he can only say that if they work hard, do a good job, behave themselves, and try to learn about the work, eventually they will be given a chance at better jobs. He cannot say if they do this and this, they will be promoted at the end of so many months . . ." Burleigh B. Gardner, *Human Relations in Industry*, Richard D. Irwin, Inc., Chicago, 1946, p. 174.

certain circumstances, it is normal for factory rules to make prediction difficult or impossible for lower strata personnel; for given the implicit but pervasive assumption that anxiety and insecurity are effective motivators, invisibly moving men to obey, employers will tend to leave undeveloped those rules which would strengthen workers' predictability and security.

More generally, Weber seems to have conceived of rules as if they developed and operated without the intervention of interested groups, groups, moreover, which have different degrees of power. Certainly bureaucracy is a man-made instrument and it will be made by men in proportion to their power in a given situation. For this reason, careful examination will be given to the role of the plant manager, to his relations with his supervisors, and their relation to ordinary workers, in an effort to see how this system of differentially distributed power relates to the growth of bureaucratic organization.

Summary

The objective of this research is to clarify some of the social processes leading to different degrees of bureaucratization, to identify some of the crucial variables, and to formulate tentative propositions (hypotheses) concerning their inter-connections. A theoretical model will be essayed which outlines a range of diverse concepts that a theory of bureaucracy, more maturely conceived, will have to encompass. Some portions of this model will rest upon more evidence than others; but since this is a case study of only one plant, nothing is to be gained by viewing any of the generalizations proposed here as more than a potentially fruitful hypothesis.

In studying patterns of factory administration, questions of economic policy are approached by a back door, as it were. At least since Weber's time, it has been all too clear that economic options could not be kept isolated from administrative questions; economic and administrative choices are but two facets of the same hard problem. For example, it is no longer mean-ingful to take a stand either in favor of "socialism" or "capital-ism," unless the administrative content of these terms is filled in.

It is not the sociologist's task to *recommend* alternative policies and to insist that some administrative options are "better" than others. But if he is not a proper catalyst of social change, neither ought a sociologist to serve as a justifier of received patterns, legitimating them with *post factum* omnis-cience as the product of "inevitability." If the sociologist may not expatiate upon what "ought to be," he is still privileged to deal with another realm, "the realm of what can be." [24] It some-times seems that students of bureaucracy are all too ready to agree with Franz Kafka's judgment: "Such freedom as is pos-sible today is but a wretched business." Underlying their pes-simism is a limited conception of the choices presently available; a choice is seen only between a utopian and hence unattainable vision of democracy, on the one hand, and an attainable but bureaucratically undermined, hence imperfect, democracy, on the other hand. But the options thus stated have been ampu-tated, for there is no real choice between the possible and the impossible. Such diagnoses serve only to generate diffuse dis-satisfactions with the present, but suggest no solutions for the future.

The methods of this study, and the policy alternatives to which they lead, are of quite another sort. The assumption here has been that examination of concrete situations will detect alternative arrangements, and a variety, not a singularity of solutions. These by their very existence demonstrate that they

---

24. The full quotation is, "Machiavelli sought to distinguish the realm of what ought to be and the realm of what is. He rejected the first for the second. But there is a third realm: the realm of what can be. It is in that realm that what one might call a humanist realism can lie. The measure of man is to ex-tend this sphere of the socially possible." Max Lerner, Introduction to *The Prince* and *The Discourses*, The Modern Library, New York, 1950, p. xlvi.

"can be," and thus empirically enrich the available policy alternatives. Concretely, this study suggests that there is a choice that may be made, a choice between two *possible* alternatives, between punishment-centered and representative bureaucracy. The study which follows, then, is shaped by the conviction that if the world of theory is grey and foredoomed, the world of everyday life is green with possibilities which need to be cultivated.

Chapter I

THE PLANT AND ITS

COMMUNITY SETTING

THE EMPIRICAL CORE
of this study consists of an intensive analysis of one plant owned
and operated by the General Gypsum Company.* This Company has many plants scattered throughout the country, with
main offices located in Lakeport, a middle-sized city near the
Great Lakes. The plant was studied for some three years, between 1948 and 1951. It is situated sixteen miles northeast of
Lakeport, just outside the village of Oscar Center. In 1948
it employed about 225 people, 75 in the mine and 150 in
various surface departments. From the standpoint of Com-

---

* All proper names here are pseudonyms, used to protect the anonymity of
the Company and its personnel.

pany people, the plant's two basic operating divisions are the sub-surface mine and the surface factories.

The miners work in two shifts; the first is from 7:00 A.M. to 3:30 P.M., while the second starts an hour later, to allow the fumes left by the final blasting to clear, and continues until 12:30 A.M. Most personnel at the plant work a six day week, eight hours a day, wages being computed on the basis of a forty hour week. A local of the Gas, Coke, and Chemical Workers of America is bargaining agent for all but office and supervisory personnel.

The Technological Process

Gypsum rock, composed of calcium sulphate in the main, is the material with which processing operations begin. Blasted out of the walls of mining rooms, about eighty or so feet beneath the surface, it is scooped up by "joy-loaders," and piled onto "shuttle-buggies" which then carry it to trains waiting nearby. The trains bring the roughly hewn gyp to the foot of the mine where it is weighed and crushed into more manageable chunks. From here, if immediately used instead of being stored, the rock is pulverized into a fine powder and dehydrated, a process known as "calcining."

It may, then, provide the main ingredient for wall plaster after a "retarder," which inhibits its setting, and other substances are added. Most powder, however, is used to make gypsum wall board. (Wall board is, of course, used ultimately in the construction of homes and offices as an insulating and room-shaping material.) For this purpose, the powder is conveyed to the "board plant" which, from the point of view of Company people, is the heart of all their activities. It is fed into a mixer along with other ingredients, such as paper pulp and foaming agents, and is churned into a paste.

This paste is poured onto a moving sheet of paper, and is somewhat smoothed out by hand. It then passes between two rotating cylinders which compress the paste to a desired thickness, cover it with a top sheet of paper, and seal its edges. It is now somewhat like a long—but inedible—sandwich. As a continuous strip of board, it is conveyed over rollers slowly enough to allow it to set partially before it reaches a mechanical knife several hundred feet distant. Near the end of the rollers, it is cut into sections of varying length, and rolled onto alternate decks of a multi-tiered steam heated dryer, through which it passes in about an hour. Upon emerging from the dryer, the board is inspected, bundled and loaded at the "take off point."

Three other activities carried on at the Oscar Center plant deserve mention. The first consists of maintenance activities, the bulk of which is localized in the repair shop on the surface. Because it is difficult to bring bulky machinery—such as the buggies, loaders, or trains—to the top, there is another repair shop in the mine.

A second distinctive operation takes place in the "sample room." Here ingenious little boxes are designed and constructed which are used by Company salesmen to demonstrate the insulating qualities of the board. This room, however, is not integral to the plant's operations, since it might just as easily be located in another plant. It is helpful in the sale of the company's products, but not in their manufacture.

Finally, there is the office building where the plant manager's and personnel director's offices are located, the records are stored, payroll preparations are made, and communication with the Lakeport office is maintained. The office building stands apart from the cluster of dusty production units and, during summer, is bordered with a flower bed that further marks it off from the others.

The Adjacent Towns

The great majority of men working in the plant live in the towns of Oscar Center, Oscar, Pinefield, West House, Tyre, or

Beeville, on the periphery of Lakeport's metropolitan area. These communities are all less than 5,000 in population, while Oscar Center itself has about 700 residents. A sketch of Oscar Center may provide insight into how the workers live in these communities.

Oscar Center has a "dominant family" who will be called the Klugers because that is not their name. Adolph Kluger has been supervisor of the town for the past ten years, but despite this political eminence, is not thought to have a lot of "class." There are, for example, rumors that his brother Felix was charged with issuing bad checks and was expelled from his University. Adolph himself is thought to bear a striking resemblance to Hitler and, in fact, many townsmen refer to him by that name.

Adolph's father before him had also been town supervisor. The older Kluger had been elected on the Republican ticket, the town being some 85% Republican. Kluger senior is said to have passed his job on to one of his cronies, Bill Schekne, with the understanding that Schekne would turn it over to Kluger junior, when the latter came of age. The story has it that Schekne reneged on the agreement and, instead, sought to install his own son as supervisor in 1938. "But the people wanted a change of name," said one townsman. "They have an antagonism to a superior ruling class." Because of the older Schekne's hold over the local Republican machine, Kluger junior was compelled to run on the Democratic ticket as an "independent Republican," a somewhat desperate expedient which proved successful.

The Lutheran and Catholic Churches are predominant in the town, though a sprinkling of other denominations are present. The community is largely of Germanic origins, along with some Poles and Hungarians, who do not live within the village itself. Formerly, the Lutheran Church gave one sermon a month in German, but it has now discontinued this practice. One respondent, an educated and young person, spoke of the community as adhering to "Nordic" values, being quite "thrifty, religious, God-fearing, and anti-Semitic."

It is a rather straight-laced community in which,' for example, dancing is still not "quite right" in the minds of the elders. The single most important association for the men is the Volunteer Fire Department. This group holds meetings and card parties once or twice a month, and also has a drum and bugle corps.

The town takes keen satisfaction in its baseball team, and is particularly prideful when able to support a hard-ball team. Like most of the local communities, it belongs to a soft-ball league which was started by the former head of the town's Lutheran Church. The General Gypsum Company's workers have a regular team entered in the league competition, though it is considered by some to consist of a "bunch of soreheads."

"Everyone belongs to the Fire Department," and the young men play on the baseball team and date the same girls. "The feuds that exist, exist between families. The family is definitely the important unit. The old man is boss, and the women are submissive. There has rarely been a divorce out here. The families are quite interlocked by marriage. Our parents felt the kids should all work, not loaf, so we all used to caddy." Often the children do not see Lakeport until they go to high school. The families "don't go to Lakeport because they feel it's too big and noisy." They may, though, go to nearby Inport for a weekend outing, or to watch the ships go through the locks.

"There really isn't anyone that stands out. Everyone lives about the same level," insists a young girl working in the plant office. "You get to know everyone." One's status in the community is determined in large part by length of residence. "Many families have been here for 25 years and are still considered newcomers." And some families came as early as 1800.

At the bottom of the social pyramid are the "new arrivals."

These newcomers evidently achieve some degree of integration rather quickly through the "get acquainted" parties held by the Community Council, and through other club activities. At the top of the social pyramid are two groups: (1) the old farm families and the "pillars of the church," and (2) the few professionals such as the doctor and ministers. In between peak and base, the vast majority of inhabitants are found, ranked by community members in terms of their occupation, farm-holdings, length of residence, and moral rectitude.

At this time, non-farming occupations are pursued by well over a majority of townsmen. Most of these, however, either live on a farm, still own one, were born and spent their youth on one, or would like to buy a farm. In addition, many are economically dependent upon local farmers.

The people "like their comfort"; they wear loose clothes and the men shave twice a week. They "live in the kitchen" and like heavy foods which are cooked in large amounts. "They eat an awful lot." In the evening they sit around, drink beer, or listen to the radio.

Many men are avid hunters and do a lot of coon hunting and track scenting. "Even though they won't blow their money on anything else, they'll spend up to $150 on a good coon dog." They have a hunt club whose announced purpose is to protect the local wild life. Most men have at least one shotgun; "they seem to love guns." The women can only "get out on Saturday nights." They tend to their babies, cook, clean, or visit with the neighbors during the day and about once a month do sewing at the church.

The fresh perspective of a plant worker new to Oscar Center may further highlight some of the area's distinctive characteristics:

"I'd lived in Lakeport all my life, but I like Oscar Center and my wife is crazy about it. We wouldn't move back to Lakeport for anything. When you go from Oscar Center to Lakeport it seems as if you're walking into a clothing closet. The houses are so close to-gether and everything is closed in. I think it is swell out here. When we first came here my kids felt pretty bad but after two weeks they couldn't be forced to move back to Lakeport. Now they've got plenty of room to play in.

"You are away from the noise, the crowds, and the traffic. I don't know about some of the classier sections of Lakeport, but in Big Rock where I used to live these were a real nuisance. I'm not a drinking man myself so I got tired of all the drunks and saloons. It's bad for the kids.

"There is one great disadvantage. We don't have a good sewage system or garbage disposal system like in Lakeport. It's not too bad, though. We're trying to have it fixed through the Community Council.

"The Council meets in the public school once a month or once every three months. The people get together and bring up things for the good of the town . . . You can bring up anything you like so long as it's for the good of the town. They also hold "get ac-quainted" parties . . .

"There's fewer 'catty' people in Oscar Center. There's not so muc of the 'knife you in the back' feeling. People aren't trying to ge something on you.

"Quite a few of the men from the plant live in town. Most of the people on my street work in the plant. That's Pine Street. Almost all my neighbors work in gypsum. We've all got something in common. When you meet someone you can discuss the plant with him. You see everybody you know, and you do a lot of talking. Everybody knows everybody else. There's nothing like that in the city.

"We like it here. City people are not friendly. There is a different attitude here. If I may use a slang word of saying something, out here they aren't so 'snooty'."

Summing up this picture of Oscar Center, it may be said that it is still characterized by a traditional outlook and by thinking in terms of the "familiar," rather than the "best," ways of doing things. It is organized in terms of families to which even grown men are subordinated, and emphasizes family welfare and unity.

Workers With Roots

Many of the employees work in this plant because it is near their town. "This is near home," says a trucker. "It's only about eight miles and there are no curves on the way here." A mechanic in the mine, explaining why he took his job says: "I live nearby, it's nearer than working in Lakeport." A surface mechanic remarks: "This was close to home, so I decided to try it and stay close to home." "I could have had a civil service job," says a young girl working in the office, "but I didn't want to take it. This job was convenient to home."

These comments suggest that the plant workers have important ties other than to their job. Being with their families, among their friends, living in their own home, rooted in their own neighborhoods, are significant values to these workers. They are not yet men of the market, perpetually "on the make," but are still, very much, men of the community and loyal to its traditional values.

Many of the workers' families have lived in these communities for generations. Their family names mark the modest headstones in the old local graveyards, with dates going back to the middle of the last century.

Their farming ties are still vital psychologically, even if frayed economically. Some have only given up farming reluctantly, and look forward to a return. For example, an extraman in the mine comments: "I used to have a farm myself, but I lost it because of high taxes. I want to go back to farming full time. Maybe work down here in the winters, like I used to. I like being my own boss." Others say, "This is the first job I ever had. I worked on the farm before this. I still live on the farm and do some work there for my father." An oiler declares, "I live in West House . . . I've got a farm there. My grandson

does most of the farming. We raise hay, wheat, and buckwheat."
In short, the plant workers are a real part of a small, traditionalistic, rural community.

"Everybody's Sociable"

This is important to notice because it has had persisting
effects on social relations within the factory. The most signi-
cant of these is the friendly and highly egalitarian relationships
between supervisors and workers. "You see," explains a mechanic, "the bosses associate with the men. They will drink
with them at the saloon or restaurant, and there is a fine sentiment. That's something you don't see in other plants. Each of
the departments has a bowling team. The Company buys bowling shirts for the men, and the bosses bowl right along with the
men. They're sociable that way. They hunt and fish together."

A foreman, at the end of an interview, pauses for a moment
and says gropingly, "You see, the supervisors here have known
each other for a long time. They grew up together. The same
with a lot of the men. You walk around sometimes and talk
over old times."

Because they grew up together and have known each other
for many years, the supervisors and workers developed personalized, informal relations on the job that reflect their community relations. The remarks of an "edge man" confirm this
point. We asked him why he thought everyone in the plant got
along "like one big happy family," as he had put it.

He replied:

"Probably because we are mostly all neighbors and a lot of us are
farmers. I'm a farmer myself and have a little place up here in
West House. Most everyone seems to know each other or have
mutual friends in the place. It ain't like a big city where very
often you don't know your next door neighbor. Here being neighbors sometimes means being a couple of miles apart and more. But
you will always manage to get to know each other if the other

fellow will talk at all. Everybody seems to get together; the men come in sometimes from Tyre, or Oscar Center and other small towns. And we have our bowling teams, church doings, picnics, and the women have their meetings and the like."

One worker, something of an "isolate" in the plant, also recognized the way in which plant relations between supervisors and workers mirrored their community ties, though he bitterly condemned it:

"They're not strict enough around here. The veterans come back with their gripes and don't like discipline. They think they are men and all grown up now. The laxness is mostly due to the shortage of men. Then, too, the supervisors know the men, they go out drinking with them and such. The men know the supervisors used to goof off the way they do, when they weren't supervisors. They talk about it when they're bawled out.

"The men talk right back to the supervisors here. In some plants they hide when the supervisors come. Here they don't give a ——! Some plants don't allow the men and the supervisors to associate together. Ford's, for example, like in the army. Not here though! They see each other a lot."

The nature of the workers' and supervisors' community life does much to mitigate the strains and tensions that arise from daily working problems. For one thing, a worker may not have to wait for special occasions, such as a strike, to express his aggressions. An angry worker does not even have to wait until the next day to screw up his courage and "tell his boss off." He may give vent to his resentment when he meets a fellow worker during an evening stroll, and both will stand around and "chew the boss out—but good."

The nature of the community also influences the recruiting of plant workers. The supervisory staff, having familiarity with a job applicant, or at least having ready access to intimate information about him, knows his general attitudes, his feelings toward authority, and toward the plant in particular. Those who are hostile to the plant, possible "troublemakers," are more easily weeded out in advance.

As true members of rural communities, the men in the plant focus their loyalties on local institutions. This seems to be true of their attitudes toward both the Company and their union. Insofar as the Company is concerned, much of their aggression is focused on the Lakeport main office, which they blame for innovations that they dislike, rather than on local management.

Insofar as their union is concerned, the workers' main loyalty is to their local of the Gas, Coke, and Chemical Workers, CIO. The workers' feelings are a mixture of hostility and suspicion toward those in the upper regions of the union hierarchy. In fact, when the Union's national officers removed their regional representative, whom they accused of being a Communist, the workers in the plant rallied to his defense almost to a man. The workers' complaints about their previous A. F. of L. union show a similar pattern. Their major grievance against the A. F. of L. was that their national union's representative was too far away to help them.

A significant thing about these localistic loyalties is that, if it tends to make those outside the community objects of distrust and suspicion, it simultaneously serves to make those within it more closely allied. This is not to say that there were no cleavages in the plant. The cleavage patterns in the plant paralleled those found in the community. Young versus old, Oscar men versus Tyre men, farmer against villager, and more recently, veteran against non-veteran. These were gentle tensions, barely rippling the surface, but noticeable to the observer. The more dramatic hostilities between management and labor, between worker and supervisor, had been blunted or, more accurately, had not yet fully emerged.

The Ebb of Ruralism

The social relations and values of the community are in flux. Today, the ebb of ruralism may be witnessed. Most obvious of all were changes in the economy. As early as World War I, many farmers began to move into industry, at least as a source of livelihood. The depression of 1929 hit farmers in the area even more strongly than it did industry and further accelerated this trend. Some of the railroads in the neighborhood stopped hauling freight, making it impossible for even those farmers who wished to continue to do so. World War II brought still more men, largely those beyond draft age, off their farms into industry.

The countryside was becoming industrialized and the farms mechanized. Canning, gypsum, paper, and other light industries moved in and grew. Farmers retired their horses, took to tractors, and adopted all manner of mechanical loaders, balers, and silage apparatus. Commercial farming was started; farming was becoming more of a business, like any other, and much less of a distinctive "way of life. Out of the "independent" home-sized farms an alien offspring was emerging, cash-crop farming, tied to and dependent upon a distant market.

The advent of farm machines made friendly relations among neighbors less of an economic necessity; machinery had made the farmers less dependent on each other. It was a boon to the farmer's wife, however, by eliminating her dreaded task of feeding the ten or twelve neighbors and itinerant workers who occasionally "helped out." Wartime speculation in land also increased turnover in farm ownership, bringing in strange faces and making it less likely that the farmer next door would be known.

Once the farmer's funds were deposited in the local bank, and his economic position came to be an "open secret" to everyone in the community. Today, deposits are more frequently made in a distant city bank, and neighbors know less about each other's economic affairs.

The one-time community cohesiveness gave way before the pressure of increasingly evident economic distinctions. More blatant forms of conspicuous consumption began to penetrate the community's life: Newspaper "personal" notices are less often of uniform size; the horse-pulling contest is now open mainly to those who can afford a special team of horses; donations to charity, formerly always anonymous, are today followed by the donor's name. Occasionally, the different groups conduct a social tug of war for control of the Volunteer Fire Department. Membership in the Department increasingly becomes honorific and efforts are made to keep it "exclusive." Those living on the "better" side of the town start playing bridge and join the Masons. The younger men are not the craftsmen their fathers were. The young people seem to be scattering and coming to the cities in greater numbers.

Just as the community has affected social relations in the plant, so, too, does the plant, like the introduction of industry into the countryside more generally, affect the community. Industry has played an important role in relaxing loyalties to local folkways and institutions. Since the General Gypsum Company is expanding on a nationwide level, it requires trained personnel to provide a cadre for its new plants. These come from older plants like that at Oscar Center. An executive at the Lakeport office mentioned that a local plant manager was partly evaluated by his ability to develop and supply personnel for new plants.

Workers' loyalties to the plant and their desire to get ahead in the Company will, therefore, often conflict with loyalties to the community. One worker expressed this ambivalence when asked whether he would take a job in a different plant:

"If it was a good job, I'd probably go. I'm interested in this plant because it is close to home; no matter where you go it's the same routine. If they want to give a man advancement they should give it close to home, unless they want to make him plant superintendent or something."

Workers resolve this tension in various ways. They may, for example, give up hope of getting ahead and come to look upon their jobs merely as a source of income, while deriving satisfactions largely from community life. Thus, a mill worker remarked:

"You can't get ahead here unless you are willing to go to work in 'Oshkosh.' Me, I'd just as soon stay where I was born. It's better to be with people you've known a long time and will help you when you need it."

On the other hand, a worker may adopt the view that traditional patterns in his community are valueless. A younger worker, for example, says:

"You can't get anywhere by hanging around this town. The people are nice but they're old fogies—even some of the young ones. I'd go anywhere the company'd ask me to—if it meant a better job and more money."

The Company's policy of motivating workers, by promising a better job in another area, tends to bring forward those workers with the most attenuated community ties. This policy rewards those community elements who are willing to travel, leaving their homes and familiar neighborhoods, and who are generally less integrated into their localities.

To sum up the changes: With the transformation of farming into a business, class stratification in the area emerges more clearly, and intimate personalized relationships begin to wane. While the community is still very far from being fully urbanized, it is certainly less rural than it used to be.

Chapter II

THE INDULGENCY PATTERN

IN 1948 A SERIES OF changes were made in the social organization and operation of the plant, along with a set of replacements among the supervisory and managerial personnel. The organizational innovations began shortly after arrival of a new plant manager, Vincent Peele, and were soon accompanied by a series of changes among middle management. It was clear to most workers that the new manager was connected with the unstable situation which rapidly developed. Since Peele's effect upon the plant was influenced by the customs and attitudes prevailing before his arrival, these need to be considered.

What, then, did the workers think about the plant? In a

deliberately broad and general sense, did they like it or not? Which specific aspects of the plant were liked or disliked? Finally, what specific criteria did workers use to arrive at these judgments?

"They Ain't Very Strict"

Before the new manager took office, workers were almost unanimous in judging the plant as a "lenient" one, as one which was "not too strict."

For example, an edge man remarks:

"I really like to work in this place. I've worked in lots of places before I came here, shops from coast to coast, but this place is really tops. There is nobody coming around pushing you all the time. The boys at the top are certainly lax in their treatment. There is *none of this constant checking up on the job* to see if the guy is around, or piling up work on a guy to be sure he can't get finished early. *Your free time is your own."*

"They ain't very strict," says an extra man. "You can come in late, and if you give a reason, they listen to it."

A take-off man is asked: *"What are some of the company rules for the plant?"*

"Oh, I don't know . . . of course, there is no whiskey or beer allowed in the place, and as long as there is work to do, they don't want you goofing off."

"Does the foreman check up on these rules?"

"No, he doesn't bother us at all unless we leave the job for a long time when it is busy."

"You would say that working conditions were pretty good then?" we asked a car cleaner, discussing an earlier period.

"Sure they were, and they still are. There is nobody pushing you on the job and the higher-ups don't think they are any better than us."

Spontaneously and frequently, men measure the plant by comparing it with others in which they have once worked.

Management's leniency is no abstract thing to them but takes on meaning in terms of their past working experiences.

A hopper man reflects: "I used to work in a gyp plant in Tyre, the —— Company. They rode the men harder and paid them less. It was a cheaper concern."

"How does General Gypsum compare with ——?" (This was asked of a worker formerly employed by —— Aircraft.)

"I have never seen a place like this or heard of anything like it as far as leniency goes," he answered. "For example, remember how I was standing around when you came in? I do my job and whatever spare time I have is my own."

As one might expect, the older men with previous working experience are particularly quick to make such comparisons. Occasionally they complain that the young "squirts" just out of school don't know "how good they have it." The older men like to say "they use us well here."

As one old worker said:

"A few fellows complain a lot. These are the men who haven't had much plant experience. They never worked in other factories where the boss was really tough."

Rational Discipline

A crucial part of "leniency" was that "your free time is your own," and that there is "no constant check-up on you" by the foreman. "When there's work to do they expect you to do it," a worker said, "but otherwise they leave you alone."

Workers seemed to distinguish between, and react differently to, two types of discipline. One of these refers to disciplinary efforts having some evident connection with the work process, and which workers feel are intended to gain efficiency. There were few complaints about such disciplinary efforts. Sometimes, however, workers felt that discipline was being imposed upon them for its own sake, or merely as a way of proclaiming the superiority of those who wielded it. This second, perhaps "authoritarian," pattern of discipline was considered improper and usually aroused resentment.

In the main, then, workers defined their role as incurring "technical" obligations. Since they conceived of themselves as being in the plant, as one remarked, "to do a job," fewer tensions arose about their production responsibilities. Their obligations to "superiors" were, however, thought of as auxiliary, as legitimate only insofar as necessary to do a particular job. Most workers held the plant to be "lenient," then, because prior to the succession, management utilized discipline primarily in connection with evident production objectives.

The Second Chance

Workers were especially anxious also to commend the plant for management's willingness to "give the men a second chance." As a mechanic told us:

"Nobody ever gets fired from this plant. Maybe Bill (the super of the board building) fired one guy in all the time I've known him, and *he was given three or four warnings.* He was a bum prize fighter and would get knocked out in the first round. When he'd come in the next morning he'd get razzed by all the fellows and he couldn't take it. Then he'd punch one of the fellows. *But he was warned quite a few times before he was finally fired.*"

The Company was also praised because of its readiness to rehire men who had once quit and gone to work elsewhere. A hopper worker told of a man who "had worked for five years before the war for General Gypsum and had left for Chevrolet. They were, however, glad to get him back."

Or, as a mechanic remarked:

"I've worked in lots of plants, but never have I seen them as congenial as here. For example, take my boss. He used to be a welder and, during the war, while the war plants were paying higher wages, he asked the Company for more money. The Company said they couldn't do it, so he quit. But now, they've hired him back and made him a boss. Have you ever seen that sort of thing else-where?"

Again, a young worker at the take off end insisted:

"They ain't very strict. You can come in late and, if you have a reason, they listen to it."

In these contexts, leniency seems to mean lack of personal vindictiveness. They warn people before firing them, rehire them even when they might be viewed as having been "disloyal," and listen to "reasonable" excuses. Instead of seizing every opportunity for penalizing workers, management was viewed as reluctant to utilize punishments.

Job Shifting

Another characteristic of the plant, warmly applauded by many workers, was the relative ease in shifting jobs. These comments by a miner are typical of many:

"I've worked here for two years. I've done just about everything in the mine but electrical work."

As an edge man put it:

"I think a fellow's chances to advance are better now than they ever were. He has more to back him up. He has the union behind him. *He can shift around and learn things or find a job he likes.*"

To some workers, easy job shifting meant a chance to sample a variety of jobs before settling down into one; to others, job shifting was a way of learning the business and thereby improved their chances for advancement and economic security. Job shifting may be particularly gratifying to workers of rural origins, because the rural concept of skill is nearer that of the craftsman's, with its emphasis on learning all sides of a trade.

The Sample Room as Hospital

Another evidence of the Company's leniency, to which some workers pointed with satisfaction, was their treatment in the event of injury. Accidents are an important, and often a traumatic part, of the factory environment. The manner in which a company treats an injured worker is, therefore, a significant yardstick widely used by workers to evaluate a company. It is frequently taken as the dividing line between a "decent" and a "cheap" company.

Workers are aware that the Company is *legally* compelled to compensate them if they suffer a disabling accident while on the job. This, therefore, carries little weight; instead they look to other expressions of the Company's attitude toward the injured.

We asked a mill worker, operating a sand-drying machine:

"What would happen to a fellow who did have an accident?"
"He'd get fair compensation but as soon as he was in fair shape they'd probably put him in the sample room. Of course, that is, if he wasn't too badly injured. Why if anyone gets hurt, *even at home,* they transfer him to the sample room, where he can sit down."

One mechanic felt that the Company's generosity had been proved irrefutably when they transferred a worker to the sample room who, in "coming out of the saloon, broke his ankle."

The sample room has been known throughout the plant as the "hospital." It has had a continuously rotating personnel of additional workers recruited from those recuperating from injuries. Since most of the work there is light, and can be performed while sitting, the injured worker who is unable to return to his regular job may earn a higher income there than he would obtain from accident compensation.

"Government Jobs"

Further indication of what workers mean by leniency is found in references to the Company's assistance with home repairs, or the personal use of material and machinery.

"We can get some nails, a piece of wood, from the storehouse, if we want it," says an electrician. "If one of the fellows needs a table fixed, he brings it into the maintenance room and when one of the fellows gets a minute, he fixes it on company time."

A union official and mechanic remarked:

"They have a rule that if a worker wants to take home any glass, tin, nails, screws or wood, all he has to do is to get a slip from his foreman and the gateman or big boss won't say a word. They (top management) know that the foreman will have enough brains not to give too much, but just enough to help a fellow out. Why it's the same with the farmers around here. They don't kick about the dust or smoke, but when they want any welding done on their equipment, they bring it in and the Company does it. The Company is like that in other things."

Not only were raw materials freely made available to workers, but they also were able to get quantities of the plant's finished product, gypsum board, without charge.

Flexible Application of Rules

Until Peele's arrival there were comparatively few rules in the plant, and fewer still that were strictly enforced. The union president remarked, for example:

"According to law, you're supposedly entitled to a twenty minute lunch hour. There is no regular lunch hour for the men on the two shifts; they eat any time they can. But they're lax about this if you take five minutes more or less."

The union president was being cautious. It was well known, for example, that the miners spent about an hour a day eating. Another worker, somewhat franker, said:

"If you ever go over to the lunch room at 9 o'clock, you will find the whole gang from the warehouse eating. You see they work as a team and it's the same with the maintenance men. Yet the fellows don't take advantage; they're reasonable."

The Company was also very flexible about the time of punching in or out. Workers were allowed to punch in a little earlier if they wanted to accumulate some overtime and, occasionally, if they had something special to do in the evening, they were allowed to punch out early.

There are many other examples of flexible application of rules at the plant. One of the most interesting, which we shall examine more closely in a later section, involved the "no smoking" rule. For the most part, this rule was enforced only when inspectors from the insurance company made their infrequent tours of the plant.

Management Responsiveness

A final element influencing workers to judge the plant favorably, prior to the succession, centered on the administration of the safety program. When asked what kind of things were discussed at the safety meetings, a wet end, extra man mentioned:

"We ask questions and bring up problems, but not only about safety."
"What else?"
"About the process. A while ago we had a mix that hurt our hands and made them sore. We asked for rubber gloves and got them right away. That's the sort of thing I mean . . . some places have a lot of red tape about safety suggestions, unless they come through the proper channels or are written down correctly on some form or

other. Out here, Bill (board plant super) will do anything that's reasonable."

This is indicative of still another source of job satisfaction important to many of the plant personnel. Under certain circumstances workers do not want to be "left alone" by management; in a situation in which they have grievances they desire an opportunity to express themselves concerning these complaints and, moreover, they will evaluate management in terms of the speed and adequacy of the response which management makes. Workers have a long memory about management's response to their suggestions. One worker, for example, telling how he happened to get a trip-hammer said, *"About three years ago* I suggested to the boss about getting a hammer and *pretty soon* they did."

Criteria of Leniency

How does "good" or "lenient" come to be defined in the particular ways exposed by the above discussion?

First, observe that "leniency" is not construed by workers as giving "tit for tat." When workers are given something they already feel to be rightfully theirs they do not speak of leniency. Instead, this approving judgment is reserved for management behavior which gives something that it might not have to, or when it gives up something for which no compelling claim could be made.

For example, management would be within its legal rights if it kept workers busy every minute of the time for which they are being paid. But management did not choose to exercise this legal privilege.

The case of the sample room, and its use as a "hospital," further illustrates this. Management did not *have* to allow injured workers to earn money at jobs in the sample room. Management could, legally, have insisted that injured workers remain at home, collecting only their compensation, until they were ready to resume their regular jobs. But, again, the Company did not "stand on its rights."

It was because management's actions did not appear to strive for a return on every cost, for a gain against every outlay, that workers felt it had a "proper attitude." It was management's expression of this attitude that allowed workers to feel that they were being treated "humanly."

To suggest that workers felt management behavior was lenient when the Company did not "stand upon its rights," is however, to consider only one side of the matter. Leniency is not merely forebearance but consists, also, of positive Company actions which conform with sentiments shared by workers.

Suppose, for example, management allowed workers to take enough gypsum board so that they could set themselves up in business with it. Or suppose management allowed workers to use their free time to sell candy and soft drinks in the plant. Or suppose further, that management gave a "second chance" to a worker who had deliberately smashed a machine. Workers would not view such Company behavior as "leniency." They would be likely to view management as a "sucker" and would claim that such a worker was "taking advantage" of management. In other words, it is not merely relaxation of managerial prerogative that evokes judgments of leniency, but only such forebearances which conform to workers' sentiments.

Nor is this the whole story. There are cases of managerial behavior which are not compelled by law or company rule, and which are in conformity with workers' sentiments, but are, nevertheless, not viewed as "leniency." For example, if a mine supervisor voluntarily shares the risks of his men in a dangerous situation, he gains the men's esteem, but is not viewed as lenient. One reason for this is that miners in the plant have no doubt that this is a relevant way of judging their foreman.

They are convinced that it is only "just and right" that a fore-man should "take his chances with his men."

Another way of putting this is that workers do not define management's role as entailing obligations of lenient behavior. "Leniency" is a judgment rendered by workers when super-visors temper the performance of their managerial role by tak-ing into account obligations that would be relevant in other relationships. Thus when workers lauded management for al-lowing the injured to work in the sample room, or permitting workers to take Company material and tools for personal use, or giving those who violate managerial expectations a "second chance," they were employing criteria legitimately applicable to the relations among *friends* and *neighbors*, rather than in a *business* and *industrial* context.

There is a second set of sentiments underlying the workers' notions of leniency. This is a belief that men should actively take charge of the events that impinge upon their lives, rather than passively submitting to them as they occur.

For example, workers' favorable judgments of the plant be-cause it did not employ a "constant check up," their reiterated assertions that here "your free time is your own," suggest that the workers were seeking to strengthen their control over their working environment. Workers defined situations as "good" when their area of discretion was enlarged, or at least retained, by minimizing the amount of time they are subject to the super-vision of others. Moreover, as the discussion of "rational dis-cipline" implies, workers also strive to influence the kind as well as the amount of supervision exerted.

The emphasis on "job-shifting" also seems to be partly mo-tivated by the worker's drive to control his own working ex-periences and environment, for in some degree, job-shifting is utilized as an "escape" mechanism, allowing workers to elude an unpleasant job or an uncomfortable supervisory relation-ship.

Summary

The Indulgency Pattern is, then, a connected set of concrete judgments and underlying sentiments disposing workers to react to the plant favorably, and to trust their supervisors. It is an important, though not the only, source of job satisfaction experienced by the workers, motivating them to fill the roles for which they were employed, expressing a commitment to a set of beliefs as to how the plant should be run, generating loyalties to the plant and Company, and expressing preferences for certain patterns of social relationships rather than others.

PART TWO

"It must be considered that there is nothing more difficult to carry out, nor more doubtful of success, nor more dangerous to handle, than to initiate a new order of thing."

MACHIAVELLI, *The Prince*

Chapter III

TURNING POINT:

ENTER THE SUCCESSOR

THE INDULGENCY PAT-tern was typical of the plant before the advent of the new manager, Vincent Peele. Almost immediately after his arrival, however, Peele made many changes which drastically disturbed this pattern. These changes will be examined in this chapter while, in the next, an explanation of why Peele behaved as he did will be proposed.

The "MacIntosh" Case

Soon after Peele took office he discharged William MacIntosh, who had worked at the plant some twelve years. MacIntosh was fired, as it was formally explained, because he had taken a full case of dynamite from the mine. Defending himself, Macintosh replied that he had taken the dynamite with the consent of a mine foreman, Mike Sigfried.

Sigfried, though, denied that he had given his permission, or that he had any knowledge of the matter at all. When the case came before an arbitrator, Peele insisted that even if Sigfried had given MacIntosh permission to take the dynamite, the latter's discharge was proper. There are certain things that a foreman has no authority to do, Peele held, and one of these is giving away company property.

The arbitrator's report indicated that it was quite *customary* for supervisors to give workers gifts of dynamite as "favors." The report mentioned that another worker, testifying on MacIntosh's behalf, had stated that during the previous summer, "he saw Sigfried give 15 sticks of dynamite to another man who asked for it for fishing and that a few days later the man brought in some fish to Sigfried in the mine . . . (Still another) corroborating witness was Peter Schutze. He testified that in July 1945 he had asked Sigfried for some dynamite and that Sigfried told him to take it, while he was not looking . . . On another occasion, Sigfried gave him a new grinding wheel."

There was reason, then, to accept MacIntosh's explanation at its face value. In any event, it was the type of thing that could easily happen, since it was in conformity with established plant practices.

In the light of Peele's subsequent actions, MacIntosh's discharge for behaving in this custom-honored fashion may be understood, therefore, as the opening shot in the new manager's attack upon the indulgency pattern. For one of the important manifestations of the Company's leniency was the "favors" which it allowed, the "government jobs," and the personal use of material and tools.

Peele's testimony at the hearing clearly announced that these informal patterns were illicit, that he would no longer permit foremen to honor them, and that, henceforth, foreman-worker relationships were to be bound by the formal regulations of the Company. By punishing MacIntosh for "cashing in" on his informal privileges, Peele made him "an example," a warning to other workers of what they could expect, should they continue adhering to the old informal patterns.

Peele's action symbolized the beginning of a rigorous application of the plant's formal rules; the era of mutual favors was history. Mourning for the past, workers began to contrast the favors now allowed them with those once bestowed under the previous plant manager, "Old Doug." If you wanted any gyp board from Doug, they explained, "he'd let you have a truckload. But *now,* if you want any board, it will be delivered to your home—*with a bill!"*

The "Day" Case

Several months later the old "Personnel and Safety" manager, Bill Day, was demoted and returned to his previous position as foreman of the Sample Room. A new personnel manager, Jack Digger, was brought in from the "outside." It was difficult to determine the reasons for Day's demotion; Day himself had been given no explanation. While talking with an interviewer, Day voluntarily raised the question:

"You want to know why I have been changed? Well, I can't give you the reason either. It happened over night . . . I had no reason to expect that I would be changed at all. I asked Vincent about it. I said a man likes to know these things . . . But he just came up to me and said, 'Bill, you know there are going to be some changes around here and I want you back to the job as foreman in the Sample Room.' "

The "mystery" surrounding Day's demotion was never satisfactorily pierced. However, if the motives for demoting Day are difficult to demonstrate, the organizational consequences are not. These consequences can be suggested by contrasting the old personnel manager with his replacement, Digger.

First, it may be noted, Digger had completed high school and had gone on to acquire a year of pre-law training. Day, on the other hand, had completed little more than grade school.

Day was brought up on a farm and was, as he put it, conservative by nature and conservative in his work. If his closest co-workers had judged rightly, he had disliked "paper work." As they added, "He regarded everything that happened as the exception to the rule." Digger, though, enjoyed paper work; he demanded careful completion of the job application forms, requiring many details that Day had usually overlooked.

While Day was "lax" in his job as safety manager, Digger unhesitatingly ventured into even the remote recesses of the mine in fulfillment of his tasks. Generally, Day was a worker among workers, easily and informally relating himself to his subordinates; Digger, however, was every inch the captain of his ship.

A verbatim report by one of our research team gives a picture of Digger in action:

"I had to report to Johnson (supervisor of the board building) to find out if I could interview him. I found him in his office with Peele and Digger working on new job classifications. Digger had a very direct manner and had taken command of the situation. He said to Johnson, 'Get out your list, I want to check off the names.' Johnson got the list out. Digger asked questions about who held what jobs. Johnson replied in a "yes" and "no" manner. Digger then gave Johnson the list of men he wanted classified for new jobs.

(Later) "In the sample shop, Digger came in asking for Day. He had a wood item he wanted painted. He gave it to Day, followed him around as he got the paint, watched him get it, and then stood over Day while he did the painting. Nothing was said by Day."

Even in their style of dress, Day and Digger presented a revealing contrast: Day was usually dressed in old, mended, work clothes, while Digger sometimes sported slacks and a checkered jacket, or G. I. coveralls, which lent him a neat, military appearance.

Shortly after his demotion Day developed a "nervous stomach" and never returned to the plant. Many of the workers said about Digger, "I don't like him . . . He thinks he owns the plant." Others said he should be given a chance to show what he had. In the main, though, there was widespread sympathy for Day, particularly after he became ill. Many held that his demotion foreshadowed further replacements, which would set aside others who had worked their way up prior to the new regime.

Without doubt, a one-sided picture has been given here of Digger. He had many commendable qualities, including a winning smile; his efficiency and loyalty to the Company were beyond question. But it has not been the intention to draw a life-sized portrait. Only aspects relevant to the research have been considered and, in this limited context, the meaning of Day's demotion is clear: A college educated, authority conscious, rule-oriented individual was substituted for an informal, "lenient" man who had little taste for "paper work." The unexplained, impersonal demotion of Day signified that the era of the "second chance" and the flexible application of rules was gone, and that a new order, oblivious to the indulgency pattern, was emerging.

The Personnel Manager

This change of personnel managers portended other changes in the operation of the plant. The personnel manager occupies a crucial position through his influence on the recruiting process. It is within his person that complex social forces crystallize, expressing themselves as "criteria of personnel selection." These criteria of selection are never purely technical but always include certain unofficial values concerning the applicant's social and psychological makeup. Both the formal and informal criteria can, by virtue of their sifting effects, profoundly influence the social characteristics of the plant personnel and their subsequent functioning.

What were Bill Day's informal criteria of personnel selection; what were some of the social affects they had on the plant, and how did they compare with those of his replacement, Jack Digger? We can let Day speak for himself. He was asked:

"Is there any particular type of man you would give preference to in picking somebody to work here?"

"You bet there is. I will pick a farm boy anytime over a city man, and I will tell you why. It is because from the ground up there is a willingness to work in the farm boy that you will never find in a city boy. When a fellow is brought up on the farm he learns a lot of things about his work, like watching his crops come in; and his pride comes in when he realizes the extra effort he took in sowing and fertilizing his crops have paid off. When you learn this sort of thing from boyhood up, you have something; a workmanship no city man can ever achieve. Well, I don't say the city man couldn't achieve it, but that the city man couldn't get the chance.

"The same would hold true in making boards here or in any other business, where the farm boy isn't interested so much in the pay, as pay, but rather as recognition of a job which he feels he has done well. This willingness to buckle down and work, and the pride in his work, I feel, is the key factor in a job, and picking a man for the job. There is, as I said, the element of conservative planning in the farm boy that you will not find in the fittest city man. Of course, there are other things to consider in picking a man too. I always consider a man's intelligence, his working ability, and you can soon tell if a man has got the stuff to stick to a job. Then I would find out through the grapevine how his record was."

"What does this grapevine amount to?"

"Why, I always tried to hire local help on the recommendation of the other men in the plant, who grew up with him or who knew him in some other way. Of course, this isn't always the best way, not always, so I have to check other qualifications along with this. You have to check several ways to be sure."

Day's criteria of personnel selection meant that local community people, especially farmers, people adhering to traditional values and, in turn, respected by their community, tended to enter the plant. "City" people were frowned upon. The established values, particularly their stress on family connections, found their way into Day's criteria of personnel selection.

Partly for this reason the plant was filled with relatives and friends. Mere examination of the names of the personnel reveals a strikingly high proportion of people with identical family names. At least 84 workers in the plant were related to each other, if family names are used as a basis for judgment. Comments of the workers themselves indicate the frequency of family ties among plant personnel. A trucker says, for example:

"They have lots of fathers and sons or brothers here. Sometimes three or four work here."

In short, the plant was enmeshed in a network of kinship relationships. This is important in understanding the social patterns that predominated before the entrance of the new plant manager. For a man cannot easily behave in an impersonal, sternly rule-prescribed fashion toward his kinsmen, or for that matter, toward his old friends. As a mill foreman explained:

"You can't ride the men very hard when they are your neighbors. Lots of these men grew up together."

Thus the high incidence of family relationships and old friendships, cutting across status lines, as it often did, lent support to the indulgency pattern.

Day's criteria of personnel selection may be compared with Digger's, whom we asked:

"Aside from skill, what characteristics do you think are best in a worker you'd want to hire?"

"Initiative. I tell a worker, 'Get to it. Climb up, go try and get my job or Peele's job.' I give them something to shoot for. He must think and use his head. I put him on his own. Success and advancement is up to him. I guess schooling never hurt anyone."

"What's your policy about hiring relatives?"

"We show no partiality. Everyone is treated the same. Relatives don't cut any ice, By and large, we have no policy on hiring relatives."

Digger's criteria of selection, his mention of "git up and git," his "impartial" attitude toward relatives, express an impersonal and competitive emphasis—an emphasis likely to corrode the friendly solidarity required by the indulgency pattern.

Twilight of the Indulgency Pattern

Aside from the cases of MacIntosh and Day, there were other, less dramatic, indications that Peele's actions were uprooting the indulgency pattern. One of these hinged on the increasing amount of paper work which he introduced. Whereas in the past this work was held to a bare minimum, Peele's new directives called for weekly and daily reports from foremen and building supervisors. In this manner, he secured a more careful check on production results, and on accidents and breakdowns. The new reports required that greater effort and care be expended, for the front office could now detect failures more quickly. In its turn, this constant check on the foremen necessarily constrained foremen to check up on the workers. As they perceived the source of the increasing pressure on them, the workers said: "As the super goes, so go the foremen."

Along with the new reports came increased restrictions that slowed down job shifting and curtailed conversation groups and loitering. Formerly, rest periods on some machines had left workers temporarily on their own, and they had used this time to circulate through the factory, free to converse with other men. The new restrictions banned this. Talking, horseplay, and freedom of movement, which for years had been characteristic of working conditions at the plant, were gradually forbidden.

Among the noteworthy innovations which Peele introduced was a paper form entitled, "Warning Notice." On it were directions calling for the delinquent worker's name, his department, clock number, and the date. Beneath this was printed:

"This will confirm our conversation of today, in which you were informed of the following:"

There then followed a check list of possible offenses, in the following order: Defective work, tardiness, absence, disobedience, carelessness, intoxication, laxness in safety, gambling on Company time, possession of intoxicating liquor, other.

The time and date of the offense, date of issuance of the notice, and full reasons for warning were also requested. The foreman's and plant manager's signatures were called for, and finally, the worker was asked to acknowledge receipt of the warning by signing it. Disciplinary measures were thus formalized to a much greater degree than they had been in the past.

The new manager also directed his attention to strict enforcement of the no-absenteeism rule. Hardly considered a serious offense in the past, absenteeism soon became a major issue in the plant. Notices were posted throughout the factory which stated that all absentees, who had no valid excuse, would be punished by being laid off for the same number of days they had been absent.

In addition, new rules were set up regulating the time of punching in and out of work. Before this, men who could find a "relief" were allowed to sign out early, while others could sign in early and receive overtime pay. Accordingly, checking in and out was now set to an unvarying pattern, and another privilege of the past had gone.

Another area where changes impended was the sample

room, which was the haven for injured men. Soon after Peele's arrival, however, he let it be known that he intended to stop the sample room's use as a "hospital." One of the foremen close to Peele commented:

"The sample room isn't going to be the hospital anymore. About three weeks ago Peele decided at a staff meeting that too many guys came in here with a sprained back or arm. In the future they can stay at home if they can't work. They just like to get in out of the cold and get a job at which they can sit down."

These remarks indicate, also, that Peele was viewing the workers as "goldbricks" who yearned for a soft berth; he was beginning to doubt that they were *willing* to do a "day's work."

There was, finally, the growing distinction between "know how" and "do how" foremen. The "know how" foremen, generally the old foremen, were responsible for watching a particular group of machines and for keeping both men and machines working. Placed farther away from the machines, the "know how" foremen's instructions were now given through the new "do how" foremen. The "do how" foremen worked directly with the men, moving from one machine to another in a particular area, and reported any difficulties to the "know how" foremen. The "know how" foremen now had more time available for their new paper work and for "front office" contact.

Individually, these varied changes might seem trivial. But whether they are trivia or tragedy depends on the perspective from which they are viewed. To workers accustomed to the indulgency pattern they were a source of bitter discontent, generating tensions to be considered later in this study. For clearly the things which have been described consist, in their totality, of the destruction of the indulgency pattern. They amounted to increased restriction of the worker, closer supervision and less "free time," elimination of "government jobs" and mutual "favors," increasing social distance between top management and workers, and more rigorous application of plant rules.

Turning from the question of what was being *eliminated* to the question of what was being *instituted,* these changes may be seen as evidences of increasing *bureaucratization.* While the men did not call it that, the innovations that have been described conform to the symptoms and substance of bureaucracy as these have been formulated by Max Weber and others. Formal rules that had been ignored were being revived, while new ones were established to supplement and implement the old. Emphasis upon hierarchy and status were rupturing the older informal ties. Distinctions between private and Company property, between working and private time were expanding. A cold, impersonal "atmosphere" was slowly settling on the plant.

By way of a summary we offer the following "program note": The violation of the indulgency pattern and the emergence of mature bureaucratic organization were closely interwoven developments; for new orders do not come into existence except by supplanting the old. How the new order will fare, how effective it will be, or how people will respond to it depends, in part, on the character of the old order which it has replaced.

In describing the indulgency pattern, a "plot plant" has been inserted which can be called upon later as the story requires it. In describing the changes by which the old order was reduced to ruins, the main "character," the bureaucratic system, has been brought onto the stage *incognito.* The people in the drama do not recognize him; but his true identity is revealed to the audience by an analytical "aside." For the present, then, attention is to be focused on the emergent bureaucratic system in an effort to understand the forces that propelled it to the front of the stage.

Chapter IV

SUCCESSION AND THE PROBLEM

OF BUREAUCRACY

WITH PEELE'S PROMO-
tion to plant manager, the growth of bureaucratic organization
became pronounced. How can this be explained? As a first step,
though by no means as a complete answer, it is helpful to consider Peele as a man playing a peculiar role—the role of a "successor." Instead of examining Peele's unique personality, let
us begin by identifying the kinds of pressures and problems
which beset him because of this role. Peele's psychological
"traits" will be considered only to the extent that they relate
to conditions of sociological importance.

Before proceeding further, however, one other feature of
Peele's behavior deserves emphasis; these are the changes which

he made among middle management personnel. As already shown, Peele brought in a new personnel director, Jack Digger, from the "outside." Digger had come from the plant at which Peele formerly had been manager, a plant also owned by the Company. Beyond this, four other replacements were made to supervisory positions which had been newly opened. This rapid change in supervisory personnel, following a succession, is so common that it should be given a distinctive label—we shall call it "strategic replacements."

The problem of the present chapter can now be formulated as follows: In what ways does the role of a successor conduce to increasing bureaucratization and to an increased rate of strategic replacements?

The Successor's Sentiments

Before being handed the reins at the Oscar Center plant, Peele was called to the main office for a "briefing." The main office executives told Peele of his predecessor's shortcomings, and expressed the feeling that things had been slipping at the plant for some time. They suggested that Old Doug, the former manager who had recently died, had grown overindulgent with his advancing years, and that he, Peele, would be expected to improve production. As Peele put it, "Doug didn't force the machine. I had to watch it. Doug was satisfied with a certain production.[1] But the Company gave me orders to get production up."

With the renewed pressure of postwar competition, the main office expected things to start humming; traditional pro-

---

1. Roethlisberger and Dickson have emphasized the tendency of informal cliques of workers to limit their output in a traditionalistic way, through their beliefs concerning a "fair day's work." But restriction of output, or "sabotage" as Veblen referred to it, is not manifested solely by operatives; it is found also among managerial personnel. Veblen, of course, has long since noted this; he tended, however, to focus on the rational motives for "sabotage" among managers, neglecting the traditionalistic component.

duction quotas were about to be rationalized. A "briefing," it will be seen, does more than impart technical data. It also serves to crystallize *attitudes* toward an assignment and to raise the salience of *values* considered appropriate to the situation.

Peele, therefore, came to the plant sensitized to the rational and impersonal yardsticks which his superiors would use to judge his performance.

As a successor, Peele had a heightened awareness that he could disregard top management's rational values only at his peril, for his very promotion symbolized the power which they held over him. Since he was now on a new assignment, Peele also realized that he would be subject to more than routine observation by the main office. As a successor, he was "on trial" and, therefore, he was anxious, and anxious to "make good." Comments about Peele's anxiety were made by many main office personnel, as well as by people in the plant, who spoke repeatedly of his "nervousness."

In turn, this anxiety spurred Peele to perform his new role according to main office expectations. As one of the main office administrative staff said, "Peele is trying hard to arrive. He is paying more attention to the plant." Peele also accepted top management's view of the plant out of *gratitude* for having been promoted from the smaller plant at which he had been, to the larger one at Oscar Center. "I appreciate their confidence in me," he said, "and I want to show it."

By virtue of his succession, Peele was, at the very least, new to his specific position in the Oscar Center plant's social system. As it happened, he had come from the "outside" and was new to the entire plant. He was all the more a stranger among strangers, as yet untied by bonds of friendship to people in his new plant. He was, therefore, able to view the plant situation in a comparatively dispassionate light and was, further, freer to put his judgments into practice. Unhampered by commitments to the informal understandings established in the plant, the successor came with a sharpened propensity for rational, efficiency-centered action.

Even before setting foot in the plant, then, Peele had an intimation that there would be things which needed "correction." He began to define the plant as one needing some "changes," changes oriented to the efficiency-maximizing values of top management, and he tentatively began shaping policies to bring about the requisite changes.

The Old Bunch

When a successor's promotion is announced, he may, however, be subjected to pressures which can introduce another, potentially conflicting, element into his frame of reference. On his way up, he is likely to have incurred obligations and to have made some friends whose loyalty and help expedited his ascent. Since a succession is often a time of promotion and enhanced power, it becomes the moment of reckoning awaited by friends, when their past favors to the successor can be reciprocated.

In a succession entailing a promotion, such as this, the successor is subjected, therefore, to somewhat contradictory pressures. On the one hand, his superiors expect him to conform to rational values and to act without "fear or favor" for any individuals in accomplishing his new mission. His old friends, however, are simultaneously exerting counter-pressures, expecting him to defer to their claims for personal preferment. The outcome of these conflicting pressures cannot be predicted without considering the distinctive problems that succession engenders for the new manager.

It might be imagined that the successor would quickly resolve this conflict in favor of the demands and outlook of top management. After all, the main office has far more power over him than his friends can muster. Moreover, the successor might evade his old obligations if he is no longer among the friends to whom he owes them. (He might say, as the newly crowned

Henry the Fifth said to Falstaff, "I know thee not, old man: fall to thy prayers . . . Presume not that I am the thing I was . . .")

But when the successor enters and tries to become a part of his new plant, he faces another difficulty which soon leads him to look with favor upon the claims of his old friends. The difficulty is that, as a new manager, he is left with a heritage of promises and obligations that his *predecessor* has not had an opportunity to fulfill. For example, when a mechanic was asked about his chances of becoming a foreman, he answered un-happily:

> "I don't know what the chances are here. I wasn't approached last time. But when Doug was here, he asked me, and I said I would like it very much and would appreciate it . . . He asked me, but then he died and we got this new man, Mr. Peele."

The successor finds that his predecessor has left behind him a corps of lieutenants who were personally close and loyal to him. When the old lieutenants find that the successor, either because of ignorance or deliberate decision, fails to respect these old obligations and their informally privileged position, they begin to resist.[2]

One expression of this was found in the behavior of the old office manager, Joe Cook. Cook had been with Doug for a long while and had worked closely with him. When Peele came, Cook continued on as office manager. But to Cook, Peele was

---

2. Other industrial studies have also emphasized that succession periods often induce widespread tensions. For example, "A new boss inevitably disrupts (established informal understandings) . . . The employees feel held off and frustrated in trying to find out what is wanted and in trying to secure the customary satisfaction of their wants. Inevitably this prevents them from relying with confidence upon a new superior . . ." *Technology and Labor,* by Elliott Dunlap Smith with Richmond Carter Nyman, Yale University Press, New Haven, p. 125. Instead of dealing only with the responses of "employees" in general to the successor, we have found it useful to distinguish the responses made by rank and file operatives, on the one hand, and the "old lieutenants" or supervisory staff, on the other.

not the man that Doug had been, and he proceeded to make Peele "look bad" in the eyes of the main office executives.

For example, when the main office would telephone the plant, Cook frequently would take the call in Peele's absence. When asked to put Peele on the phone Cook would make some effort to find him, but would finally report that he couldn't contact Peele. Instead of *"covering up"* for Peele—as he had for Doug—by pretending that Peele was in some inaccessible part of the mine, Cook would intimate that Peele had not let him know where he could be found. The main office was allowed to draw the inference that Peele was acting irresponsibly.

Since they are often placed in strategic positions, the old lieutenants are able to do substantial damage to the successor—if they want to. Another of the reasons why they were willing to do, so was the old lieutenants' belief that the new manager was not the legitimate heir. In this plant, there was a widespread conception of the proper line of succession to the position of plant manager; the supervisor of the "board building" was commonly viewed as "next in line" for promotion to manager. The old lieutenants, therefore, considered one of their own group, Johnson, the board building super, as the legitimate heir to the managership. When deprived of what he felt to be his just aspirations, Johnson became disaffected and hostile to Peele.

On one occasion, for example, Peele had to be hospitalized during a heated siege of wage negotiations. Johnson was then appointed as acting plant manager, with responsibility for conducting discussions with the union. From management's point of view, he played an extremely ineffectual role in the negotiations, not attempting to "handle" or "control" the situation even when it headed toward a strike. For these reasons, Peele became particularly critical of Johnson, disparaging him as the "least strict" of all the supervisors in the plant.

The old lieutenants are, also, often in a position to mobilize rank and file sentiment against the successor. An illustration of this involved Ralph Byta. Byta was a neighbor of Doug and had been induced by him to come to work at the plant. Doug had promised Byta quick advancement which, because of Doug's sudden death, did not materialize.

About four months after Peele's arrival, Byta was elected president of the plant's union. Byta's new position was now much more invulnerable than those of the other old lieutenants who held supervisory offices. He could not be replaced or fired, but had to be "dealt with." As Byta stated with disarming frankness:

"The good men know that a union's the best way to get ahead. You can't walk into the Company and ask them for a raise for yourself. It's different, though, if you represent 150 men. *Then, too, if the Company sees you're a leader—and the Company sees it!— well, maybe you can get yourself a raise.*"

Nor was Byta's expectation a fanciful one; it had solid justification in the Company's previous actions. As a member of the main office staff explained:

"Some of our foremen are ex-union presidents . . . The union can pick out a good man for president. If you want a good man, pick the president of the union. If you have good morale, the men elect responsible people to union leadership."

When first elected, Byta played the role of a militant and was characterized by management as "bitter." Some months following his election Peele had a "man to man" talk with him, after which Byta was viewed by management as much more "reasonable." Byta's case, then, is another example of the resistance of the old lieutenants to the successor. For his part, Peele quickly detected this mounting resistance. As he put it:

"Every foremen had set ways. When I wanted to make some changes (in procedure), the supervisors told me, 'Doug used to do this and that.' I didn't make many changes and I'm satisfied with the changes I've made. The foremen are getting smoothed off now."

Peele needed to bring the resisting old lieutenants "into line" in some way; it is partly for this reason that the successor's old friends cease to be a source of embarrassment to him and become, instead, a reserve of possible allies. For it is among them that he first looks for loyal and willing subordinates with whom he can replace the intractable old lieutenants. If he fulfills his friends' claims, he can now justify this as a means of securing personnel enabling him to satisfy top management's demands for heightened efficiency.

The Workers' Resistance

The old lieutenants' resistance finds its counterpart among rank and file operatives, when the successor's new measures are put into effect. As the discussion of the "Rebecca Myth" will indicate later, the operatives resist because they resent the dissolution of their old prerogatives and the crumbling of the indulgency pattern.

Like their supervisors, the workers too may challenge and deny the legitimacy of the new manager. Whether or not this occurs depends, in part, on the specific yardsticks used to evaluate a manager's "right" to hold office. In general, though, a succession provides a suitable occasion when threatening questions about the legitimacy of a successor will be generated and entertained most readily. In a society such as ours, with its accent on achieved, rather than ascribed, status, especially in the industrial sphere, the manner in which a manager obtains and then uses his office is a crucial measure of his legitimacy. In this plant, if a manager accepted workers' traditional privileges, if he did not "act superior," workers were disposed to accept his authority as legitimate. If, moreover, the manager showed a readiness to "stand on his own feet," without obsequious dependence on the main office, he would, all the more quickly, be taken to the workers' hearts.

Influenced by his main office briefing, however, the successor prejudged some of the workers' established privileges as impediments to efficiency. He was, too, inclined to wait for the main office to resolve the plant's problems. Main office administrators recognized that Peele's dependent and procrastinating behavior was, in some measure, compelled by his status as a successor. As one of them said, "A new plant manager is more prone to lean on the top administration than a more experienced one."

Workers viewed this pattern of behavior as "unmanly." It created a situation in which they did not know where they stood, and in which they felt powerless. For example, a mechanic remarked:

"The main office reads the labor law for its own benefit and Vincent Peele doesn't dare to read it any other way. The workers get hooked in any deal like this. *We got nobody out here to give you a down and out yes and no. Nobody here has any say-so.*"

A supervisor concurred, saying:

"Vincent is a stickler for running the plant according to the main office. Vincent says that if that's the way they want it, that's the way they get it."

These were almost exactly the words of Digger, Peele's new aide:

"I'm not interested in what went on before. The way the Company wants it, that's the way it's going to be."

A union officer summed up the workers' contemptuous feelings about Peele's behavior by saying:

"Peele can't do too much without getting Lakeport permission . . . The saying around here is that Vincent can't take a s—— without calling Lakeport first. We come in and ask him for something and he tells us to *wait* while he thinks it over. Then we come back in *several days* and he has the answer. He's telephoned Lakeport in the meanwhile."

For these reasons, therefore, workers challenged Peele's legitimacy. Since any human relationship is stable to the extent that the behavior of each party is adjusted to the expectations of the other, and "rewarded" by his responses, it is clear that the succession had shaken the stability of the worker-manager relationship at its very foundations. For by virtue of his preoccupation with *top management* expectations, the successor acted with little regard for the expectations of the *workers in his plant*. Since the successor primarily sought the approval of the main office, the workers' ability to "control" him and influence their relationship was impaired. If, in effect, the successor would not accept the workers' approval as "legal tender," it became necessary for them to buy what they wanted from him, namely the restoration of the indulgency pattern, by minting a more compelling coin, disapproval and resistance.

The Rebecca Myth

A common indication of the degree and source of workers' resistance to a new manager is the prevalence of what may be called the "Rebecca Myth." Some years ago Daphne DuMaurier wrote a novel about a young woman who married a widower, only to be plagued by the memory of his first wife, Rebecca, whose virtues were still widely extolled. One may suspect that many a past plant manager is, to some extent, idealized by the workers, even if disliked while present.

Bill Day, for example, had made many complimentary remarks about Old Doug, but another supervisor who had overheard him, said sourly:

"Sure, that's today. But you should have heard Day talk when Doug was *here*. My wife used to know his, and the things Day's wife used to say were plenty."

Day's idealized image of Doug was typical of many; for the workers' reminiscences about the regime of "Old Doug" were scarcely less than a modern version of "Paradise Lost." [3]

Though the world of mythology has a weakness for heroes all shining, and villians all fearsome, nonetheless, even myths are instructive things. For the many-threaded stereotypes of Doug and Peele, which the workers wove, reveal the sharp impact which the successor's policies had upon them.

Almost to a man, workers in the plant were in the spell of a backward-looking reverie. They overflowed with stories which highlighted the differences between the two managers, the leniency of Doug and the strictness of Peele. One tale contrasted the methods which Peele and Doug used to handle the problem of absenteeism. In the words of one worker:

"Among other things, Vincent is cracking down on absenteeism. He really lays the law down on this issue. Usually there are some who take off after payday for a day or so; mostly among the miners. But Vincent doesn't stand for it anymore. Doug used to go right out and get the men. It was funny. If a man or a couple of men were out, the foremen called Doug about it. He would hop into his car, drive down to their house and tell the men that he needed them. And nine times out of ten, they would go back with him. Vincent doesn't stand for it, and he has let it be known that any flagrant violations will mean that the man gets his notice."

An edge man complained about Peele's method of "checking up" on workers:

"Some of the men were saying that he was snooping around at three in the morning, but what probably happened was that he broke up a crap game . . . Old Doug never used to come around much and

---

3. In another connection the Lynds have commented on this phenomenon. "Middletown is wont to invoke old leaders against new leaders who threaten to leave the 'safe and tried middle of the road.'" Robert S. Lynd and Helen M. Lynd, *Middletown in Transition*, New York, 1937; cf., W. Lloyd Warner and J. O. Low, *The Social System of the Modern Factory*, New Haven, 1947, for a pithy account of the functioning of the Rebecca Myth during a strike.

when he did, you could just see him puffing to get back to the office."

"Peele's the opposite of Doug," said a laborer.

"He's always around checking on the men and standing over them. As long as production was going out Doug didn't stand over them. Peele is *always around* as though *he doesn't have faith* in the men like Doug."

Peele's impersonal attitudes were widely thought to be inappropriate. An electrician put it this way:

"When Doug was here, it was like one big happy family. Peele is *all business.*"

A car operator in the mine adds:

"Doug was a little more *intimate* with his men. Peele is a little stricter."

In other words, Peele's withdrawal from informal interaction with the workers was experienced as a deprivation. A foreman, fumbling for words, explains:

"I don't mean that Vincent wouldn't stop and pass the time of day with a man in the shop, if they should happen to meet. But it was different with Doug. All the men liked Doug, but most of them don't get very *close* to Vincent."

A car trimmer in the mine also said:

"Doug was more friendly. Every time he'd see me he'd say, 'Hi'ya, Jack.' Doug was more friendly than Peele."

"I'll give you an illustration about the difference between Doug and Peele," said another worker:

"When Doug was here, all you had to say to Doug was, 'Say, Doug, I need some board for the house.' 'Take a truck or a box car and fill 'er up,' he would say. 'But git it the hell out of here.' With Peele, you have to pay for any board you take."

Nor did the men feel that Peele gave them a "second chance." Even one of the mine foremen recognized this:

"Doug and Vincent just had entirely different ways. Doug always gave the men more of a chance in the plant. If he had any problems he wanted straightened out, he would go down to the mine and ask them what they thought about it . . . He wouldn't go directly to the foremen like Vincent does . . . Vincent backs up the foremen, doesn't deal with the men."

A catalog of Doug's virtues reads as follows: Never came around much; "ran the plant by phone"; gave the workers free board; related to everyone in a friendly and personal way; didn't punish men for their absences; but he was especially appreciated, perhaps, because he "knew how to handle the front office." The men noticed that he had entertained and had been on "drinking terms" with the president of the Company. They chuckled over stories that Doug used his deafness as a cover up, pretending he couldn't hear things, when he did not want to take the main office's advice.

The men saw that Peele, by contrast, was "nervous" in his dealings with the Lakeport office; they felt he was stingy, coldly impersonal or "businesslike," and much too strict about the rules.

This, then, was the content of the "Rebecca Myth" at the Oscar Center Plant. The myth seems to have served as a means of demonstrating that Doug had accepted the workers' criteria of a "good plant" and of expressing the grievances which Peele's behavior had aroused. Since, as seen earlier, so many of the workers' standards of a good plant were of dubious validity, it would not be easy to complain openly of their violation. The myth of Old Doug was an effort to legitimate the indulgency pattern; by transforming Peele's attack on the indulgency pattern into an attack on Old Doug, the workers' grievances could be given voice. The issue need no longer be "This is what *we* want"; it could be stated, "Old Doug did thus and so, and he was a good man."

The "Rebecca Myth" also had bearing on the bureaucratic system which was developing in the plant. As shown, the very things for which Doug was extolled were his informality, his lack of emphasis on formal hierarchy and status, his laxness with the rules, his direct interaction with the workers. These, typically, are traits which are the antithesis of bureaucratic administration. The one unfriendly comment heard about Doug came from a mechanic who remarked:

"Doug used to say that any fellow was a mechanic to some extent . . . and he didn't want maintenance to come in on a thing until the men had tried to fix it . . ."

This, though, only reinforces the picture; for Doug's rejection of distinctly separated and limited spheres of competence also violates bureaucratic principles of organization. On the other hand, the nicest compliments heard about Peele were that he "comes to the point" and was "businesslike"—in other words, that he behaved with bureaucratic impersonality.

"Sits Not So Easy on Me"

The new manager was caught in a tangle of interrelated problems: (1) Implementation of the efficiency goals set for him by top management and which he himself accepted. (2) As a necessary condition for solution of this first problem, he needed to control or eliminate the resistance to his plans by the "old lieutenants"; in Peele's words, "straightening out shirkers." (3) As another condition for successful solution of the first problem, he needed to handle the resistance developing among rank and file workers. (4) Finally, Peele experienced a problem, more accurately, perhaps, a diffuse "tension," on a totally different, a psychological, level. This was the necessity to cope with his mounting anxiety, which, situationally aroused by the definition of his succession as a "test," was exacerbated by the resistance he met.

Broadly speaking, the successor had two major avenues of solution available to him: (a) He could act upon and through the informal system of relations. (b) He could utilize the formal system of organization in the plant. Stated differently, Peele could attempt to solve his problems and ease his tensions either by drawing upon his resources as a "person," or by bringing into operation the authority invested in his status as plant manager.

To consider the first tactic, the utilization of informal relations in the plant: Peele could have attempted to mobilize informal solidarity and group sentiment and harness them to his goals. Such an approach might be exemplified by the appeal, "Come on, men, let's all pitch in and do a job!" He could offer his friendship to the men, or at least pretend to,[4] hoping that in return the workers would support his program. Peele did, for example, take pains to contact the men. "I talk with them," he explained, "I congratulate them about births and things like that, *if I can only get an inkling of it. Personal touches here and there help.*"

But in this case, mobilization of the informal system was a difficult, if not impossible, task for several reasons:

(1) The very program for which Peele sought to enlist the aid of informal relations by his "personal touches" was a program that violated the workers' informal sentiments. He could not very well use the informal system to uproot customs that it was organized to express and defend.

Informal solidarity premises a greater consensus of ends and sentiments than existed. Because of his role as a successor, Peele

4. This, in brief, is Robert K. Merton's concept of "pseudo-gemeinschaft." That is, "the feigning of personal concern with the other fellow in order to manipulate him the better." *Mass Persuasion,* by Robert K. Merton with the assistance of Marjorie Fiske and Alberta Curtis, Harper and Bros., New York, 1946, p. 142.

was particularly concerned with cutting costs and raising productivity. The workers, though, were much less interested in these ends and were more concerned about defending the old indulgency pattern. Peele was oriented to the future and indifferent to the past; he symbolized the initiation of new and better ways. The workers, however, stood for the preservation of the old and time-honored paths. It is difficult to maintain, and especially to create, informal solidarity in pursuit of ends which are so differently valued by group members.

(2) Even if a successor is wise to the ways of manipulation and pretended friendship, he is tongue-tied by his sheer *ignorance*. As Peele indicated, in his last comment above, his efforts to be friendly with the men were snarled by his inability to get "an inkling" of the things which personally concerned them. Successful manipulation of the informal network requires knowledge of the intimate events and sentiments which they communicate. Peele, though, was a successor knowing little of the subtle, but all too concrete, arrangements and understandings comprising the plant's informal system; because he was ignorant of the magic words of condolence and congratulation, the doors to the informal system remained unyielding. In fact, he even had grave difficulties with the informal group nearest his own level, the "old lieutenants."

The new manager, therefore, found that he had no social "connective tissue," that is, no informal social relations, between himself and the lower echelons. As he became more isolated at this point, he was increasingly aware of his own inadequate supply of news and information. A communication problem, to be considered in the next chapter, is added to those he already had.

Chapter V

THE SUCCESSOR'S DEFENSES

THESE CUMULATED PRES-
sures channeled Peele's anxiety, focusing it into a suspicion of
what was happening down below. One worker assessed the situation acutely:

"When Doug was here, it was all like one big happy family . . .
Why, Doug could *get on the phone,* call up the foremen and have
the situation well in hand. *Peele has to come around and make sure
things are all right.* Maybe that's why he's bringing in his own
men."

These remarks suggest that "strategic replacement" served
to bridge the communication gap between Peele and the rest

of the plant and, thereby, to alleviate his own suspicions and anxieties. They also indicate another mechanism used to mend poor upward communications; Peele goes out and "sees for himself," and engages in "close supervision." [1]

Close Supervision

Peele's practice of flitting around the plant released a vicious cycle which only intensified his problems; for the men resented his continual presence, feeling it to be an expression of distrust. A sample worker stated this succinctly:

"Doug *trusted* his men to do a job. Vincent doesn't. Doug didn't come around so much. He *relied* on the men."

Close supervision, which served as a substitute for informal upward communication, violated workers' beliefs that they should be little checked upon, and resulted in even greater exclusion of the successor from the informal system and its communication networks. Mere visitations to the plant, though, did little to dissolve Peele's tensions. He was well aware that the men modified their behavior upon his approach. Peele, therefore, soon took to showing up at what he hoped would be unexpected times and places. In a mechanic's words:

"Peele is like a mouse in a hole. You don't know when he will pop out."

But Peele could not be truly ubiquitous; try as he might, he could not be everywhere at once personally checking up on everyone. He was compelled, therefore, to resort to methods more congruent with his role. Although as a successor he had no secure position in the system of informal relations and communications, and could not infuse it with his goals, he still

1. This term is borrowed from Daniel Katz and Robert L. Kahn, "Human Organization and Worker Motivation," in *Industrial Productivity,* edited by L. Reed Tripp, Industrial Relations Research Association, 1951.

had unimpaired use of his official powers as plant manager. He could, therefore, make changes in the formal organization of the plant and move about, or remove, certain of the key personnel.

Strategic Replacements

Peele could deal with the problem of the resistant "old lieutenants" in a limited number of ways: (1) He might get rid of the "old lieutenants" and replace them with his own; (2) he could open up new or additional supervisory posts which he could staff, thereby affecting the "balance of power" among the middle managers; or (3) he might decide to "pay off" the inherited obligations to the "old lieutenants."

These three solutions are not equally useful to the successor, nor are they all equally available to him. If, for example, the new manager employs the last tactic, the "old lieutenants" may simply view this as "squaring accounts." The "old lieutenants" may feel that the successor has only given them something which they had long since earned and they, therefore, may believe they owe him nothing in return.

Thus, when Peele did promote some of the older men in the plant to new supervisory positions, they were not especially appreciative. "They don't feel very good about it," said a supervisor:

"You see they have felt that *their having worked here for a long time should have earned them promotions anyhow* . . . They feel that they are being given the jobs now only because there are no experienced men left to take them. They are taking them all right, but there is still that tongue-in-cheek feeling against the higher-ups."

This "ungrateful" reaction, among men who feel entitled to their rewards, directs the successor away from choosing replacements who would be legitimate, and hence acceptable, supervisors, in terms of the plant workers' values. By the very nature of the case, the legitimate replacements will often feel that they have merely been given their due, and will not tend to respond as the new manager hopes.

The successor finds himself constrained, therefore, to choose as replacements those whose appointment is more likely to make the workers resentful. The pressures are such that he inclines toward replacements either from among plant workers whose claim to advancement is not strongly legitimate, or else from among men he has known outside the plant. As a result, he tends to handle his problems by replacing the recalcitrant supervisors or by opening up new supervisory positions.

The successor's ability to create new positions is, however, definitely limited. As a new manager he is especially hesitant to initiate anything that would require main office approval, particularly if it entails increased costs. Yet this is involved in opening up new supervisory positions.

An escape from the above difficulty is possible if new equipment and machinery are being installed in the plant. The simultaneous introduction of new machinery and new managers probably occurs with a frequency greater than that due solely to chance.[2]

In this plant, about a million and a half dollars worth of new equipment was being installed in the board building, at just this time. With the anticipated increase in scope and speed of operations, a case was made out, in pure efficiency terms, to expand the supervisory staff. For example, it was pointed out that the increased speed of the new machines made for greater waste if a breakdown occurred, and thus more supervisors were

---

2. This is partially supported by the findings of Smith and Nyman, Ibid. For example, "An extensive labor saving installation commonly involves the elimination of some unfit employees and even executives." p. 68. In this case Peele's succession was due to Doug's death; it just so happened, however, that new machinery was also introduced shortly prior to Doug's death and heightened main office concern with efficiency, in order to make the new machinery pay.

PATTERNS OF INDUSTRIAL BUREAUCRACY

needed to prevent this. The addition of "know how" and "do how" foremen was justified in this way.

It is not being suggested that the successor merely "rationalized" his status-generated needs for additional supervisors in terms made convenient by the technological innovations.[3] Regardless of the new manager's motives for requesting additional supervisors, the introduction of new machinery did allow for the expansion of the supervisory staff, which consequently helped the successor to handle the "old lieutenants."

The gains which accrue to the successor, if he solves the problem of the "old lieutenants" by replacing them with new ones, are now clear. No budgetary increase is required and, in consequence, main office sanction, if needed at all, is less complicated. It is hard for the main office to judge from its distance whether or not a man at a local plant deserves to be fired; it is comparatively easy for them to estimate whether an increased dollar outlay is justified. A decision about the former problem is, for this reason, more likely to be left to the discretion of the plant manager. Thus replacement of the old with new supers, as a method of handling the "old lieutenants," is a more reliable and controllable solution for the successor.

Nor need he replace the entire group of "old lieutenants," even if this were feasible; for by firing some he creates anxiety among those who remain and extracts conformity from them. As Peele noted when asked:

"You had some difficulty with the supervisors . . . ?"

"Yes, I had some trouble straightening out shirkers. Some of them thought they were going to get fired. *I could work on these guys.* But others, who didn't expect to get fired, were. Each foreman is just a little bit *on edge* now. They don't know whether they're doing right. A new plant manager is going to make some changes— to suit my own way. I had to watch them. I made those changes."

---

3. The role of technological and market pressures in inducing tensions will be examined in *Wildcat Strike, op. cit.*

In short, the use of replacements enables the successor to accomplish several things: (1) He gets rid of some of those who were "shirking"; (2) he silences others and forces acquiescence from them, and (3) he can create new lieutenants, from among those he brings up, who will be grateful and loyal to him. This can be seen from an interview with one of Peele's replacements:

"Who was the plant manager at the time you began working here?"
"Why, Fier was top man then and after him Farr, Doug Godfrey, and now Vincent."
"How would you compare the four men as bosses?"
"They were all good men if you did the job."
"Would you say any was a little more strict than the other?"
"Oh, maybe a little, one way or the other, but you expect that. Vincent comes around more than Godfrey did, but none of them was really strict."
"How would you say the men generally felt about them?"
"I don't think there was any feelings against any of them. I've never heard a word against Vincent."
"Would you say then that the men feel the same way about Vincent as they did about Doug?"
"I think that maybe the men think a little *more* of Vincent because he really sticks up for the men, and I don't mean only the foremen, but all the men."

Unlike his references to the preceding plant managers, this supervisor called Peele by his first name; he was reluctant to give voice to the near-universal criticisms of Peele's strictness; he imagined that Peele was better liked than Doug. Evidently his appointment to a supervisory position by the successor made him a staunch adherent of the new manager.[4]

4. The connection between succession and strategic replacements has not gone unnoticed by other industrial sociologists. There has, however, been a tendency to explain strategic replacements primarily as a consequence of efficiency needs and the technical inadequacy of the old supervisors. For example: "The new manager did all in his power to develop sufficient ability in the super-

The New Informal Group

In obligating new lieutenants to himself, through the use of strategic replacements, the successor establishes extra-formal ties with them which he can draw upon to implement his goals. In effect, strategic replacement enables the new manager to form a new informal social circle, which revolves about himself and strengthens his status. It provides him with a new two-way communication network; on the one hand, carrying up news and information that the formal channels exclude; on the other hand, carrying down the meaning or "spirit" of the successor's policies and orders.[5] Beyond its purely communication functions, the new informal group also enables the successor to control the plant more fully; for the new lieutenants can be depended on to enforce the new manager's changes and punish deviations from them.

Finally, the new informal group also served to ease Peele's personal anxieties. A new manager commonly becomes very

---

visory force to measure up to the new requirements. But as these requirements were raised, first one supervisor then another proved incapable of being developed to meet them . . ." (Therefore) in the long run nearly the entire original staff was dismissed . . ." Smith and Nyman, Ibid., p. 128. This analysis omits consideration of two things which we have held focal: (1) The function of strategic replacements in resolving the new manager's status problems, which are generated by his role as a *successor;* (2) the existence of certain elements in the situation which constrain the successor to meet his problems by dismissing the old supervisors, rather than utilizing other problem solutions. Smith and Nyman recognize that "to attempt to meet the situation by replacement is perilous. Extensive or unjust discharges cause the remaining management and employee body to fear the changes and in secret to work against it." Ibid., p. 129. If this is typically or at least frequently the case, as Smith and Nyman suggest, then strategic replacements frustrate the intended improvement of efficiency. We must, therefore, attempt to account for the repeated coincidence of succession and strategic replacements in terms other than the utilitarian emphasis on efficiency consequences.

5. This last point deserves emphasis, for, no matter how model a bureaucratic structure the successor may finally create, its formal rules will be enmeshed in and in need of reinforcement by a framework of supporting sentiments and attitudes. Cf., Reinhard Bendix, "Bureaucracy: The Problem and Its Setting," *American Sociological Review*, Oct., 1947, for a discussion of this point.

friendly with one of his strategic replacements. This became Digger's role and, soon after his arrival, he was known to be Peele's confidant. Digger and Peele's relationship was widely resented in the plant and became one of the men's most outspoken grievances. Disturbed by Peele's failure to establish friendly connections with them, the workers, with more than a touch of envy, complained: "Digger and Peele are as thick as thieves."

Digger provided Peele with an opportunity to unburden himself at a time when few men wanted to have anything to do with him. Digger gave Peele support and approval when most of those near to him "hated his guts." In this way, Digger played an important cathartic function for Peele, serving to ease his fears and anxieties. Digger helped Peele, but at the cost of heightening the workers' awareness of Peele's impersonal and unfriendly behavior toward them. Moreover, since he felt confident of Peele's favor, Digger could behave in an "arrogant" manner, leading the workers to complain that "he acted as if he owned the plant." This, in turn, only swelled the workers' hostility toward Peele.

Succession and Bureaucracy

Disposing of the "old lieutenants" takes time. If the new manager is at all sensitive to what is going on, he does not wish to be accused of failing to give the "old lieutenants" a "chance," nor of seeking to install his favorites with indecent haste. He has to spend some time looking for possible allies and lining up replacements. In the meanwhile, the breakdown of upward communications to the new manager grows more acute. It is, in part, as an outgrowth of this crisis that the successor elaborates the system of "paper reports," the better to "keep his finger on things," and to check up on the unreliable "old lieutenants."

At this time, he also began to introduce and emphasize adherence to the "rules." Barred from effective use of the informal system of controls, the successor was compelled to rely more heavily upon the formal system. As an observant main office executive noticed: "Peele will follow along in *organizational* lines, while Doug handled things on a *personal* basis." The comments of the Company's labor relations director provide a clue about the role of succession in this change:

"*New* managers always tend to rely more on the rules. They call us up and ask us if we have lists of rules which they can use. *They are unsure of themselves and they need something to lean on.* After they're on the job somewhat longer they're less worried about the rules."

These remarks tend to reinforce the contention that there is a close connection between succession and a surge of bureaucratic development, particularly in the direction of formal rules.

To appreciate why this is so, it is necessary to consider another of the dilemmas in which the successor finds himself. It has been shown that the new manager's role disposes him to a great dependence on the main office. Yet his position is such tht he must attempt to conceal this dependence, and attempt to act with a semblance of autonomy.

Some of the latter pressures stem from workers' feeling that a manager should "stand on his own feet." The main office staff, too, is ambivalent about the successor's dependence on them. The main office prefers a manager who will heed its advice on matters of major policy; but within these limits they want a manager to be independent. "We have about twenty-five plants to handle," explained a Lakeport administrator. "We just can't spend all of our time on any one plant." Nor does the main office especially esteem a manager who "doesn't talk back once in a while."

Thus the new manager must, somehow, seek techniques whereby he can be sure that his decisions are in conformity with main office expectations; techniques which will, at the same time, allow him to make these decisions with a minimum of contact with main office people, quickly, and with the appearance of independence. These appear, in part, to be the specific functions performed by the rules which the successor seeks from his main office. Once he has the rules, he need no longer telephone it about every problem that arises in the plant. The rules, further, provide a framework which he can use to justify his decisions should the main office ever examine or challenge them.

Nor are the rules useful only in the successor's dealings with the main office; they also help to make his behavior a bit more palatable to people in the plant. When Peele did something which he knew the workers would not like, he often justified it as due to main office requirements. The workers would then criticize the main office for the new pattern, blaming Peele only because he "didn't have guts enough to fight back." Thus one worker commented:

". . . it has always been the plant policy not to have men who are relations, especially father and son teams. But while Doug was here we did that quite a bit. He was pretty easygoing on that. But now that Vincent is here, it isn't being done."

"Why do you suppose that this is so?"

"Vincent is more strict on conforming to Company rules than Doug was."

In other words, Peele was seen as bringing the plant into line with established Company rules. Some of the aggression that would have been directed at Peele was thereby deflected onto the main office. In general, the Lakeport office was aware of this and accepted it as a way of relaxing relationships between plant workers and local management, encouraging the latter to "put the blame on us."

Like all other solutions which Peele adopted to handle the

problems of his succession, the development of formal rules also had an anxiety-allaying function. The rules define the new situation into which the successor has entered, allowing him to make decisions with a minimum of uncertainty and personal responsibility. Moreover, there is reason to believe that the rules had, more specifically, a guilt-relieving role for Peele. Some of the things which Peele had done could not be easily condoned, even by himself. His failure to give Day a warning before he demoted him, or an explanation afterwards, involved the infraction of values which Peele had never deliberately set out to violate, and to which he was still oriented. The belief that he was only doing what he must, softened Peele's doubts about his own behavior. As he remarked:

"Some of the men probably think I'm a mean cuss, but I've got to follow our Company policy like everyone else. If I don't, someone else will."

The Rate of Succession

The Oscar Center plant had about six managers from the time of its inception, an average of about one for every four years of its existence. These changes suggest the importance of another specific dimension of succession, the rate of turnover among plant managers. In a case study such as this, however, since it extends over only a small period in the plant's lifetime, it is impossible to do more than allude to the possible significance of varying rates of succession and their effects on patterns of administration.

Even a cursory contrast with previous societies suggests that the rate of succession in the modern factory is "high." In part, this high rate of succession, particularly in the pinnacles of authority, is made possible by the development of the corporative form.[6] In fact, the corporation was, in some measure,

---

6. It is interesting to note that the problem of succession in strategic offices appears to be becoming a matter of conscious and public interest among busi-

deliberately designed to enable business organizations to persist beyond the life of their founders

Where authority may have to be transferred frequently, personalized loyalties to those in office may impede succession, as noted in the discussion of the "Rebecca Myth." Contrariwise, it is easier to transfer authority when workers' loyalties are attached to the office, and the rules of which it is composed, rather than to the person who occupies the position. Bureaucratization is, therefore, functional to a group subjected to an institutionally compelled "high" rate of succession while, in turn, a high rate of succession operates as a selecting mechanism sifting out or disposing to bureaucratic modes of organization.[7]

As this was a plant with a history of some twenty-five years, it was not totally lacking in bureaucratic procedures. Nor was Peele devoid of bureaucratic intentions prior to his arrival. On the contrary, the plant had experienced a degree of bureaucratization before Peele came. Moreover, the new manager was oriented to values which might, in any event, have led him in a bureaucratic direction, regardless of the circumstances of his succession.

The role of a successor, however, confronted Peele with

---

ness executives. Apparently, though, pressures are being exerted to define this problem primarily in terms of its pecuniary consequences, rather than in its impact on the organization as a social system. Thus in the November, 1949, *Fortune,* The Mutual Benefit Life Insurance Company had the following advertisement:

"Am I really that old?" was my first thought.

"Jim, you're too valuable to lose. The firm's going to insure your life. . . ."

"Don't let these gray hairs fool you, J. D.," I quipped half-heartedly.

"They don't, Jim," he reassured me. "But this is a special kind of insurance that's going to do both of us a lot of good. . . . This plan protects our company against the loss of valuable key men like yourself. It provides cash to attract a capable replacement, and it cushions our possible losses while he's breaking in."

7. Some of John Commons' writings suggest the connection between the rate of succession and rules on a more general level; he spoke, for example, of the "set of working rules which keep on working regardless of the incoming and outgoing of individuals." *The Legal Foundations of Capitalism,* Macmillan Co., 1932, New York, p. 135.

distinctive problems. He had to solve these problems if he wished to hold his job as manager. In the process of solving them, the successor was compelled to use bureaucratic methods. Peele intensified bureaucracy not merely because he wanted to, not necessarily because he liked bureaucracy, nor because he valued it above other techniques, but also because he was constrained to do so by the tensions of his succession.

Underlying Assumptions

The assumptions underlying the analysis thus far can be summarized as follows: Bureaucratic behavior was conceived of as a problem-solving type of social action. This led to an inquiry about the nature of these problems; how were they conceived or formulated? We then had to specify who formulated these problems; that is, what was this person's status, and how did his status influence his formulation of problems and choice of problem-solutions?

Since groups possess forms of stratification, it cannot be tacitly assumed that all individuals, or all positions in the system of stratification, exert equal influence on those decisions from which bureaucratization emerges as planned or unanticipated consequence. Pedestrian as this point is, Weber's analysis of bureaucracy largely ignores it. But bureaucratic behavior in a factory must either be initiated by the manager, or at least finally ratified by him or his superiors. What has here been essayed is an analysis of some institutionally derived pressures, convergent on the position of a new plant manager, which made him accept and initiate bureaucratic patterns.

Thus the relevance of *status*-generated tensions and perspectives is accentuated. Instead of assuming that bureaucracy emerged in direct response to threats to the *organization as a homogeneous whole,* the analysis proceeded from a different premise; namely, that the adaptation of an organization to a threat is mediated and shaped by powerful individuals. It was assumed, further, that to the degree these powerful individuals perceived the "needs" of the organization, they became "problems" which were molded in specific ways by status tensions. As a result, the adaptive efforts which are made may be divergent from the "needs" of the organization as a whole.

Peele's bureaucratic innovations cannot be understood in terms of their contribution to the stability of the plant as a whole. Nor were "strategic replacements" or "close supervision" mechanisms that brought the entire plant into equilibrium. At the very least, each of these three defense mechanisms did as much to disturb, as to defend, the integration of the plant. These paradoxical consequences were explained by taking into account the dilemmas and tensions engendered by the peculiar role of a successor.

Growing Points

If Peele's bureaucratic behavior, especially his development of bureaucratic rules, is usefully viewed as a problem-solution, what was the nature of the problem as he perceived it? A brief recapitulation of the plant situation, as Peele first came upon it, will reveal this.

When he arrived, Peele found that some workers preferred to punch in early and accumulate a little overtime, or punch out early on special occasions. He discovered that the miners believed that a certain amount of absenteeism was permissible, and, in fact, was a customary way of showing that "down here we are are own bosses." The resistance to Peele grew wider and more acute when he attempted to eliminate these practices.

As his "mouse-in-the-hole" behavior attests, Peele began to lose "faith" in workers and middle management, commencing to "check up" closely on both groups. He did not "trust" his subordinates, and he doubted whether they would perform their roles in accordance with his expectations. In fact, as he said explicitly of the "old lieutenants," they were "shirkers."

So much, for the present, concerning the orientation and outlook of those who initiate or ratify bureaucratic measures. Aside from this point of departure, analysis of the succession process also brought into view certain aspects of the organizational *situation* out of which the bureaucratic patterns grew. These, too, provide growing points for subsequent expansion, indicating a range of specific variables important in the later discussion.

From the standpoint of their effects on the plant as a social system, the following seem to be the most crucial tension-provoking features of the succession situation:

(1) *Interaction of Bearers of Different Values:* The successor was oriented to rational, efficiency-enhancing values, while workers were oriented mainly to the traditional, custom-honored sentiments of the indulgency pattern. The successor's outlook was structured by the main office's emphasis on rational administration; thus there was a value-cleavage emerging along status lines, that is, between top managers and the workers.

(2) *Ambiguous Canons of Legitimacy:* Whether or not the expectations held by workers were legitimate, or were properly applicable to the plant situation, was uncertain even in the workers' view. They were not so sure that their expectations were a solid and justifiable basis for action.

(3) *Unrequited Expectations:* The workers expected the new manager to conform to the indulgency pattern, even though unsure that this expectation was legitimate. The successor, though, was more concerned about his superiors' efficiency-centered expectations and, therefore, was not responsive to subordinates.

(4) *Decline of Informal Interaction Across Status Lines:* The new manager had fewer personal ties with workers.

(5) *Hiatus in the Chain of Command:* The successor could not rely upon the "old lieutenants" in supervisory positions to support and enforce his new policies.

(6) *Shortcircuited Communications:* Because of the inaccessability of the informal system to the successor, as well as the hiatus in the chain of command, the new manager's sources of information were meager.

(7) *Challenge to Managerial Legitimacy:* Both the "old lieutenants" and the rank and file of workers doubted the legitimacy of the successor. They did not merely resist him because they thought they could get away with it, that is, on purely expedient grounds, but because they felt that he was not a "proper" manager and did not *deserve* to be supported.

(8) *Degeneration of Motives for Obedience:* Both supervisors and workers had fewer sentiments of loyalty to Peele than they had to Doug. They resisted his program of changes and the policies he formulated.

PART THREE

"So far as it impinges on institutionalized patterns of action and relationship, therefore, change is never just 'alteration of pattern' but *alteration by the overcoming of resistance.*"

TALCOTT PARSONS, *The Social System*

Chapter VI

THE ORGANIZATION OF

MINE AND SURFACE

THE TWO PRODUCTION spheres, mine and surface, were sharply contrasting parts of the total work system at the Oscar Center plant. The workers themselves saw these two divisions as vitally different in many ways. Miners and surface men, workers and supervisors, all viewed the mine as being "in another world."

Access to the mine could be secured by either of two routes: One way was to take a battered, gate-enclosed elevator at the surface, down to the mine's "foot." Another, was to walk down (what to a sedentary researcher appears to be) an interminable length of rough, wooden staircases, under a low roof which necessitated frequent bending and careful footwork. A vault-like spiral of rock entombed the staircase as it criss-crossed downward. While descending, the air grows moister, and trickles of water seemingly ooze out of nowhere.

At the bottom, or "foot" of the mine, the rough offices of the mine supervisor were hewn into rock, and here, too, were the miners' locker rooms and the maintenance men's machines and equipment. The rooms were separated from each other by unfinished walls, adorned by an occasional pin-up girl and desultory office notices. Dominating the scene with its roaring noises was the rock crusher. Into the rock crusher railroad cars dumped large lumps of gypsum which came from the mine. These trains also doubled as personnel carriers, bringing the crews through several hundred feet of tunnel to the mining rooms, which were the "face" and spearhead of mine operations.

The face might be reached, also, by walking through the tunnels, bent over to avoid the low hanging roof, eyes alert for the trains' electrical cable. This power line was powerful enough to knock a man down should it so much as graze his miner's helmet. After picking a path over stray rocks and between puddles, the appearance of the peopled mining rooms was a welcome sight.

At the "face," in these mining rooms, the men worked in near darkness, while moving beams of light from the lamps in their helmets formed ever-changing patterns against the darkness. Generally, the light was focused on objects, gyp rock and machines, while the men peered out of the darkness which enveloped them. A low ceiling, three and one-half to five feet high, often forced the miners to work bent over, and sometimes on their knees. The noise created by the machinery in operation, which was most of the time, made communication among the men at the face difficult. The roar of the crusher at the foot was matched by the clang of the joy-loader at the face as it scooped up the gyp set free by the miner's blasts. It was frequently necessary to shout in order to be heard, and even this occasionally proved inadequate.[1]

Hierarchical Administration

The very manner in which the research team obtained interviews in the mine was revealing of its distinctive social organization. The procedure for securing respondents in the mine was in sharp contrast to that required on the surface. On "top," for example, we felt constrained never to slight a foreman or supervisor when making contacts for interviews. We experienced a need to acknowledge the surface foreman's authority continually and to secure surface respondents only with their cooperation and full knowledge. In the mine, however, while we occasionally contacted the superintendent or foreman, in order to secure respondents from among miners, we often as not went out and got them by ourselves. Somehow, we were not worried about "slighting" a mine supervisor. It seemed permissible to have a direct relationship with a mine worker, whereas our initial contacts with factory workers had to be mediated by their supervisors.

These varying experiences in rounding up respondents suggested that the authority hierarchies in the mine and surface

---

1. The above description of the mine was deliberately rendered in a subjective way, expressive of the researchers' feelings about it, because, as it turned out, we learned a good deal about the mine not merely by observing it, but also by recording *our own* reactions to the situation. Perhaps the most crucial of the responses that the mine elicited from the research team was the belief that the mine was not, and could not be, bureaucratized. Somehow, very vaguely, and without questioning at first, the absence of bureaucratic procedures in the mine came to be *taken for granted*. It was only as the novelty of mining operations wore off that this belief came to be taken as problematical, as a datum which had to be explained and whose significance required clarification. In sum, we found that significant hunches could be derived, not merely from observation of the mine and miners, not merely from watching how they related themselves to each other or to their jobs, but also from the manner in which they related themselves to us and the kind of feelings they invoked in *us*. This is an aspect of the research process which some sociologists have called "recipathy," and has yet to be systematically explored.

were different. More specifically, this led to the hypothesis that the authority hierarchy was less fully developed in the mine than on the surface. This was confirmed by many other observations. The socialization tensions of the new miner, for example, pointed in a similar direction. As one miner stated:

"New men in the mine are nervous; they are always looking over their shoulder for a boss. They learn differently in a few days."

A master mechanic in the mine expressed the miners' feelings about authority:

"The men (i.e., the miners) don't want supervisors who are driving. Some of them have been in the mine for twenty or more years, and they don't like any fellows telling them how to get off. They don't produce for a tough foreman. They don't give a damn. After they've been here for awhile, they don't worry about anything."

This attitude, however, could not be explained by the fact that "some of the men have been in the mines for twenty or more years." There were some men on the surface who had been with the Company that long but who would never express such a sentiment. In general, surface workers "don't stand up to" or "talk back to" their supervisors to the same extent that miners did. Moreover, the miners' statements did not reflect laziness or carelessness. On the contrary, it was not uncommon for miners to assert that the only thing they were concerned about was getting enough "empties" (i.e., empty cars on which to load the gyp).

The miners' behavior reflected informal norms of conduct which tended to resist almost any formal authority in the mine. Far from deferring to supervisors, a pattern typical among surface men, miners looked upon them in much the manner that the stars of a show look upon the stagehands.

The facility and directness with which one miner could enlist another's assistance, especially if the latter were idle, was also typical of his disregard for authority. It was informally understood when, and whom, a miner could ask for help. For example, the rock crusher operator could not be asked for aid when the load was roaring through the crusher. Also noteworthy was the fact that when help was requested, the miner requesting it did not need to claim *delegated* authority; that is, he did not usually say, "Old Bull asked you to help me."

If a miner wished something done, he usually went *directly* to the man who could do it. After searching around and finding him, the miner would discuss the matter and get his consent. The miner *might* then go to his supervisor and get his permission, after telling him what had already been arranged. Similarly, Old Bull, the head of the entire mine, might tell a miner to go to the supply room and ask for something. The miner would go, but usually he would not mention that it was Old Bull who wanted the supplies. Nevertheless, these would be given to him without question.

On the surface, there was a more fully developed hierarchy; more serious attention was paid to going through the "right channels." Normally, the surface supervisors were annoyed at men who "walk around" or left their place of work without permission. They suspected that informally arranged work reciprocities were techniques by which one worker "covered up" for another.

Spheres of Competence

Another respect in which the mine differed from the surface was the comparatively greater diffuseness of spheres of competence in the former. On the surface, for example, the maintenance men jealously asserted their prerogatives, and demanded that repairs be made only by them. Similar claims were never put forward by maintenance men in the mine. Instead, it was common for the miners themselves to make repairs which, on the surface, would have been left to the maintenance crews. One miner commented, for example:

"One day we had trouble with the shuttle-buggy. Old Bull came in to see what it was. He said, 'Let's tear it off and put it together,' and we did it in an hour. If we had waited for the mechanics, it would have taken three to four hours."

A serious mine accident took place during exactly such an incident. A machine broke down and one of the foreman and some workers set about repairing it. While these repairs were taking place, some roof rock suddenly caved in, smashing the foreman's spine.

The comparatively greater irregularity of the miner's lunch period gave members of a mining team a chance to relieve each other. In this way, miners rotated from one job to another, and not merely to jobs on the same prestige or skill level. They thereby acquired a variety of skills and learned how to master a number of different jobs.

Official Responsibilities

In general, too, the obligations placed upon a subordinate were more diffuse in the mine than on the surface. For example, a group of five "extra" workers would line up in the morning before Old Bull's office. "One of you fellows," he would bellow, "go and clean out the rock crusher!" He would not specify which one of the five it should be. Again, if an extra man were sent to help out a team, he usually was not told in advance what he was to do.

Much less effort was made by the miners to conform to a planned work schedule. The track-laying gang, for example, would be sent out with only general instructions to lay track. They would usually not be told how much track to lay in one day or when to complete the job. After a day's work, the supervisor might ask the track gang when they thought the job would be done. Could it, perhaps, be done in two weeks? Someone would answer, "Maybe. If we get cooperation."

Diffuse work obligations might be thought to derive from

the physical and technical peculiarities of mining; that is, since the amount of gypsum rock available is beyond control, and not entirely predictable, this might be the basis of vague work responsibilities in the mine. Track layers, however, were much less frequently confronted with natural resources over which they had no control. Nevertheless, they adhered to a relatively unspecified work program. On the surface, by contrast, specific workers were instructed to do a particular job in a definite time; a certain number of feet of board per minute had to be run, and a certain amount of plaster had to be prepared at a given time.

Orientation Toward Rules

"Down here," said the miners, "we have no rules. We are our own bosses." New miners might wonder, "Isn't there a whistle or bell?" The older workers told them, "We quit when we're through." In general, miners balked at leaving a job up in the air. To them, jobs should have a beginning and an ending. Not only did the miners have a higher absenteeism rate than the surface men, but the absenteeism of the miner, his refusal to conform to certain plant work rules, was *accepted* by workers and supervisors alike as traditional behavior.

Impersonalization

Finally, the mine possessed a much less "impersonalized atmosphere" than the surface. In a typical period, for example, ten "warning notices" were issued throughout the plant. Of these, nine were given to workers in the surface board plant. In the mine, however, the formal warning notices were practically never used. If a mine supervisor had a grievance against a worker, it was customary for him to express it immediately, in a face-to-face way, using unadorned, direct language. Occasionally, too, Old Bull would write a note to a worker, leaving it attached to his time-card, where it would be found at the day's end. But the formal warning notice, with its check list of misdemeanors and its prescribed place for the worker's signature, was rarely employed in the mine.

The greater impersonality among surface men was largely directed against the expression of aggression between people on different status levels, workers and supervisors. Miners, however, whether supervisors or not, expressed their feelings about the person or thing which aroused them, in forceful and eloquent detail. When, for example, one of the car trimmers failed to close a switch as instructed, the supervisor yelled, "What the hell's wrong? Why didn't you close that damn switch?"

Contrast this with the surface foreman who, when asked what he did when he felt about ready to blow his top, said, "I take a walk, cool off, and come back and reason with the man." Another surface foreman ended a dispute with two men by ordering them to "take a walk and when you've cooled off, come back." The car trimmer, who had not closed his switch, told his foreman to "take it easy"; but the surface men took a walk.

Several observable differences between the mine and surface have been presented: (1) The miners' resistance to hierarchical administration; (2) the lesser emphasis which they place on delimited spheres of competence; (3) their relative deemphasis on, and, in fact, positively hostile orientation toward some work rules; (4) the comparatively small degree of "impersonalization" of super-worker relations in the mine. In short, the pressure for discipline or unquestioning obedience to authority was greater on the surface than in the mine.

These elements, be it noted, are the stuff of which bureaucracy is made and, in their totality, warrant the conclusion that bureaucratic organization was more fully developed on the surface than in the mine.

The problem now is to explain these different degrees of

bureaucracy on top and bottom. The process by which this shall be attempted is as follows: The mine and surface will be compared with respect to: (a) their "physical" characteristics, and especially the dangers that are a function of these attributes; (b) their beliefs and value systems; (c) their informal social organization. When the differences between mine and surface, in regard to these three elements, are clarified, the effects of these differences on the development of bureaucracy will then be considered.

Danger in the Mine

Of all places of work that can fill a worker with fear and anxiety, a mine is among the foremost. Its darkness alone is enough to oppress even the staunchest soul; its dim, deserted rooms are a gloomy reminder that it is all too possible to get lost there. These fearsome qualities, though, are to varying degrees *controllable*. The miner's lamp can dispel the darkness; his caution and good judgment can relieve the fear of getting lost. More formidable, however, is the dread of the cave-in, the falling rock which can pulverize a man or squash him against his machine.

To a greater extent this kind of danger is unpredictable and *uncontrollable*. It is impossible to foretell when, where, and upon whom the rock will crash. These mine hazards reflect themselves in the plant's accident statistics. Out of a total of fifty recorded injuries for the entire plant during 1947–48, for example, thirty-one occurred in the mine. The rest were distributed through five other divisions of the plant. In other words, the mine had some sixty per cent of the recorded accidents, even though it employed only about thirty-three per cent of the men.

The miner's beliefs and his social organization would be simply impossible to understand without some appreciation of the dangers pervading the mine. A surprisingly large part of the miner's life, not only within the work situation but outside of it as well, constitutes an effort to cope with, and reflects adjustments made to, this danger.

In this respect, the gypsum miner's problems are essentially similar to those of other miners. To some degree, though, the gypsum miner is more fortunate than others. For example, there is little danger of gas or dust explosions in gypsum mines. In general, they are safer and cleaner than coal mines.

But mining in any form, and particularly sub-surface mining, has long been "one of the most hazardous of all occupations . . . The accident frequency rate in all mining is currently about three times and the accident severity rate about seven times as great as the average for general industrial work in the United States." [2] A world-wide study of mine safety, conducted by the International Labor Office in 1939, states:

"Since the beginning of the present century some 200,000 men have been killed and at least fifteen million more or less seriously injured underground in the coal mines of the world. Every year sees an addition of some 5,000 deaths and 400,000 injuries to the total." [3]

Not only is mining a dangerous occupation from the standpoint of the safety expert, but ordinary people also know and think of it as perilous. These two are separate facts, however connected they may be. It is one thing to state that mining is, objectively, dangerous; it is quite another to indicate that people perceive it as such, and to examine the chain of consequences that flow from this awareness.

There can be no question but that the miners themselves were fully aware of the mine's hazards. As a mine mechanic reported:

2. D. Harrington, J. H. East, Jr., and R. G. Warncke, *Safety in the Mining Industry*, U. S. Government Printing Office, 1950, p. 31.

3. Report to the Preparatory Technical Conference, *Safety Provisions for Underground Work in Coal Mines*, V. I. National Legislation; (I. L. O., Geneva), 1939, p. iii.

"I have seen a man with a hole through the hand muscle, between the thumb and first finger, where a point of rock pierced it. Another man had almost a 300-pound rock fall on his back and hurt it. They have to be careful all of the time, because, as you see, it can mean their lives. *If you are a miner you think about it all the time. The old fellows tell you about it right away."*

There are other ways in which the miner was reminded of the danger in the mine. Izzaboss, the welder in the mine, commented on one of these:

"Out in the old rooms, where the props are rotting, the roof keeps on caving in. Maybe you'll hear a fall sometime. It scares you. I never get used to it. You can hear it boom so, way off . . ."

The pervasive awareness of the mine's dangers is further suggested by the fact that on each seven man mining team there was one "prop" man, whose major formal responsibility was to watch the roof and prop it up.

Most miners, moreover, believed that a large part of the accidents were unavoidable, particularly those due to cave-ins. Who got hit was a matter of chance, but it was widely believed that some one inevitably would be hurt. As a mine brakeman remarked:

"In this place it stands to reason you got to be lucky if you're going to get out O.K. Some old timers, like Joe D——, got out well. It's always there. You got to think all the time. Down here nothing gives. The cars are made of iron, and the floors are rock. You've got to give."

"Can't you avoid accidents by being careful?"

"It stands to reason it's going to get you in the end. You are going to get careless sometime."

The feeling that accidents were unavoidable and uncontrollable was expressed by an extra man at the mine's face. Shortly after a cave-in, he said:

"You know about that fellow last night? The roof fell in on him. He wasn't doing anything. *He couldn't do anything about it.*"

A problem immediately presents itself: If the men were in continual and conscious dread of the roof rock, how could they work? Constant fear of the roof would prevent them from working with their customary energy and singlemindedness. (The reader is invited to look up at the ceiling under which he reads this. Notice, especially, any of its cracks or flaws. Let him ask himself whether his continued reading would be disturbed if he believed that this ceiling could, momentarily, collapse on his head.) There had to be some way, then, in which the miners made peace with their distracting fears so that they could concentrate on other things. By what means was this accomplished?

Chapter VII

THE MINERS' BELIEFS

MINERS HANDLED THEIR anxieties in several ways, one of which was the fatalistic acceptance of danger as ultimately unavoidable; "it will get you in the end." Yet this attitude of resignation was only one side of an ambivalent response to the dangers of the mine, for they adhered also to a set of beliefs which focused on adjustment possibilities, and strengthened their hope of coming out uninjured. These beliefs were expressed in time-worn stories, passed down by word of mouth through generations of miners.

One familiar myth functioned to emphasize the predictability of the mine dangers, and the benevolence of natural forces. This was the legend about the rats, who, like those in sailors' stories, supposedly made a mass exodus when danger was imminent. A new rock crusher operator was treated to this story shortly after he came into the mine. As he said:

"One of the old timers was telling me that the rats in the mine know when the roof is coming down, and they head for the shaft. Then it's time to get out."

In this story, the miners seemed to be asserting that nature is not a wholeheartedly malicious force, but does give some warning to those attentive to her signals. Of similar implication were the miners' references to the "talking roof." "Sometimes a piece of rock comes down all of a sudden," said a car trimmer. "Sometimes, though, there is a warning. As we say it, 'The roof is talking to you!'"

The miner's interest in the character and conditions of his natural environment was expressed again in the manner in which he singled out, with reiterated emphasis, the temperature in the mine. With an almost rehearsed uniformity, and with unrehearsed spontaneity, miner after miner asserted that the temperature in the mine "was fine," and that it rarely varied from sixty degrees. This, said the miners, was just the right temperature in which to work. The miners were quite right in saying that "it's nice and cool all year round," and, indeed, there are few accounts of mining which make no mention of the salubrious temperature.[1] The interest here, however, is not in meteorological facts, but in social facts; meteorology cannot explain why men *talk* about the weather, and what this talk means, however much it may be able to predict the weather. Here the miners' attention to the weather can be seen as part of their more general interest in the natural forces in their working environment. While the weather is for many people

---

1. For example: "In general, mine workers in reasonably well conducted mines, especially in bituminous coal mines, have almost ideal working conditions as regards temperature and humidity." D. Harrington, et al., Ibid., p. 86.

an unpredictable hindrance, the miners claimed it as their reliable aid, allowing them to work at an even pace all year around. This, it should be added, was a shared and selective perception of the mine climate, for in actuality there were many *negative* things about the mine climate, such as dust-laden air, acrid fumes, and puddles of water, which were given only occasional comment, and ordinarily did not become a salient definition of the mine environment.

These items of mining folklore reflect the miner's concern with the natural elements in his work situation, and kindled a lingering optimism that served to counterbalance inclinations to passive resignation. There was one story which seemed to express both sides of this ambivalence. This was the tale about a worker who got lost in the mines many years ago. His skeleton was reputedly found by "Sundown," one of the Indian miners.[2] After Sundown told this story, he was usually asked, "Was he dead?" Sundown would then solemnly reply, "Well, I carried that fellow all the way back to the foot, and he never said a word." This would bring a hearty laugh from the old-timers, who enjoyed scaring the "snowbirds" (as newcomers to the mine were called), and wanted to warn them not to get too far away from the lights. The relevant part of this tale, however, was in the epilogue, when the snowbirds gathered round and asked, "How did this fellow die, anyway?" They were then told that the lost miner took his own life by snapping a dynamite cap between his teeth. The desperate moral of the story is made when the lost miner is portrayed as a "guy with guts," who "did not sit around" passively, waiting to die of starvation, but mastered his fate by choosing to die at his own time.

All of these stories, in actuality, relegated the miner to a passive role, however much they defined the situation as predictable or selectively focused perception on the adjustment

---

2. There were about six workers in the mine who came from a nearby Indian reservation.

possibilities. They still consigned the miner to the mercy of natural forces; he might be watchful for their signs, but was impotent to alter the tragic events they foretold. Was there, though, anything the men did that placed their safety in their own hands, and which imparted a feeling that they could control their own fate?

The Propping Complex

Once the question is raised, the answer is obvious. The miners propped up the roof. Propping consists of the following operations: The men take a log, previously cut to standardized sizes, and steady it on the ground. Then a wedge-shaped piece of wood will be hammered tightly into the space between the roof and the upper part of the prop. Paradoxically, those parts of the mine which were most intensely worked were also most sparsely propped. The miners explained that if they propped close to where they were working, the props would get in their way and they could not work.

The prop, of course, did not only safeguard the miner's physical safety, but also served the important psychological function of enhancing the miner's feeling of control over his situation and his sense of security. Partly for this reason, the propping complex was interwoven with elements of folklore. These mythical elements are not altogether different from those which "primitive" people use to extol the unique potency of their tribal medicine man's "charm." For example, the miners liked to recount stories about narrow escapes which hinge on the presence or absence of a single prop. One story was told about the "last" prop in a mine which was so potent that after it was removed the entire mine caved in, from the ground down.

The above story indicates that miners tended to think of the prop as *holding back* the roof. There can be no doubt that props can hold back some relatively small rocks which would otherwise hurt the miner. Mining engineers, however, said that props could not hold back a serious cave-in, and that the prop's main function was to give warning of an imminent fall. The prop may do this by visibly bulging and spreading at the top, when the roof begins to settle on it and applies pressure. But the ordinary miner emphasized the holding and controlling, rather than the warning function of the prop.

Like primitive people boastful of their witch doctor's powerful magic, the miners wove a network of folklore about their prop man's personal prowess. In particular, they most enjoyed talking about his physical strength. One tale about a prop man related how he and his wife were once spending their evening in a local tavern. Two fellows were said to have "tried to make her," whereupon the outraged prop man smashed them both to the floor with a few well placed blows.

The prop man exhibited his strength daily, as he hammered in the wedge over the prop with long, powerful blows. Occasionally the men stopped work to watch him perform, and would turn to each other and make appreciative comments about his strength and skill. The miners expected that the prop man should be powerfully built and obviously muscular, for in a sense, they conceived of him as an Atlas who held up the roof. "The prop man has to be a strong fellow," said one miner, "the strongest one we've got." Should a miner without the requisite physique apply for the job as prop man, the others would "kid him out of it" and discourage him.

The prop man's efforts strengthened the miners' feelings that the unpredictable dangers of cave-ins could be controlled. He provided the miners not only with physical safety, but with psychological security as well. For this reason, the prop men were usually among the most popular men in the mine, and were regarded frequently as the most important members of the mining team. "We couldn't get to first base without these guys," said a miner. Because of these feelings, the miners had, during one period, repeatedly asked that the wages of prop men be raised. Top management, however, failed to recognize their genuinely important anxiety-allaying role. Management, as one executive explained, had to take into account the going rates for that type of work in the local area. Since management perceived the prop man solely in terms of his *formal* occupational responsibilities, it considered him entitled only to the comparatively low wages of an unskilled worker.

Typically, prop men learned their techniques in some informal apprenticeship, by working closely with and watching a regular prop man; they cling to and pass on the particular methods they have learned. An incident will illustrate the traditional attitude toward propping: A mechanically inclined "snowbird" had been reading a mining journal at the foot, when he noticed an advertisement for a new prop-setting machine. Upon returning to the face, he mentioned this to several miners, who refused to believe him. They insisted that the "snowbird" come back to the foot and show it to them. When the miners saw the advertisement, they looked at it in disbelief, and finally commented that it was not practical anyhow, and would require as much work as hand-propping.

If not actually impregnated with magical sentiments, the propping complex does seem to be functionally similar to magical ritual; for like magic and religion, propping also seems to "arise and function in situations of emotional stress: crises of life, lacunae in important pursuits . . . (and serves to) open up escapes from such situations and such impasses as offer no empirical way out . . .[3]

That the mine is a sphere somehow alien to the mainstream of contemporary industrial folkways is suggested by many surfacemen's wondering references to the miners as a "strange lot." They experienced the miners' deviance as beyond the normal range of non-conformity to which they had become

_____

3. Bronislaw Malinowski, *Magic, Science, and Religion,* Free Press, 1948, p. 67.

accustomed. This is, perhaps, part of what surfacemen meant when they said, "Miners live in another world."

The miner's strangeness derives, in no small measure, from his need to come to terms with a work environment harboring unpredictable and often uncontrollable dangers. This he accomplished by selectively focusing on the beneficent aspects of the surrounding natural forces, and by adhering to a received set of skills, the propping complex, which props up, not only the roof, but the miner's hope that he can master his environment.

Two Orientations: Custom vs. Efficiency

The miners' custom-rooted beliefs clearly contrasted with the more "up-to-date" and "rational" outlook of surfacemen. The surfacemen's work stories possessed little of the stereotyping of the miners' legends; moreover, surfacemen viewed the advent of new machinery in their sphere, at least in the early phases of its introduction, as the harbinger of new opportunities. They anticipated, in particular before Peele's arrival, that the new machines would bring greater chances of promotion for them. Byta, the union president, expressed a typical surface view when he said:

"Now with the expansion, chances for advancement are a little better. The new (board) machine will turn out 125 feet of board per minute . . . Now, there's some chance for advancement."

Furthermore, surfacemen liked the new machines because they permitted the plant to be kept cleaner, another status-enhancing property. Generally, miners were less likely to define technological changes as a promise for a better future, as the propping machine incident indicated. When new loading machines were first introduced into the mine, and did away with "mucking" (i.e., hand loading), they met with a mingled reaction, partly hostile. There were some suspicious old miners who adamantly refused to use them at all. On the surface, though, it was not uncommon for workers themselves to propose technological improvements. In these cases, suspicions centered on whether the Company would pay a proper cash reward for the suggestions.

There were, of course, traditionalistic attitudes toward production among surfacemen. In the main, though, these were directed at the *rate* of production, especially at a continually fluctuating rate, rather than at the actual procedures themselves. Certainly, the degree of rationalism was not uniform on the surface. The higher one went in the plant's authority system, for example, the more intense the rationalistic orientation. At the summit, the production manager in the main office expressed a crystalline rationalism. Asked whether he was, in general, satisfied with conditions at the Oscar Center plant, he replied:

"I'm not satisfied with conditions at any plant. Things could always be better."

In general, though, surface workers had more rationalistic attitudes toward production methods than miners. These basically different perspectives on top and bottom reflected themselves in the stereotypes with which mine and surface workers invidiously appraised each other. One surface supervisor presented a summary critique of the miners' work habits, and in so doing, revealed the values of his own group as well:

"*There is most absenteeism in the mine.* Elsewhere it is about even. (This is) mostly because of the class of people you have down there. There's more *drinking* done by the miner than by anyone else. You know, they also got about fifteen Indians down in the mine, too. *These fellows don't look ahead. They work for what they need, and when they make it, they knock off.* It's sort of a tradition with the miners to knock off now and then."

This picture, stripped of its moral overtones and exaggeration, is an essentially accurate portrayal of the modally different work motivations of miners and surfacemen. The miners' work motivation was ordinarily infused with a traditionalistic concern for maintaining his standard of living. He was less intent on accumulating material possessions, getting the latest model car, or impressing his neighbors with a well kept house. It was, for example, frequently possible to predict which houses in Oscar Center belonged to miners simply by noting their unpainted and unrepaired exteriors; this, despite the fact that miners' take-home pay always averaged higher than surfacemen's. Miners' work habits were more likely to be directed to the satisfaction of their immediate needs. Surfacemen, however, believed in "steady" work practices, and they insisted that money should be saved, "not burned up." They strove to have "something to show for their work" and to "put aside a bit for a rainy day." Of course, this is not to say that miners, unlike surfacemen, were disinterested in money. Both groups were, indeed, candidly interested in money. In fact, this was one source of their joint solidarity, which they sometimes deployed against management. But money *meant* something different to miners than it did to surfacemen. To surface workers, money connoted security, competitive advantage, and the wherewithal to live according to middle class standards. To the miner, however, money was a source of "independence," and an instrument for satisfying desires often *forbidden* by middle class values. If the surfaceman wanted to compete with and impress his neighbors by buying a new car, the miner preferred to "set one up for the boys." He wanted to be a *good* fellow, not a *better* one.

The surface workers' attitudes toward miners were embedded in strong feeling tones. It may be suspected that they were so zestfully critical, in part, because they were envious. The miner boozed, he gambled, he stole—"They would steal the eyes out of a dead man's face"—he whored around disgracefully, the surface stereotypes maintained. And in all this, the miners were held to be a brotherhood whose sins were all the more appealing, it may be guessed, because they were performed in unmarred solidarity:

"The miners are all for themselves, but they stick together to beat the Company. They always help each other. They always cover up for each other."

In short, the miners were viewed as acting out every desire which surfacemen had to check rigidly in the interests of middle class virtues such as security, competitive success, and respectability.

On the other hand, however, miners did not express an equally vehement deprecation of surface people. The miner had his complaints about those on top, but they were less tinged with moral indignation. One of the more interesting of the miner's critical conceptions was that the men on top failed to work as hard as they should. Miners often maintained that they could not bear to work on the surface because of the slow pace to which surface men adhered.

The above pages have broadly distinguished between miners' custom-oriented and surface workers' rationalistic belief systems, noting especially the greater importance of traditional and stereotyped patterns in the mine. These observations are merely one further confirmation of those made by Carter Goodrich some twenty-five years ago in his pioneering study in industrial sociology, *The Miner's Freedom*. As Goodrich then stated, ". . . the remark of a shrewd foreigner that 'custom predominates in coal mining more than any other industry' . . . has long been accurate in everything but its English." [4] Though the generation following Goodrich's study has seen the "cake of custom" begin to erode, these more recent

---

4. Marshall Jones Company, 1925, p. 115.

observations of gypsum miners indicate that it is still an essentially valid point in contrasting mine and factory workers.

Insulation of Mine and Surface

The foregoing comments have indicated a variety of tensions between miners and surfacemen. How were these held in check so that they were not a constant source of disruption?

The most prominent mechanism easing these strains seemed to be the mutual *insulation* of mining and surface workers, so that each had relatively little interaction with the other. The supervisor in the sample room stated this explicitly:

"The mine and surface workers have nothing to do with each other. Even back in town miners stick together and surface men stick together."

And a hopper worker echoed him:

"I don't know much about the mine. There's not much business between us and the miners. We don't have much in common with them."

This last comment suggests that one of the most effective insulating devices was the stereotypes that miners and factory workers held of each other. Surface stereotypes portrayed miners as a "lower class" of people, with whom they had little in common. Thus their motivation to interact with miners was weakened.

Another insulation between top and bottom was, of course, the physical barrier between the two work areas. It was comparatively easy, for a board worker to walk over to the mill or sample room, visit with the men there, and see what was going on. To get down to the mine, however, he had to descend a lengthy staircase whose crude construction compelled slow movement. By the time he returned to his work place he might have aroused his foreman's ire for having been gone too long.

A trip to the surface, for the miner at the face, was practically impossible for much the same reasons. The miner would
have had to get to the foot of the mine, usually by walking
through the long tunnel, before he could ascend to the surface.
Moreover, the miner at the face was a closely integrated member of a mine team which depended upon him continually.
His absence would have been noticed almost immediately.
While most surface workers did not work in such tight inter-
dependence with others, many of them were reluctant to visit
the mine, even when time permitted, because of their fear of
unfamiliar mine dangers.

There were other ways in which the mine and surface were
effectively segregated. One of these was the separate seniority
system for each work division. A worker accumulated seniority
only in one sphere, either the mine or surface, but not in both.
If, for example, a mine worker bid for and obtained a surface
job he lost whatever seniority he had acquired in the mine,
and had to start at the bottom of the surface's seniority list.
The same was also true for a surface man transferring to the
mine.

Finally, the differential residential patterns maintained by
miners and surfacemen also served to segregate them from each
other. Miners tended to live in or around Tyre, a comparatively larger community in the immediate area, while surface
workers were more randomly spread throughout the vicinity,
with some concentration in Oscar Center. Thus, even in their
leisure hours, it was easier for miners to interact with other
miners than with surfacemen.

This segregation of miners and surfacemen was commonly
recognized in the plant. Though largely due to the differences
in their value systems, the insulation of miners and surface
workers, in its turn, reinforced and maintained these differences. This insulation was a mutual, two-way affair. If the surface workers were thereby guarded against contagious contact

with miners' traditional beliefs, so, too, were the miners secured against infection from surfacemen's rationalistic and middle class orientations.

Informal Solidarity

A differentiating factor most readily observable in the mine,
but relatively undeveloped on the top, was informal group
solidarity. The miners' comparatively greater solidarity was expressed by a number of their characteristic modes of behavior.

If, for example, a miner fell ill or was injured, his friends
would, quite commonly, go around to other miners, even to
those on another shift, to get up a collection to help him out.
No parallel actions on the part of surfacemen were observed.

Again, if a miner was seriously injured by a falling rock,
the miners, like those in bituminous coal, would often drop
tools and walk off the job. This unprompted group action expressed a complexity of sentiments: fear, hostility toward the
Company and, also, solidarity with the injured worker. Spontaneous group action of this sort would seem to indicate a high
degree of informal cohesion.

Nicknames

The tensility of their informal relations was also suggested
by the many colorful nicknames and diminutives which miners
sported. The head of the mine was known as "Old Bull," while
others were called "Boysie," "Blackie," "Woodchuck," "Gorgeous," "Spider," "The Whistler," "Stocha," "Old Jack,"
"Moonbeam," "Chief," "Big Spike," "Little Spike," "Butterfly," "Luke," and "Yo-Yo."

In the mine, a worker would sometimes be called by a
pseudonym; for example, "Nick's" real name was Jacob. In one
case, a man's real name was used almost as if it were a nick-
name; Benjamin Neal, for example, was usually called "Benjamin Neal!"

Nicknames were most often given miners because of some evident peculiarity of speech, behavior, or appearance. "Boysie" received his name because of his habit of calling everyone "Boysie." "Butterfly" was so called since he weighed 250 pounds, while "Gorgeous" was one of the ugliest men in the plant. Nicknames were much more frequently used in the mine than on the surface. The point is that nicknames were almost always bestowed by the miners themselves. They served to integrate the worker into the informal group, signifying that his coworkers had taken cognizance of him as a distinctive individual. Often the nicknames constituted references to intimate or personal qualities, which in a more formal atmosphere would have been considered out of place. As such they testified to the presence of strongly knit mining groups, whose ties were firm enough to accept and cope with aggressive joking.

When questioned about the things which they "like most" about the mine, miners would frequently reply, "The group of fellows I'm working with." Or, as the shuttle-buggy operator answered the question, "I like the fellows. They're all cheerful and full of hell. When anything goes wrong they all pitch in and help." Miners placed a greater premium on spontaneous and informal relations with people, while surfacemen were more often concerned about their associate's status-enhancing qualities, and were seemingly less certain that informal ties would be binding and stable. When, for example, miners were asked what personal qualities they prefer in their friends, they tended to answer: good workers, those who help you, work together well, are not pikers, and are friendly, good-natured guys. More typically, surface workers wanted their friends to be: honest, fair or just, clean and loyal.

When asked what kind of men they did *not* like, surface workers were more apt to say, "suckholes," that is, people who defer to and seek approval from a superior by carrying tales. Miners were decidedly less fearful of the "suckhole." This is a further suggestion that informal ties on the surface were less potent than they were in the mine. In a similar vein, Wilbert Moore has written: "A rule clearly designed as a security measure is the very general practice of condemning the 'tattler,' 'stool pigeon,' or 'squealer,' as he is variously called. But the no squealing rule is not simply a device for protecting the individuals from supervisory discipline; it is a mark of loyalty to the informal group." [5] Fear of the "suckhole" indicates, that the informal group on the surface was encountering difficulties in extracting conformity from its members.

In the main, two factors were closely connected with the greater cohesion among miners: (1) The peculiar work and spatial arrangements in the mine and factory. (2) The more hazardous working conditions of the mine.

Spatial Arrangements

The spatial arrangements in the key and typical building on the surface, the board plant, were largely determined by the hopper, conveyor, knife, and the bundler at the take-off end. These arrangements allowed only for small potential informal groups. One of these, composed of four persons, two edge men, the hopper man and the paper man, was at the beginning of the conveyor. There was another potential informal group composed of the knife man, kiln man, and a fireman. Another group centering around the terminal point at the take-off was also possible.

At the beginning of the conveyor, the work arrangements inhibited informal interaction while at work. While the hopper man was working he was somewhat separated from the others. The steady flow of the mixture made constant demands on his attention. He used several tools to guide the stucco, or mixture, evenly between two rolls of heavy paper which screened him

5. W. Moore, *Industrial Relations and the Social Order,* The Macmillan Co., N. Y., Rev. Ed., 1951, p. 292.

from the two edge men and the paper man. The two edge men, however, worked together closely enough to allow informal interaction. Nevertheless, the hopper's comments imply that there was actually little informal cohesion in this group:

"I worked with a guy who couldn't work well. This fellow and the foreman were good buddies. They were always together, during work and after."

Furthermore, the hopper's group was directly in front of the superintendent's office. The superintendent, who the men point out was "around quite a bit," considerably affected their situation.

At the transfer point, where the lathe was cut up and shuttled over to the kiln, the knife man occasionally contacted the fireman and the kiln man. But the knife man's comments note that these contacts were infrequent:

"My only contact was with the fireman and the kiln man. Occasionally, the foreman comes down, and now and then I see the inspector. The job is a lonesome job and very monotonous. You don't get a chance to talk to the men way down here. I would like to get up and talk with the other men, but I don't get the chance. So I pick up a magazine to help pass the time."

Of the several groups in the board plant, the one at the take-off end possessed the highest degree of informal cohesion. The men expressed considerable liking for each other, and had originally taken their jobs in this plant at each other's recommendations. Their cohesion seemed to spring from their similarity of age and comparative youth. Relative to other board plant workers, they were the group with the lowest average age, being around twenty-one. None of the "take-off" workers were more than three years younger or older than twenty-one, thus lending their group a certain homogeneity. This homogeneity was reinforced by the fact that several of them had recently graduated from the same high school. They ate together on the job, and saw each other frequently after work, unlike many of the older surface workers who had long since acquired family responsibilities and interests which consumed their leisure hours.

Unlike most workers in the board plant, members of the mining teams usually worked together in closest association. The size of their work group was larger, their rate of interaction more intensive, and their expectations of informal work reciprocities were more pronounced. As to the size of their teams, the typical mine group was composed of seven men, compared with the maximum of four or five on the top. The nature of their work permitted them a greater degree of discretion. Since they themselves determined the speed at which they worked, the rest pauses they would take, and the strategy of digging the gyp out and propping the roof, the miners were in more constant communication with each other. Occasions requiring some joint decision occurred more frequently. On the surface, though, and especially in the board plant, the workers went through their routine at a rate determined by the machines which, in turn, was set by the plant superintendent without the men's participation.

Even if miners were as easily intimidated by the presence of their supervisors as were the factory workers, supervisors in the mine were simply not around long enough to inhibit the miners' informal relations. The mine had two operating points and there was only one foreman to cover these two areas, which were separated by a five to ten minute walk. Under any circumstances, one point was not supervised approximately half of the time. This was qualified by the fact that the foreman might not even spend the whole day at the face, while the mine superintendent customarily circulated through the mine about once a day. Thus the spatial arrangements of the mine were a factor to be reckoned with, in accounting for the miners' higher degree of informal solidarity.

Danger and Solidarity

The imminence and awareness of dangers in the mine enabled the group to put forth demands for solidarity, and provided ready justification for their enforcement. The focus on danger in the mine allowed cohesion-disrupting behavior to be constrained, in the *name of special safety* requirements. This may be glimpsed from the following:

"One man used to throw rocks at the cap of the man in front of him. It's dark and he could hear them clink. We told him it could put his eye out. He didn't realize it. You *have* to work together. You can't have one part against another. Of course, up there (on the surface) it doesn't matter."

A discussion with a shuttle-buggy operator indicated some of the control mechanisms which the miners used to handle deviants:

"What do you do when a guy has 'bad spells' pretty often?"
"We make it so hard for him he quits."
"How do you make it hard for him?"
"We don't help him when he needs it. We don't talk to him."

Ostracism and isolation were a much more disturbing experience to the deviant in the darkened mine than to a worker in the well lighted surface factory.

The miner had to rely on his co-workers to warn him of loose rocks, impending falls, or to dig him out speedily in the event of a cave-in. These were dangers which had no counterpart, in kind or intensity, on the surface. Thus, while the miners' control mechanisms were no different than those available to surfacemen, the miner might nevertheless use them with greater effect. As one old miner said, in the mine "Friends or no friends, you *got* all to be friends."

Not only did the dangers in the mine provide a ready

rationale for informal solidarity on the job, but there also were indications that these hazards permitted the miners a greater degree of out-of-plant sociability. The miners were not, of course, the "hellers" that the surfacemen made them out to be. There were, however, a group of miners who spent many evenings out "with the boys." They did this despite the fact that they were married and potentially subject to conventional family pressures. These miners could *evade* their family obligations more readily than could the married surface workers. This took the form of claiming that the difficulties and dangers of their work entitled them to special liberties. As one mill worker suggested:

"Miners may be heavy drinkers. Lots of them drink pretty heavy."
"Why do you think this is so?"
"Because they work hard and think they *earn the right* to spend some of their money."
"Don't their wives mind?"
"The wives don't argue. The miners are tough birds. They (the wives) have to take it."

The dangers and difficulties of mine work allowed miners to feel that they were engaged in a "manly" role and to lay effective claims to being "boss" in their own homes. The miners knew that their wives, particularly those of them who have had contact with coal mining, were well aware of the dangers in the mine and were fearful for their husbands' safety. As the shuttle-buggy operator stated:

"My wife doesn't like me to work in the mine. She is going to have a baby any day now. Maybe today. Coal mines where I used to work really scared her. She can't see much difference between them and this one."

Miners could, therefore, put forth more persuasive demands for special privileges, such as the convivial satisfactions of nearby taverns, which husbands in other occupations would be compelled to forego.

In summary, then, it has been noted that miners were members of stronger and more solidary informal groups, and that the greater cohesion of the miners was, in part, traceable to their distinctive working arrangements, and their more hazardous conditions of work.

The differences in the belief systems and informal social organization among miners and surfacemen coincided with variations in their personality structures. In general, miners were more "extroverted," spontaneous people of a highly "independent" bent. Contrasted with the average surface worker, who was more inhibited and repressed, the miners were somewhat more given to drinking, swearing, and gambling. The surface workers' frequent criticisms of the miners' drinking and profanity suggest their own greater possession of a middle class "conscience."

These differences between miners' and surfacemen's personalities were expressed even in their habits of dress. The miners, for example, rarely patched their work clothes. When they became too tattered for further use, miners simply heaved them into a corner of their locker room. Surface workers who had been recently transferred to the mine could often, however, be spotted by the careful patches on their clothing.

There were, too, definite indications that miners tended to allow themselves more ready expression of open aggression. Surfacemen, though, usually contained their hostilities, refusing them open manifestation. Finally, as was also noted earlier, surfacemen had a more passive attitude toward authority, while miners were more capable of expressing disagreements with or aggression toward authority.

Chapter VIII

MOTIVATION ON TOP

AND BOTTOM

IN THE DISCUSSION OF
the successor it was emphasized that bureaucratic patterns were
either initiated or ratified by strategic personnel in the organization. It was suggested, further, that the "successor" was motivated to extend bureaucratic methods when he developed a
specific conception of his subordinates, namely, when he lost
trust in them and defined them as failing to perform their role-
obligations. That the unequal development of bureaucracy in
the mine and on the surface might have been accompanied by
different conceptions of the role-performance or motivation of
miners and factory workers is, therefore, to be expected.

In considering one aspect of the worker's motivation, his

137

willingness to do the job, it may be asked: Were there any differences in the way in which miners and surface workers were looked upon as *producers?*

"The Miners Work Hard"

Typically, miners were seen as highly motivated to work; this was frequently expressed by workers in the following way:

"The miners make a lot of money, but they deserve it. *They work hard* and under a dangerous roof."

A crusher operator, new to the mine and still judging it in terms of surface standards said:

"A guy can only work just so fast. I could work faster, but the guys out in the mine (face), they are working as fast as they can. Did you ever watch them? They work right through with no lunch sometimes."

Contrasting top and bottom work patterns, a car trimmer in the mine claimed:

"Down here, they're a little more peppier. They seem to have a little more energy. The guys on the top look lazy and groggy. They seem to work slower."

Not only did the miners believe that they worked faster than men on the top, but they also insisted that they worked *better.* A mine mechanic, for example, complained that skill and quality-work were becoming extinct on the surface:

"One time when they posted a job, it was more than seniority that counted. Quality counted, too. It's still that way down here. On top, I guess it's getting to be just seniority."

Mining supervisors never complained about their workers' willingness to work. On the contrary, they typically volunteered expressions of confidence in the miners' motivation. As one of the mining foremen said:

"I think they (the miners) should be given the chance to show initiative. Here in the mine we give the man a job to do and he does it without being watched . . . The men have to do a job themselves. They're not controlled."

Surface supervisors, however, frequently complained about workers who wandered away from their jobs or hid out somewhere. One board plant foreman charged:

"You have to watch the men; some of them would sneak away and go to sleep if you let them."

Another, a wet-end foreman, told about a worker who had given him some trouble:

"One fellow wanted to sleep quite a bit. I talked to him two or three times and told him finally that he'd change or else it meant his job . . . A worker should stay on the job and take care of his business."

In fine, then, supervisors on top and bottom viewed their subordinate's work motivation quite differently. Those on top were highly critical of the workers, expecting them to "goldbrick" at the first opportunity; those in the mine manifested considerable confidence in their workers' willingness to produce. There is reason to believe that these different appraisals were in rough, but substantial, accord with the actual differences in motivation among miners and surface workers. This may be illustrated by two observational reports made by members of the research team. The first, reporting on miners' work patterns in an ordinary situation, indicated a high readiness to work:

I observe Chuck as he is working and he presents a pretty demonstration of a capable prop man. He works *briskly,* setting up three or four props in succession, hammering in the wedges with *powerful* drives. He then *grabs* his bar and tests the roof at several places, pulling down some pieces of loose rock. Next he checks the entire area *quickly* by walking around it and looking for bad spots. The shuttle-buggy comes up with some more props and Chuck yells at him, "You're my buddy!" The other replies, "Do the same for you some time." Every time the shuttle-buggy operator rode in, he was either *whistling* or *singing*. Chuck comes over to me, lights a cigarette, and says, "I used to work at Curtis, but I couldn't stand the job. *It was too easy.* There was *not enough to do.* The work here is more interesting, more variety." Chuck looks over at the shuttle-buggy as it pulls in again. "There's action for you," he says.

What is noteworthy here is that even the routine conduct of work in the mine was described with words freighted with implications of high motivation; e. g., "briskly," "powerful," "grabs," "quickly," "whistling," "singing," etc. On the surface, though, even when an emergency occurred many workers showed but little motivation. Thus one member of the research team described a production crisis in the board plant:

There was a break-down at the wet-end today. The older men scurry all over. The younger men *relax* and *make jokes.* They lean across the board machine and *talk with each other* in clusters. The foremen, though, work hard. One of the younger men *jokingly* pushes the button that lets loose a sharp whistle against the flat blast of the emergency buzzer. A foreman hustles down from the mixer. He asks, "Who done it?" One of the youths swiftly points an accusing finger at the chubby lad who is talking to him.

The above observations reveal several things already noted: The tense relations between supervisors and workers, and the low degree of informal solidarity and readiness to "squeal" among surface workers. Most relevantly, however, there was the suggestion that energetic and cooperative work efforts on the surface were not even brought about by an emergency situation. Needless to say, the situation in the mine reflected an even higher than usual degree of motivation [1] when an emer-

---

1. While this study need assume no obligation to account for the miners' high work motivation, one distinctive element which seemed to contribute to it may be mentioned. This involved the fact that miners were not "alienated" from their machines; that is, they had an unusually high degree of control over

gency occurred there. As one mine mechanic very proudly stated:

"Last week, when they had the cave-in, I worked seventeen hours straight. *But that was an emergency, and everybody helps out then.*"

Absenteeism: The Motivational Problem in the Mine

Though the miners were motivated to work, and were viewed as such, it does not follow that they were seen as equally anxious to obey. Instead, as discussion of the surfacemen's stereotypes of miners indicated, miners were viewed as somewhat undependable role-performers, given to periodic and unpredictable absenteeism. The general estimate of the miners was that when they worked, they worked hard. But it was not always sure that they would be there to work. The main problem in the mine, therefore, as consciously seen by most partici-

---

their machine's operation. The pace at which the machines worked, the corners into which they were poked, what happened to them when they broke down, was determined mainly by the miners themselves. On the surface, though, the speed at which the machines worked and the procedures followed were prescribed by superiors. The situation that occurred when a machine broke down seems especially indicative of the mastery that miners had over the technological facets of their work situation. When this occurred, everyone "pitched in." The miners did much of their own machine repair work and, unlike surface workers, did not wait for someone else, usually the maintenance men, to come and do it for them. Roethlisberger and Dickson's account of the classic Western Electric studies emphasizes that productivity is a function of the degree of participation which workers have in decisions affecting their own activities. Work at the Survey Research Center of the Unversity of Michigan also concludes that productivity is a function of the degree and extent of participation. See, John French, "Group Productivity" in H. Guetzkow (ed.), *Groups, Leadership and Men,* Carnegie University Press, 1951. It seems probable, therefore, that the miners' control over their own repair work was a distinctive factor enhancing their work motivation. Usually, in modern large-scale industry, the men who repair and the men who customarily use machines are two different groups. Thus the production worker's chance to gain an intimate familiarity with his machine is limited. When the machine breaks down, he may feel himself at the mercy of an unpredictable and uncontrollable mechanism. The conventional insistence that the worker should wait for the maintenance men to do his repairs would seem to encourage a passive attitude toward production, sapping work motivation and thereby diminishing any gains which a division of labor between maintenance and operating personnel are intended to promote.

pants in the plant, was the rate of absenteeism. As one of the mining foremen remarked:

"There's some fellows who are always taking off. A lot of men are in that class. They just don't care about having anything. They only come in four or five days in the week. You can't run a plant like that."

Did this perception of the undependability of the miners' work *attendance* arouse bureaucratic efforts, which our hypothesis as presently formulated would imply, and if not, why not? An illuminating example was the case of the "no-absenteeism" rule. Supervisors in the mine did, at first, attempt to enforce this rule. Very shortly thereafter, however, they bowed to strong informal opposition and declared that this rule just could not be enforced in the mine. In other words, they did not view strict rule enforcement as an expedient solution to the problem. This suggests the following modification in our original hypothesis: Even if supervisors see subordinates as failing in the performance of their role-obligations, the adoption of bureaucratic solutions will depend, in part, upon an estimate of whether they will *work*. The mine supervisors had to ask themselves, would the introduction of bureaucratic discipline into the mines, and an emphasis on strict conformity to work regulations, *succeed here?*

There were important features of the mining situation which made supervisors decide that question in the negative. One of these was the recurrent experiences which they had had with miners' ability to resist stubbornly. For example, when the new machines were introduced into the mine, and when some older miners refused to use them, management felt it was the better part of wisdom to refrain from trying coercion. These older miners capitulated only after they saw that others who used them made more money.

Another factor inhibiting management's use of bureaucratic discipline was the standard conception which it had come to develop concerning the miners. Among top management and in the main office, miners were widely seen as "tough birds"; as a group of men with "guts" or "nerve," who could not be "pushed around." One main office executive, wishing to illustrate just how tough an executive in another company was, told how this man had browbeaten a union executive who once had been a miner. He concluded his story by saying, "And you know how tough miners are!" Moreover, main office executives and top plant management ambivalently recounted stories about old miners who disregarded the Company's lines of communication, and demanded to see the president of the Company directly, when they had a grievance.

This image of the miners as a hard-bitten crew, who refused to play ball according to the modern rules of the game, made management feel it unwise to tamper with the miners' established work customs or to subject them to close, bureaucratic control. Management's conception of the miners encouraged them to accept the *status quo* in the mine, *forestalling* efforts at bureaucratization, however desirable these might seem.

It was not merely, however, the mine supervisors' belief that bureaucratic methods might be unworkable that inhibited them from using such methods. The mine supervisors, like their men, defined the mine as an unusually dangerous place of work and believed that men were entitled to special privileges when operating in such a setting. Mine foremen generally felt that mine hazards placed workers under special strains to which deviant behavior, e. g., heavy drinking, or absenteeism, was a permissable form of adaptation. One mine foreman put it in this way:

"They're pretty heavy spenders. They go out drinking. *Maybe they have to, to keep going.*"

This belief undermined the supervisor's conviction that (what was widely termed) the miners' "independence" deserved correction. In fact, the very label used to characterize the miners' failure to conform to conventional occupational demands, namely, "independence," signified that it was not viewed as entirely bad, but had certain commendable features seen as appropriate to their situation.

The supervisor in the mine who demanded unquestioning obedience, either to a set of general rules or to his personal orders, would have had to accept the responsibility for injuries or loss of life which might result. Since the mine supervisors were so closely identified with their men, this was difficult to do. Once, for example, when Old Bull was asked what he liked most about the mine, he blurted:

"By God, I *don't* like it! Once you get in, it's hard to get out. I've been getting out for twenty years now. *It's on your nerves all the time. It's God-damned hard to see them carry a man out."*

The industrial supervisor in a modern, private enterprise is not asking his men to risk their lives on behalf of a communal and higher goal. He cannot command his men, in the manner of a military commander in the field, to die for the "defense of the country." The mine supervisor, therefore, found it difficult to justify to his conscience, or to his subordinates, demands for conformance to rules or orders which workers claimed were dangerous.

In general, definition of the mine as an emergency-packed, dangerous place not only generated legitimations for avoidance of authority and rules by *workers,* but it also cast doubts among *supervisors* that increased bureaucratic discipline was a permissible way of solving their problems. In other words, even if a supervisor sees his subordinates as unmotivated to perform their roles, the solution he will adopt depends, in part, on whether he views this solution as legitimate. The question he has to answer is not the general one, "Are bureaucratic methods justifiable?" In brief, strategic personnel did not automatically utilize bureaucratic solutions when they perceived their subordinates as failing to perform their work obligations. They must first define bureaucratic methods as both expedient and legitimate in the situation which they face.[2]

Recapitulation

In short, the relationship between bureaucratization and management's perception of inadequate role-performance among subordinates is observable in other, more general situations than that of succession. Specifically, it was found that the mine's lesser degree of bureaucratization went together with managerial perception of the miners as more highly motivated to work than surfacemen. It was possible, however, to extend and refine the original hypothesis in the following ways:

Originally, it was indicated that management was motivated to extend bureaucracy when they perceived their subordinates as unwilling to fill their role-obligations. In the present section, other conditions leading to efforts at bureaucratization became apparent.

These were that:

Management must conceive of bureaucratic solutions as:

A. *Legitimate* in the particular type of situation involved. It may *not* be assumed that managerial personnel will always view bureaucratic methods as appropriate and justifiable under all circumstances. Moreover, management must view bureaucratic solutions as

---

2. We suspect that the reason our research team initially believed that bureaucratic solutions would not and could not work in the mine was because we vaguely perceived that the danger elements in the situation provided an effective escape clause from bureaucratic pressure. We also felt that the miner just "wouldn't take that sort of stuff." Our own response to the mining situation was useful because it suggested the possibility that other people in the situation, significant persons whose outlook could affect the organization of the mine, would see it as we did.

B. *Effective.* It cannot be taken for granted that management be-
lieves bureaucracy to be a universally successful problem-solution. Under certain conditions, management might like to
increase bureaucratization, and might even think this permissible or legitimate, but might *not* think it *expedient* to do so.
Management's judgments about the legitimacy and effectiveness
of a problem solution are not, of course, necessarily identical.
That is, management may define a solution in one way, say as
legitimate, without necessarily believing it to be effective.

Barriers to Bureaucracy

Even though management defines bureaucratic measures as
both legitimate and effective it may, nevertheless, be unable to
implement these patterns. There is, of course, a vast difference
between intentions and deeds, and it is necessary to consider
the factors which either allow these intentions to become organizational realities or which frustrate them. What conditions
either thwarted or aided managerial personnel in realizing
bureaucratic aims? The objective of this section is to show
how each of the factors in terms of which mine and surface
have been differentiated—their physical dangers, their informal
social cohesion, and their value and belief systems—bear upon
the development of bureaucracy.

The Miners' Belief System

In a general way, the miners' belief system can be seen as an
impediment to bureaucratization, largely because it was weighted
with traditionalistic emphases. Rational action and purposively
planned change are an important, though by no means the
sole component of bureaucracy. The miners' custom-anchored
behavior was deeply resistant to change, but bureaucracy is pre-
eminently part of a secular world and made for everyday
changing needs.

One specific part of the miners' belief system was especially
noteworthy: the widely held and deeply internalized belief

that "down here we are our own bosses." Insofar as bureaucracy involves submission to centralized authority and careful conformance to the lines of authority, its introduction into the mine would have violated this express and salient value on local autonomy. These beliefs assume importance because the introduction of bureaucracy into the mine would have violated them and mobilized the miners' resistance.

Two factors in particular reinforced the miners' loyalty to a set of beliefs in whose framework bureaucracy was anathema. The first of these, the mutual insulation of surfacemen and miners, has already been outlined. To the extent that these groups were mutually segregated, miners had comparatively little contact with the rationalistic and efficiency-favoring values more common among surfacemen. There were fewer individuals who could serve as models facilitating the miners' socialization into a rationalistic perspective. There were fewer interpersonal relations in which the miner's deviant behavior and outlook would receive disapproval and discouragement.

Moreover, since the board plant in particular, and surface jobs in general, were the main avenues to promotion in the Company, the miners had relatively little incentive to adhere to the beliefs of surfacemen.[3] Top management saw the production of *board,* not the mining of gypsum ore, as its major task. The board machine was viewed as the plant's "vital

---

3. It may be suggested that different kinds of incentives have different consequences for what Robert Merton has called "anticipatory socialization." Anticipatory socialization consists of practicing or taking over the beliefs and values of a group in which the individual is not a member but of which he aspires to become a member. See Robert K. Merton and Alice Kitt, "Contributions to the Theory of Reference Group Behavior," in R. K. Merton and P. F. Lazarsfeld, *Studies in the Scope and Method of "The American Soldier,"* Free Press, 1950, pp. 87-91. Thus accessibility of promotions, or the mobility rate, with which surface workers seem more concerned, would appear to be an incentive more likely to promote anticipatory socialization than wage increases, on which miners are more likely to focus. This squares with the common observation that orientation toward wage increases is more likely to be functional for a working group's solidarity than orientation to promotional opportunities.

organ," as its "money maker." As a member of the main office administrative staff pointed out:

"The board plant brings in the money. You see, that (gypsum board) is our main commodity. We can and do have board plants without mines."

The miners, then, had less interaction with people who were oriented to values which would accept bureaucratic patterns as congenial, and they had less motivation of an expedient, self-gaining sort, to adopt these values.

Mine Hazards

If the miners' distinctive beliefs impeded the introduction of bureaucracy into the mine, and engendered morally indignant resistance to it, there was one characteristic feature of the mine which could be used to legitimate and justify their resistance. This was the recognized danger of the mine as a place of work. Among the plant workers, and, likely, in larger reaches of our society, there is a far-going belief that men under stress, or in imminent danger, had certain social immunities denied them in ordinary situations. They were viewed as entitled to privileges not available to other men, such as those on the surface, who pursued safer routines. This belief provided the miners with a powerful justification for resisting work rules, or the authority of their supervisors. The comments of a shuttle-buggy operator reveal this:

"If a man is watching himself, he doesn't go into a place where the roof is bad. *He just refuses to go, even if the foreman tells him to.*"

The miner felt that he could resist authority in a situation involving danger to himself; he did not believe that foremen could legitimately order him to do something which might result in injury. Stated differently, miners maintained that a foreman's authority might be justifiably challenged if he asked a man to do something dangerous. As one joy-operator said, "A man should do what he's told (by a foreman) *unless he thinks it will endanger his life."* [4]

Similarly, mine dangers were also used to excuse the miners' absenteeism. As a shuttle-buggy operator claimed:

"Men don't stay out too often, because they have families to support. Once in a while, a guy does get drunk and can't make it to work the next morning. Sometimes if the men are too tired because of the 'night before' *they might get hurt at work, so they stay at home."*

Or, as a painter on the surface remarked:

"They can't stop the miners taking off. The men get their pay and take off. *Hell, it's no fun working in the mine. Too much danger. I don't blame them."*

Not only were safety conditions believed to justify absenteeism, but dangers in the mine placed workers under pressure from which they were held to be *entitled* to some occasional "release." This came out clearly in the comments of an ex-miner who, because of his advanced age, was now working in the sample room. He explained simply, "Miners get drunk due to conditions of work."

In sum, the physical dangers of the mine operated as an "escape clause," allowing miners to claim exemption from supervisory authority, from certain work rules, and from the demands of middle class morality. Definition of the mining situation as particularly perilous permitted miners to legitimate resistance to authority and to the disciplined control so

---

4. Carter Goodrich refers to an arbitration hearing involving two miners who had refused to obey their supervisors, on the ground that they were being ordered to work in an unsafe place. The union representative defended the men, declaring, " 'By heavens . . . I would not let any mine superintendent or mine foreman determine for me whether my life was safe to work in a place or not:' and it was on this appeal to the logic of individual rights that the union won the decision for the men." Ibid., p. 74.

crucial to bureaucratic administration. As Max Weber recognized, bureaucracy is a method for the administration of routine affairs, or at least for problems deemed routine. The mine, though, because of the imminence of dangers within it, was viewed as a place of everpresent "emergencies."

Not only did the physical dangers of the mine legitimate the resistance to bureaucratic methods, but they also enabled this resistance to be more *effective*. The widely spread awareness of hazards in the mine had an impact on the available supply of labor. For one thing, it made it more difficult to recruit replacements for miners from among surfacemen. An edge man expressed the attitude of many surfacemen when he said:

"They take a lot of risk down there in the mine . . . I don't think any of them are too crazy about it. Some of them go down for six months and then come back up on top. It scares me; I wouldn't go down there."

This standard view of the mine depressed the upper limit of the labor supply willing to work there. In that way, therefore, the danger in the mine bolstered miners' powers of resistance to changes in their work situation. (A similar depressant on the labor supply was the low prestige accorded miners among surfacemen. In the communities from which they came, the miners were often contemptuously called "groundhogs.")

Informal Social Cohesion

If the miner's beliefs mobilized his resistance to bureaucratic methods, if the dangers of the mine legitimated and bolstered that resistance, the specific instrument which organized and disciplined it was the miners' informal social cohesion. The miners' solidarity provided them with an effective agency for defeating innovations which they disliked; an agency unmatched by anything found among the surfacemen.

In an effort to reduce absenteeism in the mine, for example, management had decreed that those who were absent without permission, or a "good excuse," would be laid off for the same number of days that they had taken. Far from inhibiting absenteeism, this rule actually encouraged it in the mine, for the miners took the regulation as a direct challenge. When several miners had been penalized in the specified way, others would deliberately take off without excuses. The result was that the number of absentees in any team was greater than usual, and the team would be unable to function.[5] Clearly the success of this resistance rested on the coordinated action of the miners, their mutual aid and solidarity in the face of Company action.

The strength of the miners' cohesion and the value they placed upon it allowed the miners to demand, and to implement the demand, that supervisors become informally integrated in their group. Thus it was not long after the miners began to resist the no-absenteeism prescription that their feelings were echoed by the head of the mine, "Old Bull," who berated the rule as "red tape" and complained:

"If we laid off a man for absenteeism, we'd have to lay off four or five all the time."

Unlike the miners, the typical security technique employed by surfacemen was the development of impersonal relations with foremen, with the object of insuring "impartial treat-

---

5. Some studies in industrial sociology have advanced the proposition that absenteeism is inversely correlated with the degree of informal solidarity. It may be suspected that this is an orientation deriving, in part, from the sanguine hope that the informal group will prove to be a sociological penicillin, curing all social ailments. Actually, however, as our comments about the *traditionalism* of miners' absenteeism underscore, a high absentee rate may go *together with* high informal social cohesion when absenteeism is a *group value*. Previous studies, limited to factory workers, could not, I suppose, conceive of workers who *valued* absenteeism. For a study of this type see Elton Mayo and George Lombard, *Teamwork and Labor Turnover in the Aircraft Industry of Southern California*, Publication of the Graduate School of Business Administration, Harvard University, October, 1944.

ment." As one surface worker indicated, the good foreman is "very level-headed and doesn't get excited when a guy makes a mistake; if the foreman is nice and friendly, *but not too friendly*, he's good." Another surface worker, this one a mechanic, remarked: "The idea is *not to be too sociable* with the foremen. Just get your work done and get out."

A truck driver elaborated on this point:

"Some of the foremen are soreheads. They should be *diplomatic*, a father to the men. They should be *fair, impartial*."

If surfacemen preferred to keep their distance from their supervisors, and conceived of a good foreman as an impartial "father," miners, by analogy, preferred their supervisors to be "brothers." The miners' security technique was to bind the mine foremen's hands with informal group ties. As one miner said:

"Take 'Old Bull'. He doesn't take the attitude he's a big shot. The men like 'Old Bull' . . . they're chums, they go bowling together; he sticks to the fellows."

The expectations of surfacemen regarding the kind of foremen they desired corresponded more closely to the conventional picture of the "neutral" foreman. The miners, however, desired an individual better integrated into the informal groups. By and large, the supervisors on top and bottom conformed to their subordinates' expectations. Those on top were comparatively impersonal and formal, while those in the mine behaved in a more personalized and informal way.

Thus "Old Bull's" conception of a good supervisor was quite similar to that of the ordinary miners'. The chief quality needed by a foreman, said "Old Bull," was that "the men have got to like him." Furthermore, the mine foremen were oriented to the values of the miners, being hostile to the no-absenteeism regulations and also traditionalistic in their attitudes toward

work procedures. As a case in point, with regard to work procedures, "Old Bull" often complained that "They (top management) are always looking for new equipment."

The mining foreman shared a hazardous job with his men.
Working in near-darkness and in a hunched position made the
display of clear-cut symbols of rank difficult, even if mine foremen wanted to make such a display. About the only informal
symbols of status-difference in the mine were the low-cut shoes
worn by foremen and supervisors, as against the workers' high
shoes.

An analogy between men working at the face of a mine
and soldiers at the front line is perhaps not too far-fetched.
Every soldier who has experienced battle conditions is aware
that officers at the front behave quite differently than they did
in the training camps. When those in authority share a dangerous situation with their subordinates, rigid and formal relationships are greatly diminished.

In sum, informal cohesion among the miners and the integration of the mine foremen in these informal groups, legitimated and reinforced as it was by joint participation in a dangerous situation, allowed the informal group among the miners
more *effective resistance* against managerial efforts at increased
discipline or bureaucratization.

Finally, it might be mentioned that the miner's character
structure also interposed a barrier to the effective use of bureaucratic methods. In general, it would appear more difficult
to force the highly spontaneous personalities, typical of miners,
to follow a pattern of formal rules and rigid discipline. On the
other hand, individuals accustomed to continual suppression of
impulse, such as was customary among surfacemen and typified
by the manner in which they handled their aggression, probably found conformance to rules and discipline comparatively
easier.

The different attitudes which miners and surface workers

had toward authority, and their different modes of handling aggression, were also of importance here. To the degree that miners, unlike surfacemen, did not conceive of authority as impregnable, they were more capable of openly expressing aggression toward it. In short, violation of the miners' values, by introduction of bureaucratic methods, could lead to more *militant* resistance in part because the miners' psychological security system did not rest as heavily upon identification with authority.

In recapitulation: It has been suggested that three elements acted as barriers to the bureaucratization of the mine. These were:

1. *The miners' belief system.* This mobilized resistance to changes which would enhance labor-discipline, rationalize production, and install methods of bureaucratic administration.
2. *Physical dangers and definitions of the mine as a hazardous work place.* These legitimated the resistance of the aroused miner, and by limiting the available reserve of labor for mine work, also increased the chances for the success of this resistance.
3. *Informal solidarity.* This also increased the effectiveness of the miners' resistance allowing for concerted opposition to management.

In fine, management's ability to implement bureaucratic measures was, in part, a function of their subordinates' motivation and ability to resist managerial efforts. The degree of bureaucratization was, in this view, explainable only in terms of a balance of *power,* of the relative strengths of opposing groups. It was by no means the inevitable outcome of an irresistible force.

PART FOUR

"If you ride a horse, sit close and tight. If you ride a man, sit easy and light."

POOR RICHARD

Chapter IX

ABOUT THE FUNCTIONS

OF BUREAUCRATIC RULES

IN SEEKING TO ACCOUNT
for the development of bureaucracy we have, so far, conformed
to the time-honored canons of the working detective; that is,
we have sought to demonstrate first, the "motives," and then
the "opportunity." In considering the first, it has been suggested that the "motives" comprise an effort to solve the problem of worker "apathy"; in examining the "opportunity," attention has been given to the recalcitrance of the human material, and to the question of whether the "victim" is cussedly
resistant or quietly acquiescent.

By analogy, we are not so much interested in the "crime"
as in the career of the criminal, and this, of course, is shaped

by more than his motives or opportunities. It depends also on what *happens* in the course of such a career. Whether the criminal escapes or is caught is no petty detail; whether he satisfies his motives or frustrates them influences the development of his career.

Similarly, we were interested in the "career" of bureaucratic patterns. Wherever bureaucratic patterns are found to be relatively entrenched, it must be assumed that their "career" has resulted in a net balance of gains greater than that of the losses, though it would be foolhardy to assume that there had been *no* losses at all. Above all, this means that the *consequences* which are brought about by bureaucratic methods of administration must be examined if their *survival* is to be understood. Here the problem is not one of motives or opportunities, or intentions and powers; it is rather a question of the practical results which sustain bureaucratic patterns once initiated. In fine, the questions are: What gains were secured by bureaucratic procedures; what problems were actually mitigated; what tensions were eased by their use?

A final *caveat:* Attention will be focused here on only one aspect of bureaucracy, the bureaucratic rules. The discussion will be confined to the functions of these rules, and no analysis will be made of the functions of other characteristic features of bureaucratic organization, such as a highly specialized division of labor. In addition to expedient considerations, this decision derived from the fact that bureaucratic rules are central to Max Weber's theory of bureaucracy. If organizations (like organisms) operate in terms of a "safety margin" factor, developing their tension-reducing mechanisms beyond the point required for routine operations, then it may well be that hypotheses about the functions of bureaucratic rules will yield hypotheses of broader generality, which are applicable to other bureaucratic characteristics.

The Problem of "Close Supervision"

The problem may be opened by reviewing a point touched upon before: If a supervisor viewed a worker as unmotivated, as unwilling to "do a job," how did the supervisor respond; how did he attempt to solve this problem? He usually attempted to handle this by directing the worker more closely, by watching him carefully, and explicitly outlining his work obligations. As one foreman said: "If I catch a man goofing off, I tell him in an a,b,c, way exactly what he has to do, and I watch him like a hawk 'til he's done it." This was precisely what Peele did when he first entered the plant as manager and found that the workers were resisting him.[1]

At first glance this might appear to be a stable solution; it might seem as if "close supervision" would allow the supervisor to bring the problem under control. Actually, however, there were commanding reasons why supervisors could not rest content to supervise their workers closely and to remind them endlessly of what had to be done. One motive was fairly

---

1. Students of industrial behavior will at once note that we have been led back to the lair of a hoary problem whose origins, however indeterminate, have a certifiable antiquity. John Stuart Mill, for example, had long since observed the connections between "close supervision" and the managerial estimate of workers' motivation to work: "The moral qualities of the laborers are fully as important to the efficiency and worth of their labor as the intellectual . . . it is well worthy of meditation, how much of the aggregate of their labor depends upon their trustworthiness. All the labor now expended in watching that they fulfill their engagement, or in verifying that they have fulfilled it, is so much withdrawn from the real business of production to be devoted to a subsidiary function rendered needful not by the necessity of things but by the dishonesty of men. Nor are the greatest precautions more than very imperfectly efficacious, where, as is now almost invariably the case with hired laborers, *the slightest relaxation of vigilance is an opportunity eagerly seized for eluding performance of their contract.*" (Our emphasis—A. W. G.) Longmans, Green and Co., Ltd., London, 1926 edition, pp. 110-111. More recently, the problem of "close supervision" has been given careful attention at the University of Michigan. One of the most theoretically sophisticated accounts of this work is to be found in Daniel Katz and Robert Kahn, "Human Organization and Worker Motivation," in *Industrial Productivity*, edited by L. Reed Tripp, Industrial Relations Research Association, Madison, Wisconsin, 1951, pp. 146-171.

obvious: The supervisor could not watch all of his men all of the time. As a surface foreman remarked, "As soon as I turn my back on some of these guys, they slip me the knife."

There is, though, one basis on which the supervisor could feel confident that workers would do their jobs even when he was *not* around; that is, if the supervisors believed that workers themselves wanted to do what was expected of them. As John Stuart Mill remarked in this connection, "Nor are the greatest *outward* precautions comparable in efficacy to the monitor *within*." [2] Indeed, it may be suspected that this was *one* of the factors alerting management to the problem of the worker's motivation; for a motivated worker made the job of supervision easier.

There is, however, another consideration that made "close supervision" a dangerous solution to the problem of the unmotivated worker. Specifically, workers viewed close supervision as a kind of "strictness" and punishment. In consequence, the more a supervisor watched his subordinates, the more hostile they became to him. Workers shared standardized conceptions of what a "good" or legitimate foreman should be like, and almost universally, these insisted that the good foreman was one who "doesn't look over your shoulder." From the workers' standpoint a "driving" foreman was "bad," and they would retaliate by withholding work effort. As a hopper worker asserted:

"If the foreman doesn't work well with us, we don't give him as good work as we can . . . I just don't care, I let things slide."

In other words, close supervision enmeshed management in a vicious cycle: the supervisor perceived the worker as unmotivated; he then carefully watched and directed him; this aroused the worker's ire and accentuated his apathy, and now the super-

---

2. Mill, Ibid., p. 111. This statement was deleted from the third (1852) edition. (Our emphasis—A. W. G.)

visor was back where he began. Close supervision did not solve his problem. In fact, it might make the worker's performance, in the super's absence, even less reliable than it had been.

Must it be supposed, however, that "close supervision" *invariably* corrodes the relationship between the worker and his superior? Does it do so under any and all conditions? What is there *about* close supervision which disturbs relations between workers and supers? To consider the last question first: Notice that close supervision entails an intensification of *face-to-face* direction of the worker. In such a context, it becomes very *evident* exactly "who is boss." This, in turn, suggests one of the distinctive conditions which underpin the strains induced by close supervision; for ours is a culture in which great stress is placed upon the *equality* of persons, and in such a cultural context *visible* differences in power and privilege readily become sources of tension, particularly so if status differences do not correspond with traditionally prized attributes such as skill, experience, or seniority.

Close supervision violated norms of equality internalized by workers, and they responded by complaining that the supervisor was "just trying to *show* who is boss." Workers' devotion to this norm was indicated also by their preference for supervisors who did not act as if they were "better than anyone else;" they insisted that supervisors, or for that matter other workers, should not behave like "big shots." In other words, they were hostile to those who put forth claims of personal superiority.[3]

Again, workers expressed the feeling that close supervision violated their culturally prescribed expectations of equality

---

3. That this is a culturally induced sentiment, as significant in a military as in an industrial setting, may be inferred from the warning addressed to U. S. Army officers during the last war: ". . . do not make the mistake of thinking of yourself as a superior individual . . . ," officers were cautioned in "Military Courtesy and Discipline," W. D. Man FM 21-50, June 15, 1942, quoted in S. A. Stouffer, E. A. Suchman, Leland C. DeVinney, Shirley A. Star, and Robin M. Williams, Jr., *The American Soldier*, Vol. 1, Princeton University Press, Princeton, N. J., 1949, p. 387.

by saying that such a supervisor was "trying to make a *slave* out of us."

Supervisors, as well as workers, were frequently oriented to the same egalitarian norms. For example, the production manager for the entire Company expressed these sentiments in the following way:

"Here's the real secret to successful human relations: The real key lies in treating your employees like human beings. *I'm no better than any one of the plant workers.* Oh, maybe I can afford a little better car, or a home in Penmore.[4] I can send my kids for a music lesson while they can't. *But these things don't make me any better than them.*"

To the extent that a supervisor was oriented to norms of equality, the continual exercise of direct face-to-face supervision might be expected to create tensions for him. As one board plant foreman confided: "Sometimes I wonder who the hell am I to tell these guys what to do."

The Explicational Functions of Bureaucratic Rules

In this context, some of the functions performed by bureaucratic rules can perhaps be more readily discerned. First, it can be noted that the rules comprise a functional equivalent for direct, personally given orders. Like direct orders, rules specify the obligations of the worker, enjoining him to do particular things in definite ways. Usually, however, rules are given, or are believed to be given, more deliberation than orders, and thus the statement of obligations they explicate can be taken to be definitive. Since the rules are also more carefully expressed, the obligations they impose may be less ambiguous than a hastily worded personal command.[5] Looked at in this

---

4. A middle class suburb in the area.

5. Mill also saw the function of rules as a definitive statement of explicit obligations. He insisted that the successful conduct of a business required two things, "fidelity and zeal." Fidelity, easier to obtain than zeal, could be partly

light, rules are a form of *communication* to those who are seen as desirous of evading responsibilities, of avoiding commitments, and of withholding proper and full performance of obligations. Comprising in one facet an explicit body of obligations, the rules serve to draw a worker's *attention* to managerial expectations and to dissolve the residues of diffuseness which may allow the worker to "hedge." Thus, on the one hand, the rules explicate the worker's task while on the other, they shape and specify his relationships to his superior. Stated in the language of the political scientist, the rules serve to narrow the subordinate's "area of discretion." The subordinates now have fewer options concerning what they *may* or *may not* do, and the area of "privilege" is crowded out by the growing area of "obligation."

It might be asked, why were work obligations comparatively diffuse in the mine, but much more explicit on the surface? An illustration previously used was the situation in which a group of workers were standing around, waiting for the mine head to assign them. He stepped out of his office and said, "One of you, clean out the rock crusher."

How was a *specific* individual chosen for this "dirty" job? This was the question asked a worker who had been through the situation. "It's simple," he replied. "We all just turn around and *look* at the newest guy in the group and he goes and does it." In other words, there existed an *informal* norm among miners to the effect that *new* workers got the dirty jobs; it was a norm to which the men were so sensitive that a mere "look" could bring the expected results. The informal group among

---

ensured when "work admits of being reduced to a *definite set of rules;* the violation of which conscience cannot easily blind itself, and on which responsibility may be enforced by the loss of employment." Nevertheless, he conceded, many things needed for business success cannot be reduced to "distinct and positive obligations." Finally, in this connection, he adds "the universal neglect by domestic servants of their employer's interest, wherever these are not protected by some fixed rule, is a matter of common remark . . ." Ibid., p. 139.

miners spontaneously and with solidarity acted to enforce its norms. The informal group and its norms, then, constituted a functional equivalent for bureaucratic rules to the degree, at least, that it served to allocate concrete work responsibilities and to specify individual duties. It would appear, therefore, that the explication of obligations provided by bureaucratic rules is particularly necessary where there is no other instrumentality, specifically an effective informal group, which does this.[6]

The Screening Functions of Rules

A second, less obvious, function of bureaucratic rules can be observed if we notice that, in part, they provide a substitute for the personal repetition of orders by a supervisor. Once an obligation was incorporated into a rule, the worker could not excuse himself by claiming that the supervisor had failed to tell him to do a specific thing. To take one example: The worker who operated a machine without using the safety guard could not "pass the buck" by saying that the supervisor neglected to mention this when he gave him a task. Since there existed a standing rule that "safety guards should always be used," the supervisor need not warn the worker of this every time he instructed him to use a machine.

Once standing rules have been installed, there are fewer

---

6. This situation is in seeming contrast to one described by William Foote Whyte in his perceptive, *Human Relations in the Restaurant Industry*, McGraw-Hill Book Co., New York, 1948. Whyte recounts an incident in which a supervisor gave an order to two women, without specifying which one was to carry it out. Whyte remarks, "For effective action, orders and directions must be definite and clear as to what must be done, *how* and *when* it is to be done, and *who is to do it.*" (Ibid., p. 261.) Our own formulations are not necessarily in contradiction to Whyte's practical strictures. From our viewpoint, however, Whyte's conclusions should be limited to situations in which informal cohesion among workers has deteriorated so that they are unable to apply pressure to get the work done themselves, or if they are *unwilling* to do so. Our earlier point, about the tensions generated by close supervision, leads us to suspect that Whyte's prescriptions of detailed orders signify the presence of a motivational problem which may only be further exacerbated by the remedy he proposes.

things that a supervisor has to direct a worker to do; thus the frequency and duration of worker-foreman interaction in their *official* capacities is somewhat lessened. Moreover, even if the super does intervene in his capacity as a superior, he need not appear to be doing so on his own account; he is not so apt to be seen as "throwing his weight around." He can say, as one foreman said about the no-absenteeism rule: "I can't help laying them off if they're absent. *It's not my idea.* I've got to go along with the rules *like everyone else.* What *I* want has nothing to do with it." In other words, the rules provide the foreman with an impersonal crutch for his authority, screening the superiority of his power which might otherwise violate the norm of equality. Instead, equality presumably prevails because, "like everyone else," he, too, is bound by the rules which the plant manager has sanctioned.

Differences in power which are not justifiable in terms of the group's norms, or which violate them, seem to establish a situation requiring the utilization of impersonal control techniques. Impersonal and general rules serve in part to obscure the existence of power disparities which are not legitimate in terms of the group's norms.[7] The screening function of the rules would seem, therefore, to work in two directions at once.

---

7. William F. Whyte has made an observation in his restaurant studies which, if reconceptualized, in effect constitutes an interesting example of this pattern. Whyte points out that tension arises between the waitresses and the pantry help who fill their orders, under several conditions: when the waitresses are *younger* than the pantry people—even though both groups are women; or when those in the pantry are *men.* It would seem that these tensions emerge because *traditional* criteria of authority in our society are being violated. That is, younger people are initiating action for older people, while our cultural prescriptions prefer that power be vested in older folk. Again, women are initiating action for men, while the culture prescribes that men should wield the power. In an acute analysis, Whyte makes the following interpretation of the "insignificant-looking spindle" on which the waitresses place their orders, and from which the pantry people take them. "Wherever the people on the receiving end of the orders are related to the order givers as males vs. females, or older vs. younger, then it is important for the pantry help to have some *impersonal* barrier to block the pressure from themselves." (Ibid., p. 75.) In other words, instead of having the waitresses orally inform the pantry help of what they want, the

First, it impersonally bolsters a supervisor's claim to authority without compelling him to employ an embarrassing and debatable legitimation in terms of his personal superiority. Conversely, it permits *workers* to accept managerial claims to deference without committing them to a merely personal submission to the supervisor that would betray their self-image as "any man's equal."

The "Remote Control" Function of Rules

It would be a mistake, however, to continue assuming that management instituted rules only when it perceived workers as unmotivated. For top management was often as much concerned with the low motivation of those in the lower echelons of its own ranks, i.e., middle management, as it was with workers'. This was quite evident in Peele's feeling that foreman and supervisors were "shirking." It was also a pattern that was more generally evident. Thus, for example, if all supervisors could be "counted on" to enforce safety regulations there would have been no need for the main office to employ a "safety engineer" to check upon safety conditions in the local plants.[8]

The problem of handling the "enemy within" was sometimes more difficult than that of coping with those in the "out-group." For at least on the factory level, in-group and out-group could stand face to face and might sniff watchfully at each other, and could place their confidence for a while in "close supervision." But what could the safety engineer, for example, do to control some twenty-five plants? How could he control the supervision of safety work throughout the entire Company

---

waitresses can now write it out and place their order on the spindle. The pantry personnel can pick the order off the spindle without coming into direct interaction with the waitresses and without seeming to take orders from those culturally prescribed as inferiors. The spindle thus masks the existence of a relationship which violates internalized cultural prescriptions.

8. Safety rules are discussed more fully in Chapter X.

by means of "close supervision" alone? (Notice that the safety engineer's problem was only an extreme case of a common problem; it was not qualitatively different from that experienced by many of the plant's middle managers).

In some way the safety engineer had to utilize a "spot check" system. That is, he made occasional visits to a plant, spending a little while there, and then moved on to another factory. If, however, each plant was to operate on a unique basis, each having its own distinctive techniques for handling safety, it would be difficult for the safety engineer to make his *own* judgment about plant conditions. He would be forced to place greater reliance on local management, which was precisely what he wanted to avoid. Insofar as he had established certain general rules applying to all plants, he could go to each one and "see for himself." He could "tell at a glance" whether the rules concerning machine guards or debris on the floor were being followed. In part, then, the existence of general rules was a necessary adjunct to a "spot check" system; they facilitated "control from a distance" by those in the higher and more remote reaches of the organization.[9]

There was another aspect of the rules which was also helpful

---

9. Some further implications of this, in the context of labor relations problems, may be seen from the comments of Frederick H. Harbison and Robert Dubin about the General Motors Company: "A rigid grievance procedure has made it easier for the corporation to control the decisions and actions of management's rank and file. Thousands of plant managers, department superintendents and foremen have been dealing with union representatives on a day-to-day basis. Many of them have been inexperienced in labor relations, and some were bound to make mistakes. *The existence of a system of rules has made it easier for top company officials to locate quickly those spots where local management has been 'off base.'*" (Our emphasis—A. W. G.) *Patterns of Union-Management Relations*, Science Research Associates, Chicago, 1947, pp. 83-84. The remote control function of bureaucratic measures has also been noted by Franz Neumann and Julian Franklin. For example, Franklin writes: "Rigid hierarchy and a precisely articulated framework of offices and functions make it possible for discretionary policy to be set at *one point* outside the bureaucracy and then to be administered automatically at all levels of the hierarchy." "The Democratic Approach to Bureaucracy," *Readings in Culture, Personality and Society*, Columbia College, N. Y., n. d., p. 3.

to control from a distance. This was their *public* character. Because the rules were publicly known, an "enemy" could be used to control an "ally." For example, when the safety engineer inspected a plant he was not averse to speaking to workers whom he himself characterized as "troublemakers." The safety engineer told of a plant tour which he had made while in the company of a "troublemaker." This worker showed the engineer that there was a pile of debris in front of the blacksmith's bench, and took him to another spot and showed him how a machine had had its guard removed. He could only do this because the rules were public knowledge, and like everyone else, the "troublemaker" knew what they were. On the basis of these observations the safety engineer could then apply pressure to the supervisors. In sum, the *public* character of the rules enabled deviance to be detected by the *out-group*. This enlargened the information channels open to the heads of the in-group, in turn enabling them to keep their own junior officers in line.

These considerations lead us to expect that bureaucratic rules flourish, other things being equal, when the senior officers of a group are impressed with the recalcitrance of those to whom they have delegated a measure of command. In other words, bureaucratic patterns are particularly useful to the degree that distrust and suspicion concerning role performance has become diffuse and directed to members of the "in-group," as well as to those on the outside; and when, as the Old Testament puts it, "A man's enemies are the men of his own house."

The Punishment Legitimating Functions of Rules

Faced with subordinates who were only reluctantly performing their roles, or at least, who were seen in this way, management was experiencing a status-threatening and hence aggression-provoking situation. The supervisor wanted to eliminate these threats when they arose and to prevent their recurrence. These were the supervisor's needs which emerged from his relations with workers when the latter began to behave apathetically ("goldbricking") or disobediently ("talking back"). On another level, the personality plane, the supervisor was beginning to "burn up" and was getting set to "blow his top." He was, in brief, accumulating a cargo of aggression with which he had to do something.

Why didn't the supervisor express his aggression and "tell the worker off"? Why didn't he *punish* the worker, thereby killing two birds with one stone; namely, unburdening himself of hostile feelings and compelling the worker to conform to his expectations? After all, punishment, or the infliction of "pain, failure, or ego-degradation" [10] upon the worker might help to bolster the supervisor's threatened status and salve his wounded ego.

There was one important drawback. Among surface workers in particular, and for the Company as a whole, supervisors were expressly forbidden, formally, to express aggression. As seen when contrasting miners with the more bureaucratized surface workers, the overt expression of aggression was taboo among the latter. Moreover the Company "labor relations manual" asserted that "A *friendly* attitude toward . . . all employees will provide the basis for sound Company-employee relations in each plant." The manual also insisted that one of the characteristics of every good employee was an "ability to *control emotion.*" In the face of these proscriptions, it was difficult to express aggression openly.

In our society, moreover, it is not permissible to inflict a punishment under any and all conditions. There seems to be a deep-grooved inscription in our culture which asserts that punishment is permissible only on the condition that the offender could know *in advance* that certain of his behaviors are forbid-

---

10. Norman F. Maier, *Frustration*, McGraw-Hill Book Co., 1949, p. 194.

den.[11] This is one of the sentiments which underlies the rejection of *ex post facto* laws in our legal structure. If it has become a formally announced legal principle that "ignorance of the law is no excuse," this has, in part, been necessary because traditional folkways informally insist that ignorance of the law constitutes an extenuating circumstance.

Within the plant, orientation to this traditional norm was expressed in several ways. First, the frequent claim that so-and-so was a good foreman because he gave his workers a "second chance," a factor in the "indulgency pattern," implied that such a foreman did *not* take the first opportunity that presented itself to inflict a punishment. Instead he used this first deviation as an occasion to *warn* the worker that future infractions would meet with punishment.

That punishments which were not preceded by warnings were only doubtfully legitimate, in the eyes of plant personnel, can be inferred from the introduction of the formal warning notice. One of the functions of the *worker's signature* on the warning notice was to forestall a claim that he had not been warned and could not, therefore, be punished. Day, the old personnel manager, complained precisely of this point after he had been demoted, saying, "Why didn't Peele tell me about it long before now, instead of just replacing me?"

Bureaucratic rules, then, serve to legitimate the utilization of punishments. They do so because the rules constitute statements in advance of expectations. As such, they comprise explicit or implicit *warnings* concerning the kind of behavior which will provoke punishment.

---

11. Here, again, there is evidence suggesting that we are dealing with a culturally induced sentiment rather than one peculiar to this factory or to industrial phenomena alone. On the basis of their wartime studies of the U. S. Armed Forces, the authors of *The American Soldier* suggest that punishment is more likely to be effective if "the men are given specific *advance* warning about the consequences of an occurrence of the offense, since *most men consider fair warning as a condition for fair punishment*." Ibid., p. 425. (Our emphasis—A. W. G.)

In actuality, the establishment of a rule explicating an obligation is frequently accompanied by a specific statement of the punishment, i.e., another rule specifying the punishment which will result if the first rule is violated. Two things, rather than one, have thus been clarified: (1) what is expected of the man and (2) what will happen to him if he does *not* fulfill these expectations. For example, the no-absenteeism rule did not merely state that the worker must not be absent without cause; it also specifically provided that he was to be layed off a like number of days for those which he took.

In brief, when rules explicate obligations, they are producing consequences recognized and intended by most participants in the situation. When rules explicate a punishment, however, they are legitimating the use of punishments, a consequence sometimes not at the center of the group's intention or awareness. The relationship between the explicational and the punishment functions of rules is like the relation between the locomotive and the trains which it pulls. Attention can all too readily be diverted to the noisy, smoking locomotive in the vanguard, while the attached trains carrying the pay load are easily neglected.

An example of the punishment function of the rules occurred in the dehydrating section of the mill: There were a number of large vats, used to heat and dehydrate the gypsum into powder, which occasionally needed to be cleaned out. A rule specified that the man who went down into one of these vats must wear a harness with a rope leading up to the top; there was also supposed to be someone at the top holding onto the rope and watching the man inside. These precautions stemmed from the fear that a man at the bottom of a vat could be killed by fumes or smothered by a cave-in of the "cake" covering the inside of the vat.

One day a main office executive passed through the plant on an inspection tour and noticed a rope leading down into a vat. He looked over the side and saw a worker cleaning it out, but there was no one around at the top watching the man and guarding the rope. Immediately the executive looked for the man's foreman, who was not to be seen. After a search, however, he discovered the foreman doing exactly the same thing, cleaning out a vat without having someone watch him. The executive then "raised hell" with the foreman and took it to higher plant authorities.

In short, the first thing the executive did when he discovered the infraction of vat-cleaning rules, was to look for someone to punish and blame. Instead of calling the man up from the vat, he left him down there. Instead of doing something to forestall an accident, the manifest function of this rule, he exploited the situation as an opportunity to inflict a punishment.

The rules thus channel aggression, providing permissible avenues for its expression and legitimating the utilization of punishments. To the extent that possible objects of punishment and aggression are members of the "in-group," as suggested in our discussion of the "remote control" function of rules, it becomes all the more necessary to legitimate meticulously the use of these control measures. For, by and large, aggression and punishments directed toward in-group members are not preferred patterns of behavior in our culture and require especially unambiguous justification. Bureaucratic rules are thereby particularly functional in a context in which reliance upon the in-group has been shaken.

The "Leeway" Function of Rules

Another commonplace pattern observable in management's [12] application of bureaucratic rules, which is related to their punishment function, was the curious rhythmic quality with which rules were *enforced*. Sometimes demands for rig-

---

12. Later chapters will emphasize that these functions of bureaucratic rules were not peculiar to management, but apply also to workers.

orous conformance to a rule would be made, but would later lapse into periods of disinterest when the rules were ignored or only fitfully observed. For example, occasionally the plant guard would carefully examine packages which workers brought out of the plant, while at other times these would be given only cursory inspection. Sometimes punctual "punching in" would be rigorously enforced; at other times lateness would be given only casual comment. What was the significance of these periodic alternations? A clue to part of their meaning may be found in the *contexts* in which enforcement or relaxation of rules occurred.

Usually, it was noted that a fever of enforcement occurred when small tensions between workers and their supervisors began to coalesce into more definite rifts. A case in point was the "no-floating around" rule which specified that workers must stay at their work-place, except to go to the washroom or to eat. When foremen felt that things were going smoothly in their group, that their men were "doing a day's work" and were friendly and "cooperative," they would allow their workers to "sneak off" for a smoke, and they would make no caustic comments if they wandered over to talk to a friend. If, however, a man or the group as a whole was felt to be "goofing off," or was becoming "snotty," foremen were then more likely to invoke the "no-floating" rule.

By a strange paradox, *formal* rules gave supervisors something with which they could "bargain" in order to secure *informal* cooperation from workers. The rules were the "chips" to which the Company staked the supervisors and which they could use to play the game; they carved out a "right" which, should supervisors wish to, they could "stand upon." In effect, then, formal bureaucratic rules served as a control device not merely because they provided a legitimating framework for the *allocation* of punishments, but also because they established a punishment which could be *withheld*. By installing a rule, management provided itself with an instrument which was valuable even if it was not used; the rules were serviceable because they created something which could be *given up* as well as *given use*.[13]

The Apathy-Preserving Function of Bureaucratic Rules

Nor is this the last of paradoxes. For though bureaucratic rules were fostered by situations involving worker apathy, or its semblance, the rules actually contributed to the preservation of work apathy. Just as the rules facilitated punishment, so, too, did they define the behavior which could permit punishment to be *escaped*. The discussion of the "leeway" function of rules has considered the importance of this from the supervisor's standpoint, but it was also significant for the worker as well. The rules served as a specification of a *minimum* level of acceptable performance. It was therefore possible for the worker

---

13. This is an aspect of the functioning of bureaucratic rules which tends to be neglected by those who, like Julian Franklin, emphasize the discretion-narrowing role of bureaucratic measures. Thus Franklin writes: ". . . the aim in organizing a bureaucratic structure is to narrow the area of discretion and, as far as possible, to reduce the process of administration to a series of routine actions." Ibid., p. 3. Our comments are not necessarily in contradiction to Franklin's, since he is here, I presume, speaking of the manifest functions of bureaucratic techniques with which we ourselves concur (as indicated by the discussion of the "explicational functions" of the rules): in examining the "leeway function," however, we have been talking of their latent functions—the unrecognized and unintended consequences. Here, as in our discussion of the apathy-preserving functions of the rules, we are talking about unanticipated consequences generated by distinctively bureaucratic characteristics. This is a rather different direction than the one taken by Philip Selznick in his study of the TVA, where the "existential" dilemmas of organization—the universal ills to which the organizational flesh is presumably heir—are painstakingly examined. Our focus is on the ills specific to bureaucracy, whose universality we more than doubt. Selznick's study, more generally, can be conceived of as concerned with the reverse side of the penny. He is largely attending to the forces that generate discretionary drives and that subvert the formal ends and organization to "narrower" interests. He finds these, however, not in peculiar bureaucratic traits, but in the above mentioned existential dilemmas. For our part, we have been focusing, in the main, on forces that sustain formal ends and bureaucratic patterns. Where we note tensions which subvert them, we are concerned, in particular, with their origin in distinctive patterns peculiar to bureaucracy. See Philip Selznick, Ibid.

to *remain* apathetic, for he now knew just how *little* he could do and still remain secure.

For example, after Peele had ruled that workers could not "punch in early" and accumulate a little overtime in that way, one mill worker said acidly.

"Well, if that's the way he wants it, that's the way he wants it. But I'll be damned if I put in any overtime when things get rough and they'd like us to."

Said another worker:

"O.K. I'll punch in just so, and I'll punch out on the nose. But you know you can lead a horse to water and you can lead him away, but it's awful hard to tell just how much water he drinks while he's at it."

This, of course, is the stuff of which "bureaucratic sabotage" is made. "Bureaucratic sabotage" is deliberate apathy fused with resentment, in which, by the very act of conforming to the letter of the rule, its intention is "conscientiously" violated. The worker's feeling and attitudes toward his work were thus essentially left untouched by the bureaucratic rules. The worker could, as it were, take any attitude toward his work that he wished, so long as he conformed to the rules. The rules did little to modify *attitudes* toward work, but were significant primarily as guidelines for *behavior*. In the last analysis, it would seem that proliferation of bureaucratic rules signify that management has, in effect if not intention, surrendered in the battle for the worker's motivation. In his study of *Social Organization,* Charles Horton Cooley came to much the same conclusion:

"Underlying all formalism, indeed, is the fact that it is psychically cheap; it substitutes the outer for the inner as more tangible, more capable of being held before the mind *without fresh expense of thought and feeling.*" [14]

14. C. H. Cooley, *Social Organization,* Chas. Scribner's Sons, 1919, p. 349. (Our emphasis—A. W. G.)

And again:

" . . . the merely formal institution does not enlist and discipline the soul of the individual, but takes him by the outside, his soul being left to torpor or to irreverent and riotous activity." [15]

Thus bureaucratic rules may be functional for subordinates, as well as for superiors; they permit "activity" without "participation;" they enable an employee to work without being emotionally committed to it.

This function of bureaucratic rules is of peculiar importance since it suggests one of the inherent sources of bureaucratic rules' instability; for the rules do not seem to *resolve* the very problem, worker apathy, from which they most directly spring. Insofar as formal rules merely "wall in," rather than resolve, worker apathy, it may be expected that other mechanisms more competent to muster motivations will challenge and compete with them.[16]

Bureaucratic Rules and Close Supervision

What does this mean in terms of the problem of "close supervision?" It implies that bureaucratic rules do not elimi-

---

15. Ibid., p. 343.

16. It may well be that this is one of the organic contradictions of bureaucratic organization that make it susceptible to infiltration and displacement by "charismatic" elements, which involves loyalty to leadership based on belief in the leader's unusual *personal* qualities. Weber vaguely explained the vulnerability of bureaucracy as a breakdown of its efficiency in the face of new problems and accumulating tensions. He did little to analyze the specific nature of these tensions and tended to focus on their origins in the environment, neglecting their inner-organizational sources. We are suggesting, in effect, that bureaucratic authority is supplanted by charismatic when it is no longer possible to bypass the question of motivation. Charismatic leadership, it has been widely noted, has an ability to arouse new enthusiasms and to ignite irrational sources of motivation inaccessible to the bureaucrat. Indeed, some observers have insisted that this is one of the distinctive characteristics of modern totalitarianism. Thus George Orwell, in his *1984*, brings this novel to its climax when his hero is being tortured not merely to confess, nor to conform—but to *believe*.

nate the need for "close supervision" but, instead, primarily function to reduce the tensions created by it. Insofar as close supervision springs from management's perception of workers as failing to perform their role-obligations and as being unmotivated, the institution of rules in no way suffices to resolve this problem. The rules do not recharge the worker's motivation, but merely enable him to know what management's expectations are and to give them minimal conformance. Thus the tensions originally spurring supervisors to use "close supervision" remain untouched.

It is, instead, the secondary problems created by close supervision that are somewhat mitigated by bureaucratic rules: With the rules, the supervisor is now enabled to show that he is not using close supervision on his own behalf, but is merely transmitting demands that apply equally to all (the screening function); the supervisor is now more able to use a "spot-check" system to control workers with whom he cannot have frequent interaction (the remote control function); he now has a clearcut basis for deciding, and demonstrating to his superiors if need be, that workers are delinquent in their role-performances (the explicational function); he now has firm grounds for punishing a worker if he finds him withholding obligation-performance (the punishment-legitimating function); or he can relax the rules, thereby rewarding workers, if they do perform their role obligations as he wants them to (the leeway function). In general, then, the rules reduce certain role tensions.

To repeat: These various functions of the rules largely serve to mitigate tensions *derivative* of "close supervision," rather than to remove all the major tensions which *create* it. Indeed, the rules now make close supervision feasible. The rules thus actually perpetuate one of the very things, i.e., close supervision, that bring them into being. The dynamics of the situation are of this sort:

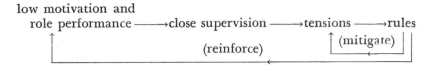

low motivation and
role performance ———→close supervision ———→tensions ———→rules

One may well wonder how bureaucratic rules could be
perpetuated and sustained, if they actually removed the tensions
leading to close supervision, rather than mitigating the tensions
stemming from it. For if this happened low motivation would
be raised to a satisfactory level; there would then be less need
for close supervision; hence fewer tensions would be generated
by it, and, in consequence, there would be less need for these
tensions to be reduced by bureaucratic rules. To put it more
sharply, bureaucratic rules seem to be sustained not only because they mitigate some tensions, but, also, because they *preserve* and allow other *tensions* to persist. If bureaucratic rules
are a "defense mechanism," they not only defend the organization from certain tensions (those coming from close supervision), but they also *defend other tensions* as well (those
conducing to close supervision).[17]

---

17. This seems to have some bearing on certain more *general* problems involved in the functional analysis of organizations, which can be elucidated by
comparing our approach with that employed by Philip Selznick. (See Selznick,
"Foundations of the Theory of Organization," *American Sociological Review,*
Feb., 1948, pp. 25-35). Selznick emphasizes the utility of concepts describing
organization defensive mechanisms. He suggests that organizations develop recurrent defensive mechanisms, in a manner analogous to the human personality.
These mechanisms, he holds, reduce tensions to the organization from threats
which impinge upon it from its environment. Selznick illustrates this with the
concept of "cooptation": Thus when the leadership body of a group loses the
consent of a segment of the group over which it claims authority, a tension is
established. One of the defensive mechanisms which may then become operative
to reduce this tension, according to Selznick, is the "cooptation" of a prominent
member of the dissenting segment onto the leadership body. This "formal"
cooptation may extract increased consent from the sub-group, thereby reducing
the tension experienced by those claiming authority. For example, an imperial
colonial administrative body may coopt a tribal chief to the imperial administrative organ. Now, in what sense has the tension been reduced? One thing
seems clear at least: The conditions which originally motivated the tribesmen
to withdraw consent may in no way have been altered by the cooptation. Actu-

It should not be supposed, however, that all the consequences of bureaucratic rules are equally reinforcing to low motivation and thereby to close supervision. Obviously, the apathy-preserving function of the rules does this most directly. It may be taken as "given," however, that punishments are more likely to impair motivation, and thus encourage close supervision, than rewards,[18] other things being equal. It therefore seems warranted to conclude that the punishment function is more apt to reinforce low motivation, and with it close supervision, than is the leeway function. Hence we should expect that the more a specific administrative pattern is organized around the punishment functions of rules, the more it will impair motivation and reinforce the need for close supervision.

The discussion of management's perception of both workers and middle management, and the analysis of close supervision, suggest that the extreme elaboration of bureaucratic rules is prompted by an abiding distrust of people and of their intentions. Quite commonly, such rules serve those whose ambitions do not generate the ready and full consent of others; they diminish reliance upon and withhold commitments to persons who are viewed as recalcitrant and untrustworthy. In the extreme case, they seem to comprise an effort to *do without people altogether.* This could not be stated with greater frankness than in the words of Alfred Krupp, the munitions manufacturer:

"What I shall attempt to bring about is that *nothing shall be dependent upon the life or existence* of any particular person; that nothing of any importance shall happen or be caused to happen

---

ally, the cooptation may safeguard the tensions which the tribesmen are experiencing and which led them to withhold consent. By inhibiting verbalization of their grievances, by directing attention and energies away from them, the cooptation of the tribal leader may allow these tension to remain concealed and to continue to fester. In other words, defense mechanisms may actually defend the circumstances which produce the tension itself.

18. Cf., N. R. F. Maier, Ibid.

without the foreknowledge and approval of the management; that the past and the determinate future of the establishment can be learned in the files of the management *without asking a question of any mortal.*" [19]

If the several assessments made in various parts of this chapter are assembled into a complete diagnosis, it appears that bureaucratic rules proliferate when a social organization is riven by the following tensions: (a) Managerial distrust and suspicion become pervasive and are directed, not only toward workers, but also toward members of the managerial in-group as well. (b) Disturbances in the informal system which result in the withholding of consent from the formally constituted authorities; the informal group is either unwilling or unable to allocate work responsibilities and gives no support to management's production expectations. (c) Finally, the appearance of status distinctions of dubious legitimacy, in an egalitarian culture context, which strain the formal authority relationships.

---

19. Quoted in Frederick J. Nussbaum, *A History of the Economic Institutions of Modern Europe,* F. S. Crofts and Co., New York, 1933, p. 379. (Our emphasis —A. W. G.)

Chapter X

A PROVISIONAL ANALYSIS

OF BUREAUCRATIC TYPES

UP TO THIS POINT SOME
of the factors generating different degrees of bureaucracy have
been considered. Is it, though, the mere amount of bureaucracy,
or the degree of its "maturity" that makes this mode of administration subject to hostile public complaint? More generally
stated: *What is there about bureaucracy* which elicits hostility,
fostering tensions within the organization itself or between the
organization and the public with which it deals?

Our research can only begin to answer a question as thorny
as this. As a preliminary step, *differences* and *variations* among
bureaucratic patterns must be sought, and an effort must be
made to discern *types* of bureaucratic patterns. Once these are

formulated, it will be important to see whether *all* of the types are *equally* associated with tensions and complaints, or whether these tend to cluster about *one* of the bureaucratic types.

As stated in another connection: "If . . . we are indeed living in an epoch of 'the bureaucratization of the world,' then it may well be that we have all the more need for theoretical tools which will point up distinctions among bureaucracies and bureaucrats. A single type of bureaucracy is not adequate, either for scientific purposes or practical political action, in a bureaucratized world. A type which includes within itself as much as Weber's does leaves no room for the discriminations without which choice is impossible, scientific advance difficult, and pessimism probable.[1]

Since this was a study of only one plant in a single company, it was not possible to sift out variant bureaucratic patterns by contrasting this factory with others. What could be done, however, was to examine several of the programs and rules within the plant and contrast them with *each other,* noting the variations that were thereby revealed.

The "No-Smoking" Rule: Mock Bureaucracy

Analysis of the plant rules can begin by turning to the "no-smoking" regulations. As comments of people in the plant emphasized, one of the most distinctive things about this rule was that it was a "dead letter." Except under unusual circumstances, it was ignored by most personnel.

Thus, while offering a cigarette to a worker, one of the interviewers asked:

"What about the 'No Smoking' signs? They seem to be all over the place, yet everyone seems to smoke."
(Laughing) "Yes, these are *not really Company* rules. The fire insurance writers put them in. The office seems to think that *smoking*

1. Alvin W. Gouldner (ed.), *Studies in Leadership,* Harper and Bros., New York, 1950, p. 59.

doesn't hurt anything, so they don't bother us about it. That is, of course, until the fire inspector (from the insurance company) comes around. Then as soon as he gets into the front office, they call down here and *the word is spread around for no smoking."*

The workers particularly seemed to enjoy the warning sent by the front office, for they invariably repeated this part of the story. For example, another worker remarked:

"We can smoke as much as we want. When the fire inspector comes around, *everybody is warned earlier* . . . The Company doesn't mind."

Since under ordinary circumstances no one attempted to enforce this rule, it entailed little or no tension between workers and management. On the contrary, the situation was one which strengthened solidarity between the two groups. Their joint violation of the no-smoking rule, and their co-operative effort to outwit the "outsider," the insurance company, allied them as fellow "conspirators."

It seems evident from the above quotations that *one* of the things leading to rejection of the no-smoking rule, by workers and management alike, was that this regulation was initiated by an *outside* group. The workers usually distinguished between rules voluntarily initiated by the Company or plant management and those which, for one or another reason, management was compelled to endorse. Nonetheless, there were certain rules with which workers complied, even though local management was not viewed as responsible for their introduction.

One of these regulations governed the mining of gypsum ore. It specified that different "checks" (which were little numbered placards) had to be placed on each load of gypsum that was sent up from the mine. As a miner explained:

"You get a 'Number 1' check for General Gypsum and a 'Number 5' for royalty. They (the Company) have to pay ten cents a ton to everyone whose land they use. You can see *they're not doing this 'cause they want to; it's got to be done this way.*"

Though something of a nuisance, miners were ready to conform to this rule, and did so, despite the fact that it sprang from "outside" pressure. They conformed because the system enabled them to "check up" on their tonnage output and, since their earnings were geared to this, on their income.

Enforcement of the no-smoking rule would, of course, subject workers to an annoyance which, for some of them, was more than trifling. To demand that a man give up smoking would be much like asking him to stop chewing his fingernails. As a surface painter said:

"You can't stop a man from smoking. He has to. *It keeps him from getting nervous.* You just can't stop a man from smoking if he wants to."

Had conformance to this rule been demanded, a powerful and clear-cut legitimation would have been needed. As the above painter added:

"Safety is another story. The men won't resist that. *It's for their own good. They don't want accidents, if they can help it.* It's not like smoking."

Similarly, the labor relations director at the main office remarked:

"In plants where there is a *real danger of fire,* the men can be gotten to give up smoking."

In this plant, though, since there was little inflammable material around, workers could see "no good reason" why they should stop smoking. In other words, workers do not believe that management has the right to institute *any* kind of a rule, *merely because they have the legal authority to do so.* A rule must also be legitimated in terms of the group's *values,* and will be more readily accepted if it is seen as furthering their own ends. Workers rejected the no-smoking rule, in part, because it could not be justified by rational considerations; it did not effectively attain something *they* valued and wanted.

This, however, was only a part of the picture. What would have happened, or what did people in the situation believe would happen, if the no-smoking rule would be enforced? Enforcement of the rule was generally expected to *sharpen* status distinctions within the plant. This was suggested, for example, by the comments of a foreman, who was explaining why the no-smoking rule was ignored:

"You see, they got a permit to smoke in the office. *The men feel if they can smoke up there, they can smoke down here* (in the factory)."

In brief, enforcement of the no-smoking rule would heighten the visibility of existent status differences, allowing to one group obvious privileges denied to another. This relates to the "screening function" of the rules, and their role in blurring unacceptable status distinctions. Apparently, where enforcement of rules *unveils* status distinctions, as in this case, rather than masking them, the rule is neglected.

There is a difference between this situation and the "check" system in the mine. When miners conformed to the check-regulation, their status was not impaired. Quite the contrary; for an important attribute of their status, namely their income, was made all the more secure by conforming to the checking rules. Conformance to the no-smoking regulations, however, would threaten, not fortify, the status of most production workers and even their supervisors.

Only on one occasion did management seek compliance with the no-smoking rule. This occurred when the insurance inspector made his tour through the plant. The worker who violated the rule *at this time* was bombarded with sharp criticisms by his peers. As one board worker complained:

"There are a few guys who didn't even stop smoking when the inspector comes around. They are troublemakers, and *we let them know where they get off.*"

During these routine inspections, as in the routine conduct of the "checking" system in the mine, workers viewed management's enforcement of the rule as compelled; that is, "they're not doing this 'cause they want to." The inspection was *not* seen as an occasion joyfully seized upon by management to increase its control over the workers. On the other hand, workers who *"violated"* the no-smoking rule under ordinary conditions were not viewed by supervisors as "troublemakers," giving vent to their hostilities. Instead, workers who smoked were viewed as being in the grip of an uncontrollable "human" need, for smoking was presumably required to quell their "nervousness."

Briefly, then, the no-smoking rule is a pattern possessing the following fairly obvious characteristics:

1. Usually, the rule was neither enforced by plant management nor obeyed by workers.
2. As a result, it engendered little tension and conflict between the two groups and in fact seemed to enhance their solidarity.
3. Both the customary violation of the rule, as well as the occasional enforcement of it, were buttressed by the informal sentiments and behavior of the participants.

As point "two" above suggests, this pattern was partly anchored in the "leeway function" of the rules. That is, informally friendly and cooperative attitudes toward management were evoked insofar as management *withheld* enforcement of the rules. While the above discussion has already suggested some clues as to *how* this pattern was brought about, it will be helpful to wait and consider other rules before a summary analysis, which sifts out the underlying variables, is attempted.

This pattern has been called "mock bureaucracy," for many of the bureaucratic cues were present—rules, posters calling for their enforcement, and inspections—but in the ordinary day-to-day conduct of work, this bureaucratic paraphernalia was ignored and inoperative. In terms of the plant's recognized work divisions or departments, it is evident that the mine, rather than the surface factories, more closely approximated mock bureaucracy. Finally, it may be noted that "mock bureaucracy" was the organizational counterpart of the "indulgency pattern." The indulgency pattern refers to the criteria in terms of which the plant was judged by workers as "lenient" or "good." Together, these criteria comprised an implicit description of mock bureaucracy. To put it the other way around, mock bureaucracy refers to the kind of social relations that emerge if the norms of the indulgency pattern are administratively implemented.

The Safety Rules: Representative Bureaucracy

The safety operations comprised a sphere which was more bureaucratically organized than any other in the plant. This was not, of course, the only respect in which safety regulations differed from other rules; nevertheless, it is a key factor that deserves consideration.

As a preliminary indication of the high degree of bureaucracy in this sphere, attention may be given first to the sheer quantity of rules included under the heading of safety. These were more numerous and complex than rules governing any other distinctive activity. There were, for example, sizeable lists of safety regulations which applied to the plant as a whole, while there were others which applied only to specific divisions of the factory. Thus, in the mine, there were specific rules concerning the use and handling of dynamite caps. In the mill, there were rules specifying the manner in which the large dehydrating vats were to be cleaned out. Still other rules, indicating proper procedure to be followed if a tool fell into the mixture, applied only to the board building.

Not only was the system of safety rules complex, but considerable stress was placed upon conformity to them. Unlike the no-smoking rules, the safety regulations were not a "dead letter." Specific agencies existed which strove energetically to bring about their observance. These agencies placed continual pressure upon both workers and management, and sought to orient the two groups to the safety rules during their daily activities. For example, the Company's main office officially defined accident and safety work as one of the regular responsibilities of foreman and supervisors. As the Company's safety manual asserted:

"The foreman must accept the responsibility for the accidents that occur in his department . . . (and) he should be provided with the *knowledge* (sic) he needs to carry it out." (Our emphasis—A. W. G.)

A complex system of "paper work" and "reports," so symptomatic of developed bureaucracy, was centered on the safety program. Thus, in the event that a compensable accident occurred, foremen were directed to prepare a complete report. The safety manual specified the detailed information which this report had to contain: (1) the specific, unsafe condition involved in the accident; (2) the specific unsafe working practice committed by the injured worker or some other employee; (3) what the foreman had done, or recommended should be done, to prevent a similar accident.

In addition to these reports, records were also kept of *all* first aid cases. Both accident reports and first aid records were given regular and careful review by a "safety engineer" who worked out of the Company's main office.

Another instrument designed for generating conformance to the safety program was the closely planned and regularly conducted "safety meeting." Usually, this was presided over by the "safety and personnel manager" employed by the local plant. Such meetings were supposed to limit themselves to a thorough examination of the accidents which had occurred, the analysis of the outstanding accident-producing practices and conditions in the plant, and the suggestion of ways and means of correcting them. Actually, as will be noted later, the meetings sometimes discussed other subjects having little connection with safety work.

A final indication of the extent to which safety work was bureaucratized is that it was organized by, and was the responsibility of, a specific, continually existent office, "the safety and personnel manager" in the plant. On the basis of his *superior and specialized knowledge,* he was expected to detect unsafe acts or conditions in the plant, and to call them to the attention of the appropriate foreman.

No other ongoing program in the plant was as highly bureaucratized. The "no-absenteeism" rule, for example, was not backed up with anything like the careful system of statistics and reports which were prepared for accidents. In fact, there were no absenteeism statistics kept in the plant. No other program in the plant had the galaxy of rules, special meetings, posters, inspections, or special supervisors in the main office and local plant. Indeed, until Peele's arrival, the only thing that the men in the plant thought of as "rules" were the safety regulations. As one foreman said: "It is the one thing they really work on."

In terms of the hypothesis developed in the section comparing mine and surface workers, it would be expected that a high degree of bureaucracy would result from the conjunction of two factors: (1) a high degree of bureaucratic *striving* on management's part, and (2) a low degree of *resistance* to bureaucratic administration among the workers. Both of these conditions were to be found in connection with the safety program.

Workers' Attitudes Toward Safety Work

Given a list of four sets of rules, workers were asked which of these rules they "were most likely to follow." The safety regulations ranked second as the rules workers would be likely to accept; the rule occupying third position fell far behind.

RANK ORDER	RULES WORKERS MOST LIKELY TO FOLLOW	NO. OF CHOICES
1	Bidding Rules [2]	50
2	Safety	28
3	No-Absenteeism	4
4	No-Smoking	2
		84

To the extent that workers willingly conformed to safety rules, and thereby represented only a negligible barrier to management's bureaucratization of this area, they did so for reasons which are sometimes obvious and at other times subtle. Of course workers were concerned lest they be permanently injured, mutilated, scarred, or even killed by accidents. Moreover, they might suffer also from loss of income in the event of an injury, since weekly compensation payments were less than their ordinary wages. Besides, accidents hurt; in and of *themselves* they comprised a punishment for the infraction of safety regulations.

Aside from these utilitarian motives, some workers appeared to have other, non-rational [3] incentives for accepting the safety program. To appreciate these, it must be noticed that to no small degree safety work is enmeshed in, and is an expression of, middle class morality. Consider, for example, the rule against drinking on the job or bringing whiskey into the plant.

2. These rules, which enabled workers to secure better jobs in the plant, will be discussed in a later section.

3. That is, they were non-rational with respect to the goal of *accident reduction;* they might have been quite rational with regard to other ends.

Formally, this rule functions to mitigate accidents deriving from drunkenness. But this rule can also be viewed in the context of the varying value systems of miners and surfacemen, or in the light of surface workers' stereotypes of miners as "hard drinkers." In this perspective, it is likely that the "no drinking" rule had more than an accident-preventing function, but also served to reinforce surfacemen's middle class values.

Perhaps another example will bring this out more clearly: One of the important components of the safety program was called "good housekeeping." This sponge-term included such diverse strictures as, "Keep tools in their proper place," "Sweep up regularly," "Wash and paint buildings when needed," and "Come to work neatly attired and clean shaven." Undoubtedly some of these did contribute to greater safety. Refuse on the floor, for example, might cause a worker to slip and hurt himself. On the other hand, the connection between being clean shaven, or neatly dressed, and accident prevention, seems tenuous indeed.

It will be recalled that it was the more middle class surface workers, rather than the miners, who were apt to prefer their friends to be "clean." It would seem, therefore, that the "good housekeeping" part of the safety program was more likely to appeal to those who had interiorized the middle class virtues of cleanliness, neatness, or orderliness. In other words, some workers, most probably those on the surface, were further motivated to adhere to the safety program because, to the degree that it consisted of good housekeeping, it was congenial to their values.

In addition, a "clean job" and place of work is more prestige-laden than a dirty one. Surfacemen viewed the miners as a "lower class" group, in part because the miner's job was a *dirtier* one. Similarly, many surface workers complained about the grey dust, which pervades all gypsum processing, and they asserted that this often kept men from seeking employment at the plant. To such men, safety, via "good housekeeping," was a *status-reinforcing* agent.

Still another factor in motivating workers to conform to the safety program was the manner in which this work is actually conducted. As contrasted with the "outside" initiation and administration of the "no-smoking" rule, workers (as well as management) participated in the initiation and direction of the safety program. The safety meetings were attended by workers, and they were, moreover, encouraged to make suggestions from the floor. This is illustrated by the comments of a wet end worker who mentioned:

"We have safety meetings every month."
"What sort of things do you take up there?"
"We ask questions and bring up problems, and not only about safety."
"What else?"
"About the process. We just had a 'mix' that hurt our hands, and made them sore. We asked for rubber gloves and *got them right away*. That's the sort of thing I mean."

The safety meetings provided workers with frequent opportunities for the expression of complaints and with a chance to make, and immediately see the response to, safety suggestions. As a foreman remarked, "Anything that is reported as dangerous, they take care of *right away*." There would seem little doubt that this was one of the most satisfying things about the safety program and reinforced workers' obedience to it. Like the housekeeping part of safety, this, too, bolstered the worker's status, though in a somewhat different way. While "housekeeping" enhanced the prestige of the worker's job, the safety meetings expanded his control over an aspect of the work situation.

Education vs. Punishment

Management believed that adherence to the safety program could be secured by way of "education," rather than discipline and punishment. This was a unique characteristic of safety work, distinguishing it from all other programs and rules in the plant. The safety meetings, safety posters, reports and records on accidents, were viewed as educational or fact-finding devices. Their use as punishment and control-gaining techniques was explicitly disavowed. As the safety engineer emphasized:

"For the more serious type of injury which would come under compensation, a complete report is made out . . . (but) *not as some companies do, to fix the blame.* We do it in order to gain an understanding of the causes of accidents, *so that we can better deal with them and prevent them* . . . One thing we always keep in mind is that we carry on our work to get at the causes. Lots of companies do it just to fix the blame. Discipline in its dictionary sense is education and training and *not punishment.*"

There is reason to believe that the safety engineer's comments cannot be taken entirely at their face value, and that a part of safety work involved the distribution of blame and punishment.[4] But the safety program was unique because it was carried on with the conscious intention of using methods *other* than punishment.

In a factory situation, a punishment is, at the very least, a harbinger of withheld promotions, demotions, or even of dismissal. As such, it is a direct status threat to the worker. By minimizing the use of punishments, the safety program was conducted in such a way that it did *not* present continual threats to the workers' status.

Extensions of the Hypotheses

What has been said thus far illustrates anew the role of value elements in determining the degree of resistance to bureaucratic forms of administration. That is, some workers had little resistance to the safety program, since it was in conformity

---

4. Cf., the discussion of the punishment-legitimating functions of rules in the last chapter.

with their values on personal well-being, cleanliness, and neatness.

Examination of the safety program also permits an extension of that earlier analysis. For it introduces explicitly the concept of *status* and suggests that resistance to bureaucratization will be affected by the way in which it impinges upon the status of a group. The use of bureaucratic methods is held to heighten resistance insofar as it impairs the status of group members.

Examination of one other factor in workers' attitudes toward safety can lead to further refinements of our hypotheses: When accidents occurred, workers on top and bottom tended to blame their foremen. Workers, like top management, defined the foreman's role as including a responsibility for safety. It was in this sense that a miner declared:

"A foreman's job *is to take care of his men.* If he doesn't take care of them, there is trouble."

A foreman in the board building told of the "trouble" he got into when an accident occurred on his shift:

"It's always hard if anybody gets hurt. One lad got killed on my shift. I don't know whose fault it was. It wasn't anybody's fault . . . He was off his job. He was supposed to be on the take-off, but he was playing around. *This kind of thing always comes back on the foreman.* They all asked, 'Where was you?' *And they wouldn't let me explain. They always blame the foreman.* But accidents are too quick. What could I have done?"

Sometimes, also, workers attributed an accident to the "cheapness" of the Company. Accidents were often seen as coming about because the Company wouldn't spend the money needed for proper equipment. More generally, then, workers frequently defined accidents as evidence of the supervisor's failure to perform his role-obligation, namely to "take care of the men."

In consequence, workers sought to formalize management's

safety obligations by incorporating them into the union-management contract. This contract put the onus for accidents on the Company:

"The Company agrees to all such safety devices for the protection of themselves and health of its employees as shall be mutually agreed upon by its representatives and the Plant Safety Committee."

Our earlier hypotheses, therefore, require some modification: In their last form, the hypotheses asserted that the degree of bureaucracy was a product of (a) the intensity of workers' resistance to (b) managerial striving for bureaucractic administration. The "safety clause" in the contract indicates that the reverse is also true. Namely, that it may be *workers* who perceive *management* as unwilling to fill their roles. It may, therefore, be workers who *initiate* bureaucratic forms, while on the other hand, the management group may be the barrier resisting them. Another important example of this, to be discussed later, is the "bidding" system. Our earlier statements can now be seen as only a special case of the following more general hypotheses:

1. Bureaucratic efforts emerge when either superiors or subordinates see the other as unwilling to perform their role-obligations.
2. The degree of bureaucratic development is a function of:
   a. The strength of the bureaucratic drive of either superiors and/or subordinates (for both may want it) and
   b. The strength of the resistance of superiors [5] and/or subordinates (for both may resist it).

---

5. There are several reasons why it is desirable to emphasize the *status* of initiators and resistors, at least in this provisional statement:
(1) Much of organizational analysis, from Weber onward, neglects *systematic* examination of the manner in which status differences *within* an organization affects its mode of administration.
(2) Moreover, many studies (for example, Selznick's, Ibid.) focus on a group's behavior as a response to threats from the "external" environment, thereby tending to underestimate the role of *internal* tensions.
(3) By focusing on status *differentiation*, we may, thereby, restrain the dubious assumption that all people in the situation are oriented to the *same* values. This

Representative Bureaucracy Continued

Turning attention to the other side of the coin, management's orientation to the safety program may now be considered. In this connection, at least two things require clarification:

1. What gains did *management* derive from the safety program?
2. Why did management administer this program with such a distinctive style, *emphasizing education rather than* discipline?

Management's motives for desiring a safety program often paralleled the workers', being both utilitarian and non-rational. This might be expected, if only on the grounds that line supervisors frequently faced the same work hazards as their workers. A safety program was, therefore, directly beneficial to their own bodily welfare. Furthermore, some supervisors were motivated to do something about safety because workers who might be injured would, often as not, be their friends. In addition, accidents increased the Company's premiums for industrial insurance, and when they happened, immediately disrupted production. Again, when accidents occurred they deteriorated worker-supervisor relations, for workers frequently blamed accidents on supervisors.

---

may, or may not, be the case. As we saw, certain groups of *workers,* the miners, were favorably oriented to pro-absenteeism norms. *Management,* however, either rejected this norm, or only reluctantly acquiesced to it. Attention to status differentiation may alert us to the possibility that different groups within an organization will accept different values.

(4) By focusing on management as superiors, and on workers as subordinates, we imply that there *normally* exists a power differential in favor of management; hence the degree of bureaucratization is likely to be more influenced by management's drive for or resistance to it, than by the workers'. This is, perhaps, more evident in organizations like the army or the civil service where subordinates have few or no status-defending organizations. The assertion that workers may initiate, as well as resist, bureaucratization should not be taken as a cue to relax attention to the role of "strategic persons." In either event, whether workers resist or initiate bureaucracy, it would seem necessary to broaden our view and include another group of "gatekeepers" or strategic personnel, namely, the union officials or informal leaders among workers.

Certain sections of management, like some workers, also appeared to derive value-affirming satisfactions from the "good housekeeping" part of safety work.

In addition, the safety program coincided with *humanitarian* mores which place a high value on the individual person and his life. Remarks made by the safety manager are again illustrative:

"You've probably heard of the Gypsum Association. All the gypsum companies belong to it. I was at one of their meetings, and they accepted the idea of (losing) one life a year in the mine. *We don't figure that way; we just couldn't think along those lines.*"

In the main, however, management felt that the most convincing justification for a safety program was the interdependdence of safety and production. The Company's safety manual asserted:

"During the past decade leaders in industry and commerce came to recognize more and more the *economic advantages* of organized accident prevention work . . . (we must) accept as our *guiding principle the fact that safety and efficient production are inseparably united* . . . The standard described in the following pages is based on the premise that there is an inseparable relationship between safety and efficient production . . . If . . . the safety engineer can show that compliance with his suggestions will enhance production or otherwise result in economic advantage, *he will not find it difficult to obtain the desired result.*" (Our emphasis—A. W. G.)

It is possible that management's reiterated emphasis on the connection between safety work and production was a rationalization intended to advance "hard-headed," and hence acceptable reasons, for behavior actually motivated by "soft," humanitarian mores. Whether this is so cannot be determined from our data. In any event, the *major* legitimation of safety work, from management's public viewpoint, was its usefulness to production.

There are, indeed, consequences which safety work has for production, especially on worker-supervisor relations, which are somewhat more subtle than those noted above. Safety work not only minimizes production losses due to accidents, but it occasionally provided an easily justifiable technique for *controlling workers.* The comments of a foreman at the wet end exemplify this screening function of safety rules:

"Are there any new rules in the building?"
"Well, there's no wandering around now, to the mine and mill. You can't leave your department without permission of the foreman."
"How do the men feel about it?"
"They don't like it, but they live up to it."
"Why was it introduced?"
"For *safety purposes.* A man could wander off into the mine and *he could get hurt there."*
"Can you think of a case where a surfaceman did this?"
"I can't think of an instance where it did happen because of walking around, but it's to *prevent it.* The men would walk around all the time and talk to the men in different departments."

Since this change was tied to safety considerations, which were accepted by both groups, workers' resistance to the loss of their customary privilege of walking around was inhibited. In this case "safety" was probably a rationalization; for the "no-wandering" regulation was introduced as part of the more general increase in managerial control that began with Peele's succession. One of the latent functions of the safety program was, then, to legitimate supervisory production control over workers, and to screen extensions of it.

In this way safety work was status-reinforcing for the supervisory staff. The production or "output" consequences of safety work also fortified the supervisor's status, since management on all levels was made or broken in terms of its production record.

Thus safety innovations aiding production, and thereby status enhancing for management, were therefore more readily accepted than safety proposals whose production consequences were indeterminate.

An example of a fairly *acceptable* safety innovation involved a change in the board machine. This proposal was intended to solve the following difficulty: When the plaster poured down from the hopper on to the rolling paper, it sometimes had a large undissolved "lump" in it. This lump might tear the paper when it was pressed between the rollers. The tear would then branch out, destroying yards of board, like a "run" in a woman's stocking.

As a result, when a worker saw a lump fall, he tried to pick it out with his fingers before it reached the rollers. In doing so, however, he was in danger of crushing his fingers, or his whole hand, between the rollers. Similar danger existed when a worker attempted to retrieve a tool that had accidentally dropped into the mixture.

To prevent these accidents a "release" bar was installed directly above the rollers. Like the release trigger on a washing-machine, the bar would instantly spread the rollers apart, preventing injury to the worker's hand *and* to the board. This innovation was accepted with relative ease because it aided *both production and safety.*

Management Deviance From Safety Requirements

Those safety innovations that provided no obvious production gains were, however, received with greater reluctance. As the safety engineer said:

"Now, if you take something intangible . . . (for example, if you recommend) that a union safety committee be appointed from the union members—well, that's worse. The plant managers don't like the idea."

Union safety committees were not resisted, however, merely because they were "intangible." They were opposed because plant managers saw them as status-threatening. As the safety engineer added:

"Union committees have worked out well. But there is a lot of disagreement on this from other (sic) companies. I just can't see it. These other companies holler, 'If you let them get into a discussion of safety programs, the next thing you know, they'll be sticking their nose in everything and *be wanting to run your plant for you.*'"

In brief, management tended to support safety work when this aided production and thereby garnered status gains for themselves. They resisted safety efforts when these were seen as incurring status losses.

However much safety work was justified in terms of its production consequences, these two interests did not always coincide. Since management's stake in production is so compelling, they might sometimes neglect safety considerations when these two interests diverge. One illustration of this occurred in the mine:

At one time the mine required a number of new workers immediately, in order to cope with a difficulty which was slowing production. Applicants for mine work were, however, ordinarily given a special physical examination before being allowed to enter the mine. This was a time-consuming requirement, and the workers were desperately needed. Peele, therefore, decided that "you have to relax the rules sometimes." The workers were put to work first, and given their examinations later. As a main office executive explained:

"When it comes to a question of meeting his quota of rock production, Peele is not going to worry about the rules. He might on other things, but not on the problem of meeting his production quota. *That comes first.*"

Because production "comes first," management sometimes found itself violating workers' beliefs that "supers must take care of their men." It was partly because of this that workers came to feel that management was unwilling to fulfill its safety obligations. In this setting, workers will initiate bureaucratic controls, while management may be a barrier to their implementation.

Solidarity as a Function of Safety Work

Management had at least one further incentive for supporting safety work, namely, the role that the safety program played in strengthening solidarity between itself and the workers. The safety program brought into prominence behavior patterns which, for the most part, *both* groups desired. It enlarged the "social space" in which the two groups could cooperate. In addition, the safety program, especially through the safety meetings, provided an important "safety valve"; it opened up opportunities for the expression of grievances and for their routine discussion apart from the time-consuming formal grievance machinery. As the worker quoted earlier indicated, things "other" than safety were considered at these meetings. For example, it was not unusual to hear discussion of bidding problems, of wage rates, and up-grading problems at the safety meetings.

While workers did not appear to be very conscious of the solidarity-building function of safety work, management was often aware of it. The safety engineer's remarks provide several illustrations:

"It is really wonderful how things can be worked out in this safety field. You must know Tenzman? He's regarded as a troublemaker. But when he got involved in safety work and discussed this with his supervisors, why they came away saying, 'He's not a bad guy after all.' He gained a lot of respect for himself . . . You get into industrial relations in this work. And I'm continually pleased by the things that come out of it.

"In another of our plants there were two fellows who were also known as troublemakers. Then they got on the safety committee of the union. In working along and in sitting down talking things over, it is surprising how much more highly the supervisors now regard them . . . I've found the foremen are surprised with the results also. Works out fine. *It's an area of real harmony.*"

In brief, a further function of safety work was to diminish conflict and to cement solidarity between workers and management. There were, therefore, compelling motivations for management to support the safety program; safety work implemented its rational and non-rational values while, concomitantly, it fortified aspects of its status.

The "Careless" Worker

Our hypotheses would lead us to expect that management initiated bureaucratic measures in this sphere, as in others, because it perceived workers to be failing in their role-obligations. Management did, indeed, feel this way. Its complaints usually took the form of charging workers with "carelessness," rather than unwillingness, about safety. As the safety engineer said:

"You know how people think, 'It can't happen to me' . . . It always happens to someone else, not to you."

Management thus frequently complained that workers did not put on their safety-goggles when they should, that they failed to keep their machine-guards in place, and so forth. A second diagnosis, made by management, was that safety depended upon things about which workers were ignorant. For example, it was maintained that workers might not *know* how to use their knees when lifting heavy objects. Or they might not *know* that wearing rings during certain kinds of machine work was dangerous. As an "expert," the safety man was expected to know this, and it was his job to communicate this *information* to the worker.

These, then, were the two most frequent explanations of accidents offered by management. In effect, they asserted that the worker did not do as he should and failed in his safety obligations, because he was "careless," or because he did not know what to do.

The distinctive form of these explanations can be underscored by comparing the safety situation with others. For example, foremen were never heard to say, "So-and-so was *late,* or was *absent,* because he didn't *know* when to come in or because he was 'careless.' " Safety differed from other situations in that management did not believe that workers would *want* to have an accident. Management believed that workers were often absent or late *deliberately,* and perhaps maliciously, which of course was sometimes the case. A worker was not expected, however, to have an accident as a way of vexing his foreman or of expressing resentment toward the Company. In fact, the worker who was little motivated with regard to safety might be viewed by management as highly motivated with respect to *production.* An example of this was the resistance of mill workers to the introduction of "bag rests." A bag rest enabled a worker to pick up a newly-filled bag of plaster without bending down; for in bending, the bag was brought closer to his eyes, and should the bag tear, he might be blinded by the powder. Workers resisted the "bag rest," explained the safety engineer, on the ground that it "will cut productivity by fifty per cent." A worker who resisted safety innovations or who violated safety requirements in *this* context was doing so because he *conformed to production values,* which were so salient to management. He was therefore not regarded as a "bad worker," or as one unwilling to *work.*

Because workers who deviated from safety requirements were defined as *careless,* or lacking in sufficient *knowledge,* and might nonetheless be concerned about production, management strove to secure workers' conformance to safety by the use of meetings, discussion, and posters. *"Education" appears to be a response to deviance, when the deviance is believed to spring from "ignorance" or well-intentioned carelessness. Conversely, "punishment" appears to be a response to deviance which is seen as stemming from willful, status-threatening resistance.*

In the safety program, then, there was a very different pattern of rule-administration than in the case of the no-smoking rule. The safety pattern differed from the latter in that:

1. The rules were ordinarily enforced by management and obeyed by workers.

2. Adjustment to the rules was usually obtained, not by ignoring them, but instead, by "education" and by involving the workers and the union in their initiation and administration.

3. Like the no-smoking rule, the safety program generated few tensions and little overt conflict between workers and management. Solidarity between the two groups, however, derived from their mutual *acceptance* of the program, rather than their joint *rejection* of it. Solidarity was developed through the interaction that arose in the process of securing *conformance* with, rather than *avoidance* of, the rules.

It is still somewhat premature to essay a systematic statement of how the "mock" and "representative" bureaucratic patterns come about, or why they differ from each other. By now, however, it may be understandable why this pattern has been termed "representative bureaucracy." [6] For it was characterized by the day-to-day *participation* of the workers in its

---

6. This term is taken over from the very stimulating historical study of the English Civil Service by J. Donald Kingsley, *Representative Bureaucracy*, 1944, Antioch Press, Yellow Springs, Ohio. In thinking about the names given the different bureaucratic patterns, it is well to bear in mind Ernst Cassirer's strictures on the functions of names: "The function of a name is always limited to emphasizing a particular aspect of a thing, and it is precisely this restriction and limitation upon which the value of the name depends. It is not the function

administration, though it was not in any sense an "ideally" democratic pattern. On the other hand, there were few indications that management's efforts to elicit workers' participation were importantly influenced by deliberately manipulative intentions. It should also be emphasized that the safety programs do not always take the form of "representative bureaucracy." The safety program in another company might conform to a "mock" or a "punishment-centered" bureaucratic pattern. It is *not* safety *as such* with which we were concerned, but only the social characteristics which happened to be associated with safety in this plant.

Efficiency and Bureaucracy

It was noticed that the safety program possessed a relatively high degree of bureaucratization. Can this be explained, as Max Weber has suggested, because of its efficiency? Was safety work so fully bureaucratized because this mode of administration had proved so effective? This would hardly seem to be a serious explanation, for neither the Company nor the research team had any idea of just how efficient *any* aspect of the safety program was, least of all its bureaucratic mode of administration. Actually, the Company had never worked out any measure of the effectiveness of its safety program. It could demonstrate that trends in accident rates occurred over the years, or that cycles of accidents occurred during a single year. It was not shown, however, that these variations were at all *due to the safety program,* in any respect, and least of all to its bureaucratic form.

The growth of the safety program, and its elaboration in bureaucratic directions, cannot be attributed simply to a demonstrable competence in achieving its ends. Instead, and in

of a name to refer exclusively to a concrete situation, but merely to single out and dwell upon a certain aspect." *An Essay on Man,* 1944, Yale University, New Haven, p. 135.

conformity with our hypotheses, the high degree of bureaucratization in the safety sphere appeared to be a function of (a) a strong managerial motivation to bureaucratize this area, born of the belief that workers are careless or ignorant of safety requirements, and (b) the low degree of workers' resistance to this managerial drive. This is obviously a simplification for, as was noted, *workers also* initiated a bureaucratic organization of safety work, because they believed that management sometimes failed in its safety obligations.

Chapter XI

PUNISHMENT-CENTERED

BUREAUCRACY

"PUNISHMENT-CENTERED bureaucracy" is distinguished from "mock" and "representative" bureaucracy in that responses to deviations take the form of *punishments*. This particular type is composed of two sub-patterns, depending on *who* exercises the punishment and who receives it. In one case, management utilizes punishments, directing them against workers. In the other case, workers subject management to punishments when the latter deviates. The first case can be called the "disciplinary" pattern. The second sub-type can be termed the "grievance" pattern, for the union-grievance machinery is one of the most commonly used instruments by means of which workers inflict punishments on management.

The best example of the "disciplinary" pattern was the "no-absenteeism" rule, in which a specific punishment was promulgated for violations of the no-absenteeism rule. Moreover, the formal "warning notice" made explicit provision for absences and was, in fact, more frequently used to warn workers about violations of this rule than for any other infraction.

The "Bidding System"

The "bidding system" is an example of rules enforced by "grievances." Originally incorporated into the labor-management contract at the union's initiative, the bidding rules specified that:

"All job vacancies and new jobs shall be posted within five (5) days after such a job becomes available, for a period of five (5) days, in order to give all employees an opportunity to make application in writing for such jobs. Such application shall be considered in the order of seniority in the department, provided, however, that the ability of the applicant to fill the requirements of the job shall also be considered. If no one in the department bids for the job, bidding shall be opened to other employees."

The workers were usually determined that supervisors should conform to the "bidding system." Supervisors, however, responded to the bidding rules with considerable resistance, much of it covert. They would sometimes strive to evade these regulations by posting a job at a lower rate than it should have carried. This discouraged bids from all individuals except the worker whom the super wanted for the job. He would bid for the job on the super's private advice, get it, and shortly thereafter be upgraded.

The "bidding system," in brief, involved a pattern from which local management withheld full support and which it sometimes deliberately evaded, but which was strongly supported by most workers. The grievance machinery, by which workers compelled conformance to these rules, specified that complaints must *first* be taken up directly with the "deviant" supervisor. Only if he continued to evade the bidding rules, or if no settlement could be arranged with him, could the grievance process move up to higher echelons. (This provision was functionally similar to the "warning notice," which was utilized in the "disciplinary" pattern.)

As shown in the table on page 190, fifty of eighty-four workers believed that *workers* were most ready to conform to the bidding rules. Only three of eighty-three workers, however, expected that *foremen and supervisors* would be "most ready" to conform to these same regulations.

It was also noted in the earlier table that only four of eighty-four workers believed that *workers* would be most ready to follow the no-absenteeism rule. Out of eighty-three workers, thirty-two believed that foremen and supervisors were most ready to follow the no-absenteeism prescriptions.[1] These diverging judgments indicate that the "disciplinary" and "grievance" patterns were associated with considerable tension between workers and management.

You Can't Chase Two Rabbits

Certain tension-provoking characteristics were built directly into the "bidding system." This system can be thought of as a method of "rating" which employed "multiple superlatives"; that is, it sought to maximize *two* values, namely, seniority and ability, at the same time. It was as difficult to maximize *both* of these *simultaneously* as it would be to chase two rabbits at

---

1.

RANK ORDER	RULES WORKERS BELIEVE SUPERS MOST READY TO FOLLOW	NO. OF CHOICES
1	Safety	48
2	No-Absenteeism	32
3	Bidding	3
4	No-Smoking	0
		N = 83

once.[2] Invariably pressure was exerted to drop one of the superlatives, ability or skill, and to concentrate attention on the other, seniority.

This particular resolution of the tension was influenced by the fact that most plant jobs required little or no skill. It was much more difficult to distinguish one job from the other than it was to make clear-cut discriminations in terms of seniority. The latter was readily quantifiable, and was divisible into years or months and, if necessary, even into weeks. Thus the tendency to use seniority as the exclusive criterion for promotions or transfers became accentuated. The "bidding system" therefore developed in a direction which placed management's value on "ability" under stress. On the other hand, however, it served an important apathy-preserving function for workers, by making horizontal and vertical mobility available even to those who put forth no special effort.

Twilight of Middle Management

The "bidding system" can be easily interpreted as infringing upon the managerial prerogative to transfer, hire, or promote workers. Initially, therefore, top main office management looked askance at the union's proposal for a "bidding system," seeing in it a challenge to its status. Under continued union pressure, top management later accepted bidding, in part, because it recognized that most jobs in the plant required very little skill anyhow. Actually, therefore, utilization of seniority as the basic criterion of promotions did not violate *top management's* value on skill. Moreover, it did not in practice infringe upon rights, control over plant hiring, transferring, and promoting, which it commonly exercised.

These rights had long since been delegated to the *local*

---

2. Cf. George K. Zipf's discussion of "The 'Singleness of the Superlative,'" pp. 2-5, *Human Behavior and the Principle of Least Effort,* Addison-Wesley Press, Inc., 1949. Cambridge, Mass.

plant management. Previously, much of the plant hiring and promoting had been guided by the recommendations of foremen and supervisors. By conceding to the "bidding system," top management agreed, as it were, to rescind the privileges of another group, that is, middle management. In effect, the bidding system constituted a silent transfer of power; it expanded the rights of workers at the expense of *middle* management. With the introduction of the "bidding system" there was a precipitous decline in middle management's role. Both foremen and workers agreed upon and recognized this as a consequence of the bidding rules. As a board plant foreman grieved:

"This shifting around (now possible through the 'bidding system') makes 'breaking-in' more of a problem . . . Fellows are always coming to me, saying they want to shift."
"Do you have any idea why they want to do it?"
"None of them ever tells me anything. The union compels the Company to post jobs, and we have allowed them to shift."
"How was it when the union wasn't here?"
"Then you *stayed where the foreman told you to.* You didn't move unless the foreman saw fit to move you."

A mechanic expressed the workers' viewpoint:

"I think the union's all right . . . I guess the fact is, they're pretty good. The foreman didn't like the 'bidding system' so very much. *Now, they can't get their friends in anymore."*

Or as another worker in the mill remarked:

"You don't have to pull strings . . . When there is a job open, they put it on the board and you put in a bid for the job; the man with the most seniority gets the job."

With the advent of the "bidding system," the worker did not have to "pull strings," or "play up to" his foreman, if he wanted a transfer. If relations between the two were strained, the worker could escape his foreman by bidding for a job in another building or division. When he got a job in this way, he owed his new *foreman* nothing for it; no "favors" had been done, and therefore no obligations had been incurred. In this way, the "bidding system" narrowed the super's discretionary powers and undermined his status, while strengthening the workers'. The workers were thereby motivated to support bidding, while supers were impelled to evade it. As far as the workers were concerned, the bidding rules performed a "leeway function," serving to make middle management compliant to their own *informal* practices; unless a supervisor "played ball," workers would take a job under another supervisor. They knew that if a supervisor had too many workers under him bidding for other jobs, the plant manager would begin to wonder whether the super was handling his duties properly.

Having considered the "grievance" form of punishment-centered bureaucracy, an example of the "disciplinary" form may now be examined.

The No-Absenteeism Rule

Management on all levels of authority was hostile to absenteeism. While workers had varying feelings about the no-absenteeism rule, few of them welcomed it. Since we are not paid for time off, some workers asked rhetorically, why should management complain? As already emphasized, absenteeism was traditionally valued by the miners, and they solidly closed their ranks to squash a challenge to this ancient prerogative. Many values important to workers were satisfied by absenteeism: for example, they could spend more time with their families, repair their homes, do spring plowing, hunt and fish, visit around, get drunk, or just rest. It was also a personalized and individual way of giving vent to dissatisfactions that arose in the course of working. At any rate, absenteeism was one way workers realized values that at any given moment might be more important to *them* than management's need for regular, predictable production.

The social status of workers and management alike was involved in the tug-of-war centering around the no-absenteeism rule. The foreman who was short-handed, due to absenteeism or any other reason, faced the danger of being unable to fill his production quota. No one in the plant was exempt from meeting this obligation, for "production comes first." Supervisors enforced the no-absenteeism rule, partly, therefore, because it enabled them to satisfy their chief status-obligation, keeping production going.

The no-absenteeism regulation also meant that the worker had to *account* for what he did *outside* of the plant. Under this rule the worker had, in effect, to receive his supervisor's permission to go to a wedding, attend a funeral, or stay home with a sick relative, whom he must now prove was really sick. The no-absenteeism rule challenged the workers' control over a wide range of out-of-plant behavior, bringing it within the purview of the foreman. As such, the rule was experienced as an extension of managerial power into an illegitimate area.

When the worker returned from an absence, the supervisor had to decide whether the worker's behavior was punishable. He was not formally interested in the causes of absenteeism, as he was of accidents, with the object of removing them. The investigation of an absence simply determined whether or not a worker would be punished.

The supervisor operated on the assumption that some absences were not "excusable." He believed that they evidenced the worker's "irresponsibility," marking him as a person who knowingly and deliberately evaded his obligations. The supervisor did not assume, as he did with respect to safety violations, that the absent worker was unwittingly careless, or ignorant of the requirements. As one foreman said emphatically:

"They know God-damned well they're not supposed to be out without a good excuse. What can we do with them but get tough?"

Workers responded in much the same way when they felt that the requirements of the "bidding system" had been evaded by supervisors. Since the bidding rules had been incorporated into the contract and since, time and again, the union committee had called these provisions to management's attention, their neglect tended to be viewed as malicious and deliberate. As one mill worker said in such a situation, *"They're just asking for trouble."* Like management, workers responded by getting "tough." The rules, therefore, served to legitimate the punishment of those deemed to be *willfully* deviant and deliberately aggressive.

In fine, then, the punishment-centered bureaucratic pattern was characterized by the following features:

1. The rules about which the pattern was organized were *enforced,* but primarily by *one* group, either workers or management, rather than by both.
2. Adjustment to the rules was not attained by ignoring them, nor by "educating" the deviant or involving him in the rule's administration, but by *punishing* him.
3. The pattern was associated with considerable conflict and tension.

It may now be clear that this pattern was given its name because it is organized around the punishment-legitimating functions of bureaucratic rules, and is intimately associated with "close supervision." In the next chapter an effort will be made to synthesize and compare the three bureaucratic patterns which have been examined and to relate them to the Weberian theory of bureaucracy with which this research began.

Chapter XII

THE THREE PATTERNS

OF BUREAUCRACY

BEFORE SETTING THESE
three bureaucratic patterns into a theoretical framework, and
to facilitate their comparison, they need to be stated in a more
succinct and systematic manner, indicating the variety of factors associated with each. This is done in the table on the following two pages.

Locating Bureaucratic Tensions

At the beginning of chapter ten, it was suggested that a
typology of bureaucratic patterns might provide clues concerning the specific organizational characteristics which generate
tensions and arouse complaints. Inspection of the following,

SUMMARY OF FACTORS ASSOCIATED
WITH THE THREE PATTERNS OF BUREAUCRACY

MOCK	REPRESENTATIVE	PUNISHMENT-CENTERED

1. Who Usually Initiates the Rules?

The rule or rules are imposed on the group by some "outside" agency. *Neither* workers nor management, neither superiors nor subordinates, identify themselves with or participate in the establishment of the rules or view them as their own.

e. g.—The "no-smoking" rule was initiated by the insurance company.

Both groups initiate the rules and view them as their own.

e. g.—Pressure was exerted by union *and* management to initiate and develop the safety program. Workers and supervisors could make modifications of the program at periodic meetings.

The rule arises in response to the pressure of *either* workers or management, but is *not jointly* initiated by them. The group which does not initiate the rule views it as imposed upon it by the other.

e. g. — Through their union the workers initiated the bidding system. Supervisors viewed it as something to which the Company was forced to adhere.

2. Whose Values Legitimate the Rules?

Neither superiors nor subordinates can, ordinarily, legitimate the rule in terms of their own values.

Usually, *both* workers and management can legitimate the rules in terms of their own key values.

e. g.—Management legitimated the safety program by tying it to *production*. Workers legitimized it via their values on personal and bodily welfare, maintenance of income, and cleanliness.

Either superiors or subordinates alone consider the rule legitimate; the other may concede on grounds of expediency, but does not define the rule as legitimate.

e. g.—Workers considered the bidding system "fair," since they viewed it as minimizing personal favoritism in the distribution of jobs. Supervisors conformed to it largely because they feared the consequences of deviation.

3. Whose Values Are Violated by Enforcement of the Rules?

Enforcement of the rule violates the values of *both groups*.

e. g.—If the no-smoking rule were put into effect, it would violate the value on "personal equality" held by workers and supervisors, since office workers would still be privileged to smoke.

Under most conditions, enforcement of the rules entails violations of *neither* group's values.

e. g.—It is only under comparatively *exceptional* circumstances that enforcement of the safety rules interfered with a value held by management, say, a value on production.

Enforcement of the rules violates the values of only one group, *either* superiors or subordinates.

e. g.—The bidding rules threatened management's value on the use of skill and ability as criteria for occupational recruitment.

4. What Are the Standard Explanations of Deviations from the Rules?

The deviant pattern is viewed as an expression of "uncontrollable" needs or of "human nature."

Deviance is attributed to ignorance or *well-intentioned carelessness*—i. e., it is an unanticipated by-

In the main, deviance is attributed to *deliberate* intent. Deviance is thought to be the deviant's *end*.

MOCK	REPRESENTATIVE	PUNISHMENT-CENTERED
e. g.—People were held to smoke because of "nervousness."	product of behavior oriented to some other end, and thus an "accident." This we call a "utilitarian" conception of deviance. e. g.—Violation of the safety rule might be seen as motivated by concern for production, rather than by a deliberate intention to have accidents. If for example, a worker got a hernia, this might be attributed to his ignorance of proper lifting technique.	This we call a "voluntaristic" conception of deviance. e. g.—When a worker was absent without an excuse, this was *not* viewed as an expression of an uncontrollable impulse, or as an unanticipated consequence of other interests. It was believed to be *willful*.

5. What Effects Do the Rules Have Upon the Status of the Participants?

MOCK	REPRESENTATIVE	PUNISHMENT-CENTERED
Ordinarily, deviation from the rule is status-enhancing for workers and management *both*. Conformance to the rule would be status-impairing for both.	Usually, deviation from the rules impairs the status of superiors *and* subordinates, while conformance ordinarily permits both a measure of status improvement.	Conformance to or deviation from the rules leads to status gains *either* for workers or supervisors, but not for both, and to status losses for the other.
e. g.—Violation of the no-smoking rule tended to minimize the visibility of status differentials, by preventing the emergence of a privileged stratum of smokers.	e. g.—The safety program increased the prestige of workers' jobs by improving the cleanliness of the plant (the "good housekeeping" component), as well as enabling workers to initiate action for their superiors through the safety meetings. It also facilitated management's ability to realize its production obligations, and provided it with legitimations for extended control over the worker.	e. g.—Workers' conformance to the bidding system allowed them to escape from tense relations with certain supervisors, or to secure jobs and promotions without dependence upon supervisory favors. It deprived supers of the customary prerogative of recommending workers for promotion or for hiring.

6. Summary of Defining Characteristics or Symptoms

MOCK	REPRESENTATIVE	PUNISHMENT-CENTERED
(a) Rules are neither enforced by management nor obeyed by workers.	(a) Rules are both enforced by management and obeyed by workers.	(a) Rules either enforced by workers or management, and evaded by the other.
(b) Usually entails little conflict between the two groups.	(b) Generates a few tensions, but little overt conflict.	(b) Entails relatively great tension and conflict.
(c) Joint violation and evasion of rules is buttressed by the informal sentiments of the participants.	(c) Joint support for rules buttressed by informal sentiments, mutual participation, initiation, and education of workers and management.	(c) Enforced by punishment and supported by the informal sentiments of *either* workers or management.

indicates that there is a continuum in the degree of tension and conflict associated with the different patterns.

Line 6b of the table shows that mock bureaucracy is accompanied by little or no tension, that representative bureaucracy generates a few tensions, though little overt conflict, while punishment-centered bureaucracy manifests the most tensions and overt conflict. The table signifies quite clearly, then, that the different bureaucratic patterns are *not equally* tension-provocative.

Moreover, further inspection of this table indicates those factors associated with a high degree of tension. Briefly, these are: (1) Unilateral initiation and administration of the rules; (2) non-legitimacy of the rules; that is, the larger the number of power centers withholding legitimation of the rules, the more tensions will be created; (3) Enforcement of the rules violating values held by people in different power or status groups; (4) "Voluntaristic" explanations of deviance from the rules; (5) Enforcement of the rules resulting in an asymmetrical distribution of status gains and losses, so that one group loses while another gains in status. These five factors, which are closely associated with the development of tensions in the factory bureaucracy, are given their fullest expression in the punishment-centered pattern.

If the different bureaucratic patterns are not equally tension laden and conducive to conflict, then it should be expected that they do not all equally generate criticisms and complaints. More specifically, it should be found that the epithet "red tape," commonly directed at bureaucratic organizations in our culture,[1] is more likely to be attached to the punishment-centered form of bureaucracy. This can be partially explored by

---

1. An analysis of public conceptions of red tape, setting these in the framework of a theory of social problems, rather than organizational structure, is to be found in, Alvin W. Gouldner, "Red Tape as a Social Problem," in Robert K. Merton *et al.* (editors), *Reader in Bureaucracy*, Free Press, Glencoe, Ill., 1952.

determining which pattern of bureaucracy within the factory was thought to possess the most "red tape" by plant workers. The following table indicates that, when asked which rule they thought involved the most red tape, workers more frequently mentioned those which were organized on a punishment-centered basis.

TYPE OF PATTERN	RULE	NO. CHOICES AS HAVING MOST "RED TAPE" *
Punishment-centered	No-Absenteeism	26
Punishment-centered	Bidding	18
Representative	Safety	12
Mock	No-Smoking	6
		N = 62

* Only those who indicated that they knew what the term "red tape" meant were tabulated.

Although the safety rules and the program surrounding them were far more complex than the no-absenteeism rules and the bidding system, nonetheless they were viewed as possessing less "red tape." Apparently, therefore, the sheer *degree* of bureaucratization was not as important in eliciting complaints about red tape as was the *type* of bureaucracy. In other words, there are now grounds for suggesting that it is not "bureaucracy" *in toto* that provokes internal tensions, or complaints about "red tape," but, rather, that these are more likely to arise when bureaucracy is organized along specific lines; that is, as a punishment-centered pattern.

The Bureaucratic Patterns and Weber's Theory

As suggested in the introductory chapter, the seed of this distinction between "representative" and "punishment-centered" bureaucracy was resident in Weber's work; to this extent, at least, the conclusions presented here are continuous with Weber's theory of bureaucracy. For there is little doubt that the two latent strands in Weber's work, his biforked conception of bureaucracy as based on expertise and on authori-

tarian discipline, correspond to two of the proposed bureaucratic patterns. Weber's notion of bureaucracy as administration by experts, and on the basis of their knowledge, converges
with the "representative" pattern. In the latter, for example,
the safety engineer was expected to acquire knowledge of the
facts within his sphere, such as accident statistics and other
data, and to use his technical know-how to prevent accidents.
The safety program sought to *persuade* conformance by dif-
fusing knowledge through meetings, posters, and discussions.

The second element in Weber's theory, his conception of
bureaucracy as administration by authoritarian discipline,
parallels what has been called "punishment-centered" bureaucracy. In the latter, for example, when a supervisor investigated
an absence, he did not do so in order to determine its causes.
Instead he strove to extract obedience to the rule, without concern for the causes of disobedience, and with the object of
allocating blame and punishment.

In keeping with the second element in Weber's theory, foremen felt that they had a right to impose and enforce the no-
absenteeism rule, because of *their formal position of authority*.
Supervisors rarely expressed any rationale at all for the no-
absenteeism rule. They hardly ever justified it on the grounds
that it would realize some given end, such as regularizing production or making it more predictable. Sometimes, however,
they did assert that this rule would curtail absenteeism. In
such an emphasis, however, the rule became "the basis of action
for its own sake," as Weber would put it, and was almost like
attempting to curtail accidents by installing a "no-accident"
rule.

In the punishment-centered pattern, then, the rule is treated
as an end in itself. By contrast, however, the safety program,
the prototype of representative bureaucracy, involving rules
such as "don't throw debris on the floor," was designed to bring

about another end, accident curtailment. Obedience was sought and given the safety rules, on the grounds that they would effec, tively lead to desirable consequences *beyond themselves*. Moreover, workers and supervisors at the safety meetings would discuss and assess the relative merits of competing safety procedures. There was a continual effort to improve safety techniques. No attempts were ever made, though, to rationally evaluate the "no-absenteeism" rule or to find a *better* method of regularizing attendance by workers.

In the introductory chapter, it was noted that expert or representative bureaucracy was not legitimated *solely* in terms of the possession of technical skills. Examination of the safety program suggests several other conditions that must be satisfied before those who possess technical expertise will be acknowledged as legitimate authorities. One of these seems to be a consensus on ends or values. From this standpoint, it is not an irrelevant detail to note that *both* management and workers valued and sought accident-curtailment. If "voluntary consent" is vital to this pattern of authority, it would seem that this, in turn, rests on the subordinate's belief that he is being told to do things congruent with *his own ends and values*. Examination of the representative pattern also suggests other sources inducing voluntary consent from workers. Most particularly, in this pattern the worker had some measure of *control* over the initiation and administration of the rules through the safety meetings.

If this view is correct, then it would appear that representative bureaucracy, or Weber's administration by the expert, entails a proto-*democratic* process of legitimation. For the possession of expertise is, at most, a necessary but not a sufficient condition of legitimation in a representative bureaucracy. The expert's authority is validated only when used to further the workers' ends, and when workers have a say-so in the enactment and administration of the expert's program.[2] This would hardly be worth making such a point of, were it not for the fact that the role of "consent" and of democratic processes is blurred by Weber's theory of authority.

Weber's analysis of authority, of which his theory of bureaucracy is only one part, involves avoidance of the traditional classification of modes of political authority. The classical political scientists had emphasized a trichotomy of oligarchy, aristocracy, and democracy. In establishing their classification, the early political scientists had used variations in the mode of succession to authority as the basis of differentiation.

Weber, however, classified authority primarily in terms of the *grounds* on which obedience was sought and given. He described three modes of authority: (1) The "charismatic" form, in which loyalty was attached to the person of a leader on the grounds that he possessed unusual personal qualities; (2) the "traditional" form, in which loyalty was attached to the person of a leader who served and was guided by ancient traditions; (3) and finally, the "bureaucractic" form, in which loyalty is attached to formal rules, but not to persons, on the grounds that they are legally enacted, and expedient or rational.

When viewed in the perspective of older classifications of authority, Weber's conceptions may be seen to have important consequences. His classification presents us with a set of alterna-

---

2. A clear case of this is to be found in the typical attitudes of workers toward rate-setting engineers and experts. The workers do not ordinarily make an issue of the engineers' *competence,* but challenge the *ends* to which they put their skills and disagree with the norms which are used in setting a rate. In recent times this pressure has resulted in management efforts to involve unions in rate-setting activities, thus hoping to elicit worker's consent and conformance to the rates which are set. The complicated tangle of forces which then ensues is impossible to consider here. It should be added that work proceeding at the University of Michigan is lending empirical weight to our basic assumption here; thus Donald C. Pelz states that a useful postulate in their research "is that a leader will be accepted by group members to the extent that he helps them to achieve their goals." "Leadership Within a Hierarchical Organization," *Journal of Social Issues,* Vol. VII, No. 3, 1951, p. 55.

tives from which, as if by conceptual magic, the democratic form has utterly vanished. Weber implies that democracy is not a living option. It is on this level that his work has its deepest resonance with Robert Michel's "iron law of oligarchy."

Just as Michels maintained that the masses could only form the pedestal for the rule of an oligarchy, so too did Weber proclaim the ineffectuality of the people in the face of expert bureaucracy.[3] Just as Michels emphasized that democratic forms were destined to be the facades of oligarchical rule, so too did Weber indicate that democracy must abdicate in favor of bureaucracy.[4]

For Weber, authority was given consent *because* it was legitimate, rather than being legitimate *because* it evoked consent. For Weber, therefore, consent is always a datum to be taken for granted, rather than being a *problem* whose sources had to be traced. In consequence, he never systematically analyzed the actual social processes which either generated or thwarted the emergence of consent. This investigation of one of the bureaucratic patterns, representative (or expert) bureaucracy, suggests that the problem is much more complex than Weber had indicated. Indeed, in this case, it would seem that democratic processes are the covert foundation on which this type of authority actually rests, rather than merely its deceptive façade.

It may be that "consent," springing from a consensus of ends and values, also provides a clue for further investigations of punishment-centered bureaucracy. More specifically, it seems possible that this pattern arises not merely along with, but

---

3. For example, Weber writes, "Under normal conditions, the power position of a fully developed bureaucracy is always overtowering. The 'political master' finds himself in the position of the 'dilettante' who stands opposite the 'experts,' facing the trained official who stands within the management of administration. This holds whether the 'master' whom the bureaucracy serves is a 'people' . . . or a parliament . . ." Gerth and Mills, Ibid., p. 232.

4. In particular, see Weber's essay on "Politics as an Avocation," in Gerth and Mills, Ibid.

partly *because of a dissensus in ends;* that is, obedience would tend to be stressed as an end in itself, and authority tend to be legitimated in terms of incumbency of office, when subordinates are ordered to do things *divergent from their own ends.* If the no-absenteeism rule had *furthered workers' ends,* for example, it could have been justified on these grounds. At best, however, this rule is related to management's need to regularize production and to make it more predictable—ends which are *not salient for workers.* It is in part for this reason that supervisors had only an authoritarian legitimation for the absenteeism rule, and must declare, as it were, "You do this because *I* say so."

In such a context, where the supervisor has thrown his very status behind a rule or order, disobedience is likely to be experienced as threatening to his person and his authority. Since the supervisor did not have a "good argument," with which to persuade the worker in the first place, he cannot hope to bring an open dissident into line by sheer persuasion. The situation is then ripe for punitive action, and punishment becomes an expression of the supervisor's outrage and is felt to be "the only course" left open to him.

Bureaucratic Roles: A Note on Future Research

The three patterns presented here provide a framework which may be useful in describing and analyzing a given organization, and indicate variables fruitful for the systematic investigation of real administrations. It has not been the intention, of course, to imply that each of the patterns is equally important or powerful within a given organization. Future research must take this as a problem, resolvable only by the empirical findings in each case.

In fact, it may be wise to adopt the working hypothesis that representative bureaucracy in industrial settings operates in a "social space" whose contours, opportunities, and barriers are defined and shaped by punishment-centered bureaucracy. Grounds for favoring this hypothesis, or at least warranting its submission to careful test, may be seen, if instead of discussing the "representative" and "punishment-centered" *patterns*, the typical *authority roles* within each is examined. To facilitate this, the authority role in the punishment-centered bureaucracy shall be called the "true bureaucrat," while the authority in the representative bureaucracy will be termed the "expert." [5]

The expert, it seems, never wins the complete trust and acceptance of his company's highest authorities and tends to be kept at arm's length from the vaults of power. This is revealed by several aspects of the social and cultural organization found in, but not peculiar to, this Company.

Most familiar of all, possibly, was the commonplace separation between "line" and "staff" authorities, with the usual subordination of the latter.[6] In this Company, "staff" authority was defined as "consultative;" staff people could *advise* but they could not *command*. As a case in point, recall the safety engineer who operated out of the Company's main office. As he explained, he had to "sell" local management on his ideas

---

5. In the previous section dealing with Weber's conceptions of bureaucracy and their relationship to our own, we had in effect already begun a discussion of "experts" and "true bureaucrats." These two types of authority figures had there been distinguished with respect to the manner in which their power was *legitimated*. The expert's power was legitimated in terms of his possession of expert skills, while what we here call the "true bureaucrats" had their power legitimated by virtue of their incumbency of a legal office. Further, the expert validates his authority by pursuing ends congruent with his subordinates' and eliciting their consent in the enactment and administration of his program. Rather than using a process of persuasion to generate consent, the true bureaucrat—as discussed in that section—tended to employ coercion and punishment. In the paragraphs that follow we wish to develop other aspects of the distinction between experts and true bureaucrats.

6. Research at the Institute for Social Research at the University of Michigan tends to confirm this. e. g., "Our data showed how different persons in the organization perceived the power role of other persons in the line and staff organization. As a rule, the locus of power tended to be in the *line* organization. Floyd C. Mann, "Human Relations Training through a Company-wide Study," Institute for Social Research, Michigan, (Mimeo.) 1950, p. 8.

but could not command them to be carried out. Staff authorities were thus divested of "imperative control." And normally an organization's experts are located in its staff system.

Another indication of the subordinated position of the expert was in the mobility barriers with which he was handicapped. It was widely recognized in this plant that "real promotions" were given mainly to production, that is, to "line" authorities. The expert was therefore under constant pressure to forego the active pursuit of his specialty if he wished to make headway in the Company hierarchy. Along these lines was the case of a leading Company executive. Though this man had a Ph.D. in a branch of engineering, he never mentioned or gave any indication of it whatsoever, and apparently preferred that it be forgotten.

Still another reflection of the expert's subordinated role in the power and prestige structures of the Company was implicit in the pervasive conception of the "Company man." A "Company man" was one who had completely committed his career aspirations to this specific Company. He was usually also a person who had filled a variety of responsible roles in the organization, had been with it for a long time, and indicated that *he expected to remain with it.* Above all, calling an executive a "Company man" implicitly rated him as "high" on a "loyalty-to-the-Company" scale. Company experts were not quite as likely to be spoken of as "Company men." This does not mean that there existed conscious doubts about the expert's loyalty. It suggests, however, that the inner group, among whom intimacies were exchanged and in whom most confidence was reposed, was likely to consist mainly of non-experts or of renegade experts.

A full examination of the reasons for the subordination of experts to true bureaucrats is far beyond the scope of this study. A serious analysis of this problem would investigate the expert's "loyalty rating," along lines indicated above. It would also have to be considered whether the expert's tendency to solve problems dispassionately contributes to a low loyalty rating. The expert, be it remembered, has been disciplined to appraise "many sides of a question"; his professional training inhibits the reflexive display of reassuring sentiments of loyalty to a particular company or client. The expert may all too readily empathize with his opponent's viewpoint and appreciate his technical skills, even when they are being used against his own client. As a result, it may be that the expert is not easily viewed as a thoroughly "reliable" member of the in-group.[7]

One other factor contributing to the expert's subordination in an industrial setting also deserves considerably greater study: If top management's authority was legitimated on the grounds of its expertise, which always entails a *specific* and limited area of competence, then tensions would be created when it asserted its power over subordinates who were specialized or experienced in *other* areas. Thus some workers complained when Peele sought to control the head of the board building: "What does Peele know about board production? Peele's an electrician by trade, while Johnson (head of the board building) has been at his job for years."

Perhaps enough has been said to suggest that it is the true bureaucrat who comes to man the bastions of the power system, establishing himself as the gatekeeper through whom the expert is obliged to operate.[8]

---

7. In a sophisticated analysis of the legal profession, David Riesman remarks: "This conflict between lawyer and client over the proper degree of affect which the former is to bring to the affairs of the latter is one of those conflicts between client emergency and occupational routine which has attracted the interest of Everett Hughes. As he observes, the client wants his problem given priority—yet he would be uneasy with a professional for whom his case actually was 'the first' and who had neither been trained on other people's emergencies nor could control his own emotions in the face of the client's loss of control." "Toward an Anthropological Science of Law," *The American Journal of Sociology*, Sept., 1951, Vol. LVII, No. 2, p. 130.

8. Compare F. J. Roethlisberger's comments about experts, e. g., "Coordinating the functions of these different specialists is not explicitly the function of any

There are grounds, therefore, for expecting that punish-ment-centered patterns, the sphere of the true bureaucrat, may have more than an equal share in the conduct of organizational affairs.

---

of these specialists but of a *line* executive." (our emphasis—A. W. G.) *Management and Morale*, Harvard University Press, Cambridge, 1941, p. 76.

CONCLUSION

"We have only begun to knock a few chips from the great quarry of knowledge that has been given us to dig out and use. We know almost nothing about everything. That is why, with all conviction, I say the future is boundless."

CHARLES F. KETTERING

Chapter XIII

CONCLUSION

AS A CASE HISTORY OF only one factory, this study can offer no conclusions about the "state" of American industry at large, or about the forces that make for bureaucratization in general. It is the function of a case history to develop hypotheses which may be shown, on further investigation, to have broader application. It may be helpful, therefore, if an overall view of the key hypotheses which have emerged is set forth in some more organized form. While doing so, a brief review of some of the main lines of supporting evidence may be made. Finally, indications of the "policy" implications of this work shall also be given. Hypotheses, like all human ideas, cannot be contained within an impermeable scientific package; they overflow in their implications for human conduct, and impinge upon the choices which men must make in everyday living.

Several central interests pervaded this study: What factors were associated with the expansion or contraction of bureaucratic methods of administration? That is, what led to increasing or decreasing degrees of bureaucracy? What were the problems for which bureaucracy was perceived as a solution? Once initiated, what strengthened bureaucratic organization, lending it a self-perpetuating dynamic? What gains or satisfactions did increased bureaucratization provide, and for whom did it provide these? These are the basic questions to which the hypotheses which follow are related.

Perceptions of Role Performance

1. Efforts are made to install new bureaucratic rules, or enforce old ones, when people in a given social position (i.e., management or workers) perceive those in the reciprocal position (i.e., workers or management) as failing to perform their role obligations.

Bureaucratic measures are thus a response to a breakdown in a social relationship; they are a defense against the tensions which arise when the expectations that two parties have of each other are no longer adequately meshed and complementary. More specifically, the point of the above hypothesis is that one of the parties, for whatever reason, *perceives* the other's behavior as departing from his expectations. Not only does the *degree* of bureaucratic striving vary with such a definition of the situation, but the *type* of bureaucratic striving was also related to different conceptions of deviant role performance. In other words, the frustrated party's explanation of *why* the other party departed from his expectations influenced the development of the defense that was used. Specifically, the analysis of the no-absenteeism rule and the safety rules led to the following hypotheses:

A. When one party defines the other's failure to perform in an expected way as being due to the latter's "carelessness" or ignorance—the "utilitarian" conception of deviance—his response will take the form of developing a "representative bureaucracy."

B. Where one party defines the other's failure to perform in an expected way as being deliberate and intentional—the "voluntaristic" conception of deviance—his response will take the form of developing a "punishment-centered bureaucracy."

The importance of how role performance was perceived was first noted in the study of Peele's succession. Peele was actively attempting to cope with the resistance of the "old lieutenants," as well as of the rank and file workers, whom he conceived of as "shirkers" and was unwilling to trust. Perceptions of workers' role performance was examined also in the contrast between miners and surfacemen. On the more highly bureaucratized surface, supervisors tended to view their subordinates as unwilling to work and as ready to "goldbrick"; in the less (or mock) bureaucratized mine, supervisors viewed the miners as hard workers. Thus, while only one plant was studied, the above hypothesis is supported, as are others, by observations of several discrete units of behavior.

The role obligations held to be in default by this hypothesis center around two distinct, yet closely related, systems, the work and authority systems. In the context of the latter, management called improper role performances "uppityness," "snottiness," or "insubordination." When management defaulted in its own authority obligations, workers sometimes spoke of its "cheapness" or "failure to take care of the men." In work relationships, workers spoke of improper management behavior as "pushing" or "driving"; management termed workers' failure to perform their work obligations as "goofing off," "goldbricking," or "apathy." Certain of the conditions generating bureaucratic efforts are, therefore, closely linked with a problem of abiding interest to labor economists and industrial sociologists, namely, "restriction of output." It is possible that further study of industrial bureaucracy may provide another opportunity to bridge the interests of sociologists and economists, thus contributing to a real, rather than a pious, platform for inter-disciplinary efforts.

One of the more promising points of departure for furthering convergence of research in this area is the problem of why role performance comes to be *viewed* as inadequate. Under what conditions does management perceive workers as "restricting output"? Attention in this area has commonly been directed to the question of what makes *workers* restrict output. But the actual level of workers' productivity can no more generate a pervasive social problem, such as "restriction of output," than does the actually deprived condition of Negroes, by itself, give rise to a "Negro problem." It takes two things, at least, to provoke a "social problem"; one of these is a set of existent social conditions; another is a group of people who perceive these conditions and decide that they require a remedy.

The Decision-making Process

2. Efforts will be made to install or enforce bureaucratic rules only if those measures are judged to be both
    A. *Expedient,* that is, capable of achieving desired results, and
    B. *Legitimate,* that is, morally appropriate or "right," in that situation.

In the main, warrant for this hypothesis derives from observation of the mine. There, two standard definitions of the situation inhibited sustained efforts at bureaucratization, despite the fact that miners were sometimes viewed as unwilling to fulfill obedience obligations, such as regular attendance. There was, first, the widespread definition of the mine as a dangerous place; this led mining supervisors and others to view deviant behavior among miners as a legitimate response to hazardous conditions. Absenteeism, or drinking, therefore became an expression of "independence"; consequently, bureaucratic efforts to suppress them were not viewed as clearly legitimate. Secondly, miners were viewed as a "tough lot"; hence it was also thought to be inexpedient to subject them to close bureaucratic control.

These same pressures inhibiting bureaucratic efforts were found again in a different setting—that involving the "no-smoking" rules. Supervisors did not view this rule as legitimate since there was little inflammable material in the plant. Moreover, supervisors also viewed efforts at enforcing the no-smoking rules as inexpedient, for since it was believed that smoking habits were rooted in an uncontrollable "nervousness" or in "human nature," supervisors were pessimistic about inhibiting them. Thus the mock bureaucracy in this sphere, as well as in the mine, illustrate the tendency to suppress bureaucratic efforts, unless these are viewed as both legitimate and expedient.

One problem for future investigation, emerging from these considerations, is the question of the *general* conditions under which bureaucratic measures will be defined as legitimate or expedient. In short, knowing that the "danger" situation in the mine disposes supervisors to relax bureaucratic efforts, and to define them as non-legitimate, does not help in predicting when or whether a supervisor in *another* type of work situation will judge bureaucratic efforts to be inappropriate.

Bureaucracy and Resistance

3. The degree to which bureaucratic efforts will result in stable bureaucratic routines depends partly on the degree to which those subject to increasing bureaucratization *resist* these efforts.

   A. The strength of their resistance is a function of:
     a. Their adherence to belief systems which are violated by bureaucratic measures
     b. Conditions legitimating active resistance
     c. Conditions making the resistance expedient
     d. The degree to which their status is injured or impaired by increased bureaucratization
     e. The strength of the informal solidarity among the resisters.

For the most part, these hypotheses stem from the contrast between the mine and surface. The miners, for example, tended to adhere to "traditional" values to a greater degree than the surfacemen, who were more easily adjusted to the rational and changing aspects of bureaucratic organization. The physical dangers of the mine, which were much more serious than those on the surface, allowed the miner to feel that he had a right to make his own decisions, and to resist encroachments on his autonomy that would be brought about by a centralized bureaucracy.

Similarly, these same mine dangers also curtailed the number of men who are willing to work at mining jobs; hence the ability as well as the willingness of the miners to resist bureaucratization was strengthened. Further fortifying the miners' powers of resistance was the solidarity of their informal groups. Unlike those on the surface, these were welded together by the experience of sharing a common danger and were less exposed to the disruption of "suckholes." The role of status impairment, as an inducement to resist bureaucratization, emerged in analyzing the safety pattern, where it was suggested that workers accepted safety rules partly because the "good housekeeping" program enhanced their prestige, while the safety meetings extended their power.

This cluster of hypotheses bearing on "resistance," perhaps more than any of the others, has the most elemental of practical implications. It challenges much of the current pessimism that often surrounds discussions of bureaucracy, and which is expressed in vague assertions concerning its "inevitability." There is a widespread tendency today, particularly among intellectuals, to decry the "bureaucratization of the world," a development which is viewed as irresistible.

The hypotheses tendered here, however, say that the *degree* of bureaucratization is a function of human striving; it is the outcome of a contest between those who want it and those who do not. The hypotheses imply that resistance to bureaucracy is possible, and the data indicate that it is sometimes successful. In particular, our comparative study of the mine reveals at least one case in which bureaucracy's march was not triumphant. As Robert Merton comments: "More is learned from the single success than from multiple failures. A single success proves it can be done. Therefore it is necessary only to learn what made it work." [1]

Functions of Bureaucratic Rules

4. The degree to which efforts at bureaucratization generate stable bureaucratic routines is also dependent on the on-going consequences, or actual results of the bureaucratic rules, that is, on
   A. The explication function
   B. The screening function
   C. The remote control function
   D. The punishment-legitimating function
   E. The leeway function
   F. The apathy-preserving function.

Each of the functions mentioned above was illustrated in a variety of different contexts. For example, the "explication" function of the rules was considered in comparison between mine and surface. Here it was noted that rules were more often

---

1. *Social Theory and Social Structure,* Ibid., p. 195.

needed to specify workers' obligations on the surface; for in this work sphere, workers' informal groups did not have the motivation or the strength to allocate and direct work responsibilities. The "screening" function was illustrated in the analysis of Peele's succession. When the legitimacy of Peele's authority was challenged by both foremen and workers, an emphasis on the rules enabled him to claim that he was not changing things on his own behalf, but on behalf of the main office.

The "remote control functions" of the rules were also evident in Peele's succession, where communication through rules assisted him in by-passing the resistant "old lieutenants." The "punishment-legitimating function" was illustrated by the vat-cleaning incident. The "leeway function" was observed in the operation of the no-smoking rule, which was usually ignored, in exchange for workers' informal conformance with management expectations concerning smoking behavior. Conversely, where workers failed to conform to management expectations concerning proper work behavior, foremen would enforce the "no-floating around" rule.

Finally, the "apathy-preserving" function of the rules was considered with respect to the interaction of workers and supervisors. For example, the more mining supervisors attempted to enforce the rules concerning absenteeism, the more miners deliberately stayed away from work. More generally, to the extent that workers experienced the enforcement of the rules as "close supervision," the more their indulgency expectations were violated; they then became increasingly hostile and resisted by doing as little as they could get by with.

In emphasizing these several consequences of the rules, the perseverance and development of bureaucratic patterns has been accounted for as a result of what they themselves brought about. In other words, bureaucratic organization has been seen as a homeostatic, self-perpetuating system; it has not been considered adequate to imply that bureaucratic organization persists or develops simply because it has once been initiated. That a pattern has been initiated is no guarantee of its immortality.

Hence it was necessary to consider not only those things giving bureaucracy its initial impetus, but also the factors maintaining its momentum. The development of bureaucratic patterns in this factory was, therefore, related to the results which it continued to produce, to the gains and satisfaction which it created in the course of its on-going existence.

This is no idle academic matter, of interest only to social scientists. Actually, this "theoretical" question runs over into one of the important political questions in the present day world, involving an ideological issue of international scope. For the people of more than one sixth of the earth are told by their government that the elaborate development of bureaucracy in their society is, indeed, due to "inertia." Specifically, Soviet apologists have insisted that bureaucracy in their society is explainable in terms of a "cultural lag" theory. They assert that bureaucratic forms in the Soviet Union are "capitalist survivals" and vestigial "bourgeois habits of thought." [2]

Soviet theoreticians have failed, however, to explain why these inappropriate "habits of thought" have persisted and, indeed, persisted and grown for more than a quarter-century of Soviet rule. They completely neglect analysis of the functions which bureaucracy performs in their society; they ignore the possibility that Soviet bureaucracy is attributable to the problems and pressures of indigenous Soviet institutions, rather than being the product of alien ideologies which remain mysteriously vigorous. Ideologically, of course, this "cultural lag" hypothesis serves to defend Soviet institutions from criticisms, by implying that there is nothing wrong with *them*, but that

---

2. See S. Kovalyov, *Ideological Conflicts in Soviet Russia,* Public Affairs Press, Washington, D. C., 1948, translated from the Russian by the American Council of Learned Societies.

the difficulties stem from capitalist hangovers which will die out in due time.

Tension Reduction and Tension Defense

5. Bureaucratic rules are functional insofar as
   A. They reduce status-located tensions *stemming* from close supervision.
   B. They reduce tensions of the organization as a whole, *stemming* from
      a. Interaction of bearers of different value or belief systems
      b. Ambiguous canons for judging the legitimacy of a claim
      c. Unreciprocated expectations
      d. Decline in friendly, informal interaction
      e. Hiatus in the chain of command
      f. Short-circuited communications
      g. Challenge to managerial legitimacy
      h. Degeneration of motives for obedience
   C. They defend or reinforce tensions creating close supervision.

These hypotheses emphasize that bureaucratic rules are serviceable to different aspects of the organization and different people in it. Thus bureaucratic rules are held to survive because they reduce tensions consequential to people in varying statuses and for the organization as a whole.

Throughout this study, it has been repeatedly asked: For whom, or for what, was bureaucracy functional? This emphasis stems from a critical appraisal of Max Weber's theory where it was found that he was primarily concerned with the functions of bureaucracy for the *whole* organization. This was accepted, but only as a partially adequate formulation.

In the analysis of Peele's succession, it was shown that the decisions which increased bureaucratization were largely under the influence of the plant manager. In short, bureaucracy was man-made, and more powerful men had a greater hand in making it. It has been our working assumption that these powerful individuals, like any others, do not respond directly to all of the tensions of the organization as a whole; they respond with greater readiness to those organizational tensions which threaten their own status.

In emphasizing the tension-reducing role of bureaucratic organization, it has been conceived of as a "defense mechanism." As this term is used by some sociologists, this means that bureaucratic patterns served to defend the organization from things which threaten its survival or equilibrium. But we have suggested that a "defense mechanism" does not merely defend the organization from threatening tensions, but also defends certain of the *tensions* which threaten the organization. If bureaucratic rules reduce tensions that *emanate* from close supervision they make it less necessary to resolve, and thus safeguard, the tensions that *lead* to close supervision.

More generally, the rules often seem to enable the conditions which produce tensions (such as 5, B, a-h) to persist. They seem to mitigate the tensions which these conditions produce, but do not remove the conditions eliciting the tensions. For example, the "remote control function" of bureaucratic rules may allow a manager to bypass short-circuited communications that arise from the resistance of middle management; but the rules do not by themselves motivate these middle managers to accept the plant manager and follow his orders. Again, the "screening function" of bureaucratic rules may reduce the challenge to management's legitimacy; but it does not remove the tensions which led the worker to challenge management's legitimacy in the first place.

There is a ceaseless interplay, then, between the tension and the defense mechanism; the defense mechanism arrests the tensions but allows the conditions which produce them to continue in operation. If, however, the defense mechanism actually eliminated the conditions which *produced* the tension, how could the defense mechanism *persist?* If bureaucratic measures actually remedied the conditions which produced tensions then, it would seem, there would no longer be tensions for it to resolve, no functions to perform, and the basis for its persistence would be undermined. It is, in this sense, that we have advanced the hypothesis which asserts that bureaucratic rules persist *because* they *preserve* the tension *leading* to close supervision.

It is in the framework of the cluster of hypotheses set forth above that the discussion of the succession dynamics can be best utilized. That is, it is not maintained that succession always, and under all conditions, generates bureaucratic defenses. Instead, it seems more likely that it does so only insofar as it induces close supervision and brings with it the accompanying tensions. It may be suggested that the higher the *rate of succession,* within a given time period, the more these tensions will be heightened, and because of this, the more likelihood of bureaucratic development.

It is obvious that many important questions concerning the effects of succession are yet to be explored. One of the most important of these is whether or not an "inside" successor is liable to provoke as many tensions leading to bureaucratic defenses as one coming from the "outside." It is often maintained that the difficulties of succession would be diminished if the successor were chosen from among those already in the group. It seems possible, however, that an "inside" successor would create *different* types of tensions, rather than *fewer* of them. In any event, it is probable that industrial sociology would profit from further study of this question and from an effort, also, to determine the specific pressures that lead to the choice of a successor from within, or from outside of, the group.

Bureaucratic Types

In an effort to empirically bracket off those aspects of bureaucracy that induced tensions, three types of bureaucratic patterns were described: i. e., the "mock," "representative," and "punishment-centered" forms. These differed according to whether or not they enforced the rules, and the manner in which they did so. Evidence tended to suggest that the punishment-centered pattern aroused the greatest proportion of complaints about "red tape" and incurred the greatest internal tensions. Thus the final hypothesis emerging from this research indicates that:

6. Internal tensions, and complaints about "red tape," are more likely to be associated with punishment-centered bureaucracy than with representative or mock bureaucracy.

Some of the major research problems deriving from this study are those centering on this typology of bureaucratic patterns. For example, it needs to be determined whether an "experimentally" pure form of "representative bureaucracy" would eliminate the smaller proportion of complaints about "red tape" that were found to be directed against this pattern. We also know practically nothing about the larger institutional forces underlying the various forms of bureaucracy. In our own work, there were definite indications that changes in the labor and commodity markets accelerated the emergence of "punishment-centered bureaucracy." That is, renewed postwar competition for gypsum customers exerted pressure to "tighten the plant up," and to produce more efficiently. Simultaneously, the loss of job opportunities in local defense plants which had closed down, increased the competition for jobs. This in turn enabled management to "put the bit in the workers' mouths," and utilize "punishment-centered bureaucracy." [3]

Like other of the problems considered here, the distinction between "representative" and "punishment-centered bureaucracy" has certain fairly obvious policy implications. Clearly, on

---

3. This process is analyzed more fully in *Wildcat Strike*, Ibid.

a policy level, unlike that of sheer sociological analysis, it is often necessary to choose between one or the other of the *operative* forms of bureaucracy. Which shall be chosen, "representative" or "punishment-centered bureaucracy"? This choice must, of course, be made in terms of some yardstick, that is, a set of values which are either realized or thwarted by the options available.

As a sociologist, it is not our job to make this choice. But as Wilbert Moore has stated so well, "If it is not part of the sociologist's job to save the world, or any segment of it, it may be part of his responsibility to discover alternative forms of social organization that have some chance of acceptance and survival." [4] In presenting these bureaucratic patterns, an effort has been made to fulfill this responsibility, even if only in a provisional way.

Robert Merton has observed that failure to consider alternative ways of satisfying existent social needs results in an implicit but unwarranted ideological commitment to received social patterns. There are at least two distinct implications to be drawn from this sound directive: (1) After functionally assessing a given social pattern, it is necessary to suggest generally that there may be alternative practices capable of subserving the same needs. (2) Going beyond this, *specific* alternative patterns, capable of performing equivalent functions, should be indicated. This research has been guided by the second inference. An effort has been made to multiply policy alternatives, not by speculation, but by the empirical detection and description of already existent, functionally similar patterns.

Sociologists may well take their lead from the working assumptions of medical scientists who, in practice, rarely spend their energies in scholastic definitions of "health," "normalcy,"

---

4. "Industrial Sociology: Status and Prospects," *American Sociological Review,* Vol. 13, No. 4, 1948, pp. 390. Cf., also my discussion of Moore's paper which elaborates on several collateral points, pp. 396-400, Ibid.

or in pious pronouncements concerning the inevitable imperfections of man. They attend to the reduction of disease; they seek to make men less ill, rather than perfect. Similarly, instead of issuing warnings against dangers engendered by utopian conceptions of democracy, conceptions which are in any case found rarely, instead of concerning ourselves with whether bureaucracy is or is not "inevitable," the more fruitful problem is to identify those social processes creating variations in the amount and types of bureaucracy. For these variations do make a vital difference in the lives of men. Taking this route, the sociologist will eschew the role of a mortician, prematurely eager to bury men's hopes, but will, instead, assume responsibilities as a social clinician, striving to further democratic potentialities without arbitrarily setting limits on these in advance.

Appendix

FIELD WORK PROCEDURES:

THE SOCIAL ORGANIZATION

OF A STUDENT RESEARCH TEAM [1]

THE PURPOSE OF THIS appendix is not to show how our procedures conformed to the canons of scientific method, but to describe in some detail what we actually did and how we did it. This does not mean that we were insensitive to methodological requirements. As the contrast between mine and surface may indicate, we tried to orient ourselves to the *logic* of the controlled experiment—at least as much as our recalcitrant research predicament would permit. Our case study, however, is obviously not a venture in validation. Instead, it is primarily exploratory and comprises an effort to develop new concepts and hypotheses which will lend themselves to validation by experimental methods. In short, we sought to take a beachhead, rather than to consolidate a position on it. In view of these scientifically primitive objectives, it behooves us to plainly describe our procedures, rather than to pretentiously appraise our work in terms of more mature standards.

---

1. This appendix was written with Maurice R. Stein. Mr. Stein, then a teaching fellow at the University, was with the research from its inception. He soon became informally acknowledged as "second-in-command" and assisted in the direction of the field work. Comments which refer to the attitudes or feelings of the team members stem largely from Mr. Stein's observations and are based upon his close interaction with the research group. However, Mr. Stein's contribution here is by no means limited to these questions alone. Needless to say, in this section as elsewhere, I assume complete responsibility for all errors of fact or for mistaken judgments.—A. W. G.

The Sources of Data

The most important of our techniques was an interview which, in all cases, was at least *partially* "non-directive." That is, after setting the interview on its course we allowed it to go pretty much where the respondent wanted it to—if he wanted it to go anywhere. While we started with a crude schedule which directed the interviewer's attention to key areas of hypothetical importance, this schedule was continually changed in the light of our field experience. Thus we often asked questions which emerged in the midst of the research, even though these same questions may not have been raised with previous respondents.

Sometimes, questions we had intended to ask a respondent could not be raised. This was so for a variety of reasons; occasionally a respondent had a "bee in his bonnet" and insisted upon talking about a problem that was momentarily disturbing him. When this happened we just sat and listened—and, often as not, learned a great deal. On other occasions, a respondent had to return to work before we could put our standard questions to him. And in a very few cases, a respondent was so upset at being interviewed—for reasons that were not always clear— that we spent the greater part of the interview reassuring him. Since the plant was a tightly-knit social group, we felt it imperative that not a single respondent walk away from an interview hostile to the study, if we could help it, lest he become a nucleus of spreading resistance.

In general, interviews were designed to provide two types of data: first, a picture of the plant as a social system as seen from the perspective of the people in it. We wanted to know the problems they felt they were confronted with, what they thought about their everyday work, and the people they habitually met. We wanted to see the plant through their eyes. Secondly, we had some theoretically derived hunches, as well as ideas based upon the research of other industrial sociologists, about the kind of things that might turn up, about the problems that might be found and the data needed to analyze these problems.

The interview was opened after the interviewer introduced himself and very generally explained to the interviewee that we were a research team from the University. We also explained that we were interested in learning more about factory life, and we asked them to help us. Usually, the worker had already heard about our research from a co-worker, or at the first union meeting which we had attended. But more of this later.

After this, we allowed the worker to pursue whatever he wished, dwelling on and probing those areas that our hunches suggested as important. As the men became accustomed to us, and as we learned to speak their language, we found it less necessary to use non-directive methods; we felt increasingly free to direct focused questions at them. It was our impression that the workers often viewed non-directive techniques as a form of "caution"; it seemed as if this sometimes generated a counter-caution.

In all, we conducted 174 *formal* interviews, the average one of which lasted between an hour and a half and two hours. The interviews were conducted during working hours and at the plant, and the men were paid at their usual rates while being interviewed. The interviews, therefore, often gave the men a rest from their regular routines. Perhaps for this reason there were few indications of "interview fatigue"—at least among the respondents. Of these 174 interviews, 132 were with a representative sample of the men in the plant. The sample was stratified to take into account the worker's seniority, his rank, and the department in which he worked. We were able to obtain a representative sample of ninety-two of the workers (out of the above 132) to whom we asked standardized questions concerning attitudes toward the different plant rules and toward red tape.

A second basic source of data consisted of our *observations* of the plant. We spent a good deal of time just walking around, or standing with a worker and talking with him casually as he worked. The small size of the plant enabled us to "see" it as a *whole* fairly quickly. We quickly became immersed in the plant's "atmosphere" and got the feel of it by walking through the massive heat of the kiln, breathing in the dry gypsum dust, climbing the catwalks high above the plant, poking around the tops of the enormous mill vats, riding the rough gypsum cars, lighting cigarettes as we sat, exhausted, on full cases of dynamite in the mine—a practice which miners insisted was safe, though they were always addicted to broad humor.

Aside from simply having a wonderful time—a factor of no little motivational significance—this total immersion helped our interviewing considerably. It helped us to talk, with some degree of fluency, about the complicated mechanical environment that surrounds the worker. We did not have to ask the workers, say, how the mix was beaten up, unless we deliberately wanted to play 'possum, for we had seen it. In turn, the workers saw we "meant business" and that we were not prissy white collar people who were out slumming. We showed by our *actions* that "we could take it" and that we were really interested in them. When they saw this, they met us more than half way. In the course of these observations, we naturally had thousands of brief conversations and got to know many of the workers' jobs fairly well. This, too, aided us in the formal interviewing, for by then we were not entirely strangers.

Our observational material was importantly supplemented by the fact that one of our research team, Paul Mahany, who was a skilled mechanic as well as an astute researcher, spent a summer working in the mine. Mr. Mahany was known by the miners to be a member of the research team. Nevertheless, the

miners quickly accepted him, and with only a flickering of suspicion. Since he held down a full time job in the mine, it was
not feasible for Mr. Mahany to prepare his own observational
reports. In lieu of this, we got together with him once or twice
a week, during which time he just talked to us or answered
questions about what he had seen and heard.

A third and final source of data was many thousands of
pages of *documentary material* to which we were given access—
e. g., newspaper clippings, interoffice memoranda, private cor-
respondence, Company reports, government reports about the
Company, union contracts, and arbitrators' decisions. Some of
this material was highly confidential, and we could not have
obtained it unless we had won the confidence of main office
management, as well as of the workers.

One of the factors aiding us to do this was the nearness of
the plant and the main office to each other, and of both to the
University. We could and did visit quite frequently at the
main office. We must have spent literally hundreds of hours
talking with the Company labor relations director alone. We
were thus able to establish friendly relations with people fairly
high in the Company hierarchy. It is not uncommon for main
office personnel, even where they are available, to define the
sociologist's function as one of studying their subordinates in
the factories or offices; often, however, they do not wish themselves to be studied. In this case, the main office people allowed
themselves to be looked at, just as anyone else. We were thus
better able to see the Oscar Center Plant in one of its "natural
habitats," the General Gypsum Company.

It was also because the plant was adjacent to the towns from
which it drew its labor supply, and because these were *small*
towns, that we were able to get some overall picture of the
workers' community lives, however crude. Frequently, members of the research team would spend an evening at one of the

workers' favorite taverns, playing cards or drinking beer with the men.

The Research Team

Throughout our research we faced a twofold problem: to get the data and to train the people to get the data. To get our material we had to organize a group of inexperienced, undergraduate students into a motivated and competent team. From the students' viewpoint, the research project was, at first, justifiable as a means to an end: namely, to extend their education in Sociology and in methods of research. In order to get the research accomplished, it was necessary to commit oneself to the needs and interests of a specific group of students, and to see to it that their needs were also gratified.

In working with undergraduates as a research team, it is important to remember that they have often been socialized in Sociology by faculty members who, all too frequently, have little familiarity with research techniques and sometimes less respect. Similarly, many of the textbooks the students have used communicate little awareness of the central role of research. Thus before the research was begun, considerable discussion had to be given to matters of research technique. The imminence of the "first interview," set by a mutually agreed upon deadline, produced something like an actor's "first night" jitters. Sufficient anxiety was induced among the team members to preclude too much concern with theoretical matters, which was perhaps just as well, since they had all previously gone through an intensive theoretical education.

Reading-lists of articles dealing with various phases of technique were distributed, read, and discussed. On the one hand, these articles relieved anxieties by communicating some sense of what the research process would be like. On the other hand, however, they also engendered anxieties by bringing up new things to worry about. But the sheer act of reading, taking notes on, and talking about the articles was one of the first confidence-building experiences shared by the team members. They started to get the feeling that their forthcoming experiences were not novel; that others had lived through them. They discovered also that leading "theoreticians" had also written articles about research technique. Thus research began to take on enhanced value for them, and there were the glimmerings of an *esprit de corps*.

Formally, the team was organized as a "tutorial," under the University's traditional tutorial system. This meant that all of the students were *volunteers;* though they received regular University credit for their work, none of them *had* to do this particular thing. By and large, they initially chose to volunteer for the project because they were interested in the subject of the research, liked the chance to get out in the field and away from routine class work, because they knew and liked others who had volunteered, and because they knew and liked the project director. From its inception, then, there were warm, friendly relationships among many of the members.

This good group feeling was furthered by the practice of holding meetings in the project director's home. It raised the campus "prestige" of persons in the group and began a campus tradition wherein the team members were felt to be a distinct and fortunate unit by other students in the Sociology Department. As members of the group began to wear distinctive work clothes on campus, presumably dictated by their wish to resemble the factory workers while interviewing them, this feeling of solidarity and collective difference from the rest of the students was heightened.

It is interesting to recall how the problem of wearing the right clothes to the factory was unduly exaggerated at the outset of the study. On one occasion, a student had worn a white shirt to the factory. On the way to the plant in the car, he realized his "mistake" and began to worry whether he would be mistaken for a foreman and identified with the Company management. When he reached the plant, however, he realized that somehow what he wore did not matter as much as how he *behaved.* Or, at least, it did not matter unless it made him feel conspicuous and out of place, with damaging results to his interviewing. Perhaps "proper dress," in this case, did not contribute half so much to interviewing rapport as it did to provide clearcut symbols of the research group's identity and to raise our solidarity.

Entry Into the Plant

At the outset, we decided to make entry through both the Company management and the union in the Oscar Center plant. Contact was first made with the main office's labor relations director, who was a lawyer and a man with a keen mind and considerable familiarity with the social sciences. From the very beginning, he supported the study fully and aided us in meeting other executives. His motives for wanting the study done were straightforward: He felt that he faced many problems in his job to which he did not have all the answers, and he was willing to try anything which promised to give him more knowledge and insight into these difficulties. At no time, however, did he propose that we pay particular attention to any specific problem or situation and, like everyone else, left us completely free to pursue our interests.

Somewhat contrasted with this emphasis on the long-range gains from the study was the interest of certain people in the production department to whom the labor relations director introduced us. One of these, a person from whom final permission to do the study had to be secured, liked the whole idea, but added that he hoped we would let him know if we found any foreman who was causing trouble at the plant. We explained, firmly, that we would do no such thing and told him that, from our point of view, the important question was, not what *people* were causing trouble, but rather what kinds of *social situations* created tensions. Replacing people, we added, would in our view do little good if the situations which made them behave in a "troublesome" fashion remained. The production man appreciated our viewpoint and told us to go ahead. Shortly afterwards, we were introduced to the plant manager at Oscar Center, and one side of our entry problem had been solved—or so it seemed at the time.

We then immediately made arrangements to attend a local union meeting and secure its permission to do the study. On our first visit to the plant, we sought out Byta and received his permission to explain the study at the next meeting of the union. When the time came to attend the meeting, Gouldner had a class to teach, so Paul Mahany and Maurice Stein went. Since we were all rather nervous about the outcome of this session, we got together and prepared a talk explaining the study to the workers. When the time came to deliver this talk, Mahany and Stein—even though carefully attired in old clothes and a sprinkling of army gear—were quite ill at ease.

The first part of their talk was greeted stoically until they came to the point where they mentioned that all members of the research team were ex-GI's. At this point, a worker who we later learned was the "factory drunk" shouted out: "Let's help give the GI's an education." This brought the house down. The union president then asked them what outfits they had been with.

Once defined in this way, suspicions that we might be "Company spies" were dismissed. The workers conferred upon themselves the status of "teachers" who were to help give the team an "education." Moreover, this helped the veterans at the factory to feel at one with the research team. At any rate, after the meeting the workers were quite willing to be interviewed. Thus we had made a "double-entry" into the plant, coming in almost simultaneously by way of the Company and the union.

But it soon became obvious that we had made a *mistake,* and that the problem had *not* been to make a double-entry, but a *triple*-entry; for we had left out, and failed to make *independent* contact with a distinct group—the management of that particular plant. In a casual way, we had assumed that main office management also spoke for the local plant management and this, as a moment's reflection might have told us, was not the case. In consequence, our relations with *local* management were never as good as they were with the workers or with main office management. (This statement needs qualification in that we actually got along quite well with the supervisors in the mine, while most of our tensions with local management involved relations with *surface* supervisors.) Actually, however, while the problem is easy to define, and we can readily see that local management *should* have been independently contacted, we are not so sure that there is an easy way to do this. Local plant management is unorganized and does not have a union, like the workers, who can be approached for their corporate consent. Local plant management is in no position either to agree or disagree with a research proposal, but must allow main office management to have the final word.

We would not care to propose a concrete solution to the question at this time, other than to suggest that a definite part of the research team should be assigned the responsibility of establishing, improving, and maintaining contacts with local plant management throughout a study. Once having started the study, we of course began to work on our relationship with local management but, in our view, it never attained the level of rapport we achieved with others, in part because of our mode of entry.

Aspects of the Interviewing Process

In order to get respondents—especially on the surface—we would first go to a foreman and then go with him to a respondent. We did not want to bypass a foreman, but at the same time, we did not want to be identified with Company management. Wherever possible, therefore, interviewers would ask the foreman to point out an available man that satisfied our sample requirements. Then the interviewer would walk over to the man without the foreman and introduce himself. This seemed to work out quite well.

Since the informants were to be talking about their jobs and co-workers, it was necessary that the interviews be conducted away from their immediate place of work. Many interviews were held in the "first-aid" room, which was a convenient, neutral, and private spot. Others were held outside on the grass—weather permitting—or at the tavern across the street. Since plant interviews were always conducted on Company time, this meant that we had to be careful not to take more than one man off the job in any department.

Many of the jobs, for example, the isolated knife man, were of a sort which made it easy to interview the man while he worked. For that matter, there were some jobs where interviewers were invited back to help pass the time and relieve the monotony. The early identification of such jobs was useful because it provided respondents who could be repeatedly visited, and who could help to keep us up to date on changing developments in the plant.

Other jobs involved relief operations, for example, those at the take-off end, so that it was possible to complete several interviews by adapting oneself to the relief; that is, an interview was started with the man on relief while his partner worked; when this man had to return to work we interviewed his partner. After the partner returned to work, we finished our interview with the first worker, and so on.

Other respondents had jobs which made it difficult to interview them. The men working at the mine face are a case in point. It is interesting, though, that as soon as the men realized that we were willing to make the somewhat arduous trip to the face, and to wait around for interviews at their convenience, they were actually more cooperative than any other group. In addition, the miners felt that they were the only ones who really knew the score about the Company and saw our efforts to reach them as a mark of respect for their "inside dope."

Getting interviews in the mine was quite different from getting them on the surface. In the first place, the miners' feelings about their foremen were different from those displayed by surfacemen. The miners' solidarity was sufficiently strong that being brought into their group by a foreman did not threaten them. Occasionally, it was actually helpful, because the foreman might be a respected member of the group. On the other hand, if miners disliked a foreman, they would tell you so right to his face. If miners saw a team member with a disliked foreman, they would not reject him but would, instead, try to convince the researcher that the foreman was a "s. o. b."

On the surface, however, though workers treated their foremen in a more "respectful way," they did not *feel* quite so much respect for them. Being introduced by a surface foreman never helped us, and we prevented this in the way described above. Another contrast: Surface foremen were hard to interview, but mine foremen often sought us out, if there were no one else around at the moment with whom to pass the time. There is no one pattern of interviewing relationships that can be recommended for all circumstances: In the mine we could be very friendly with mine foremen and no damage would result; but similar cordiality with surface foremen would have been disastrous.

The team members were always struck by the difference between our rapport with the miners and the surfacemen. We had good rapport with surface workers, but it was qualitatively different from that prevailing in the mine. Our relations with the miners approximated informal solidarity. While we seemed able to get all the information we sought from surface workers, we never got to know them too well as *persons*.

The differences between mine and surface interviews should not be unduly exaggerated, but there were variations of feeling-tone in interviewing typical persons in the two groups. The miners insisted that we be friendly before they would allow themselves to be interviewed. Surfacemen, for example, rarely tried to draw us out and elicit our opinions, but the miners often did. Again, the miners were far more likely to talk about personal affairs than were surface workers.

The miners regarded us as people who were *also* interviewers; surfacemen thought of us primarily as interviewers and established "segmentalized" relations with us. Before a miner was going to tell us anything about *his* feelings, he wanted to know about *ours*. This was not because they were suspicious of us, but largely because they were unwilling to accept the dependent and passive role involved in a one-way exchange. And we not only had to express our ideas to the miners, but our *feelings* as well.

Despite the fact that this seemingly violates the canons of good interviewing, we were all convinced that our best data was obtained during such moments of real interaction. Our experience suggests, therefore, that there are some persons who *cannot* be well interviewed unless the interviewer abandons an appearance of lofty detachment and impersonal interest, and unless he behaves with friendly respect. The ideal role of the impersonal interviewer could be approximated on the surface, but it fell flat in the mine. We tentatively conclude from this experience that the dangers of interviewer "over-identification" or "over-rapport" can be much exaggerated, and that it is sometimes indispensable to develop friendly ties with certain kinds of respondents in order to obtain their cooperation.

Certainly, we are not advocating that scientific objectivity be abandoned and, of course, one should avoid expressing opinions on matters of concern to the study which would bias the informant's comments. But deep rapport can be based on recognition of mutual identification on broader issues. Furthermore, it is necessary that such identifications be recognized—as we think they have been here—so that they will not interfere with analysis of the data. One of the mechanisms which prevented the interference of such identifications was our use of *collective* analysis of the data, which will be elaborated on later, so that distinctive individual prejudices which arose were canceled out by the group process. Deep rapport has its perils, but to treat the norm of impersonality as sacred, even if it impairs the informants' cooperation, would seem to be an inexcusable form of scientific ritualism.

The Morale of the Research Team

As aspect of the interviewing process, perhaps of some interest, was the fact that the head of the research team chose to get as many or more of the interviews as anyone in the team. This was noteworthy in its effects on the morale of the research team, because it forestalled any feeling that the work load was being unfairly distributed. If, on occasion, a team member would gripe about how hard he was working, another would point out that Gouldner was working just as hard. Interestingly enough, however, this "complaint" was not always voiced in an unhappy way, but often expressed a perverse sense of superiority which some team members felt toward other tutorial groups. It was clear, however, that the research director's participation in the "dirty work" was a factor that contributed to the group's morale.

There can be little doubt that the increased campus status, mentioned earlier, was another contributing element. Even more important, however, were the ongoing "social" satisfactions that the research team provided for its members. Each meeting was ended by consuming healthy quantities of "coffee and," and after the work was done for the night, a bull session went on into early hours of the morning.

Again, since the plant was some fifteen miles away from the campus, a half hour ride each way was required. This ride was also punctuated by stops for coffee and small talk. The ride back from the plant provided a useful opportunity for discussing things that had arisen during the interviews, and while they were still fresh in our minds. They provided a relaxed atmosphere for verbalizing new ideas, and a setting in which tensions inevitably engendered during interviews could be given some catharsis. It is impossible to calculate the extent to which the warmth and support of these group ties encouraged individuals to "spill out" a good idea, which in a more formal and austere group would never have seen light.

Another factor fortifying group morale was the way in which meetings were held. These weekly meetings were completely informal; each team member would read the best interview he had obtained that week, and we would all comment on it at will. The remarks were of two types: first, every point that seemed to contribute to an analysis of bureaucracy in the plant was discussed in great detail. Thus analysis of the interviews was a *collective* process which took place in a regularized way. Comments by one person often set off a train of associations among the rest of the group, and it was evident that no one person alone, nor all of the people working individually, could have originated the entire chain of ideas. In short, the very method of analyzing the interviews gave us a feeling that we were solving a problem *together,* and solidified us.

The interviews were, secondly, also discussed from the standpoint of interviewing technique; every point in the interview where it might have been improved was brought to the interviewer's attention in the least painful manner. Loaded questions and places where more probing would have been desirable were soon easily picked up by everyone. Personal stigma was removed by virtue of the fact that everyone, including the research director, submitted his interviews to group evaluation, and the inevitability of slips soon became evident. Moreover, emphasis was placed on extracting positive and constructive contributions. For example, whenever a new question spontaneously devised by an interviewer seemed good, the rest of the team would note it for their own later use. Thus, the weekly meetings promoted a sense of collective effort and collective product. Everyone was able to participate in and assimilate the ongoing analysis as it developed.

There were still other satisfactions that built up the group's morale and raised their motivations. One of these involved the type of people with whom the group interacted in the course of their work. The respondents were working class people, in the main, many of whom had personality traits seemingly different from college students. And many of these traits were immediately viewed as desirable by many members of the team. For example, they were particularly impressed with the "spontaneity" of the miners and became quite identified with them because of this.

It became a common saying among the team that "No one could criticize John L. Lewis without first knowing miners and being in a mine." From these friendships, the students developed an appreciation of an ethos which, while different from an academic atmosphere, was sometimes surprisingly more congenial to their own values and personalities. Sustained contact with the miners provided a perspective which became a basis for invidious evaluation of academic folkways, and for the cathartic expression of aggression toward them.

The team members enjoyed the freedom of movement in the mine. It was pleasant to get into sloppy clothes and throw oneself around the mine without worrying about getting dirty or looking well. Again, most team members liked the language patterns of the miners. Conversations were relaxed and profane.

Miners shouted and yelled at each other in a way not permissible in polite circles. There was a spontaneous expression of feelings too often inhibited in academic groups. In short, part of the motivation to work on the project derived from the fact that team members liked the miners and the atmosphere in which they worked; so much so, in fact, that after a while the miners became preferred respondents, and eventually arrangements had to be made to share opportunities for mine interviewing.

The Interviewing Network

We were at all times aware that getting respondents was a *social* process, taking place in a social framework which could either hinder or help us. In essence, the tactic we followed was to grope around for the informal communication centers and, having found them, to use them as a springboard for operations, gradually edging out along the communication lines.

Our first interviews were with men who worked in the "sample shop," and this turned out to be advantageous in several respects. The men in the sample shop were partly older men who had been with the Company for a long time; they were on a regular assignment in the shop because they were too old to work on the line. Others were men who had just been injured on their job and were sent here to do light work until they recuperated. The old men knew a lot and had a lot to communicate; those who had been injured and were in the shop on temporary assignment often had particularly strong attitudes which they wanted to express. Their injury somehow made them particularly cooperative respondents.

Furthermore, the sample shop was a communications center in the plant, since many of the temporary workers kept up their contacts with friends on their regular jobs. Frequently, their buddies would drop by to ask how they were getting along and would bring in news of their own work groups.

After we were accepted by the sample room workers, details about us quickly traveled back to the rest of the plant. Then, too, when the injured workers got better and left the sample room, we would meet them at their regular jobs and they would introduce us to their friends.

The sample room became our main base of operations. It provided a spot where interviewers could rest, or meet each other without feeling conspicuous. Furthermore, the first aid room, in which we frequently did our interviewing, was located in the sample shop. After a while, we came to use the sample room as a "training ground" where we could break in new interviewers as they joined the team. We would first let them interview the friendly sample room people, who had plenty of time and willingness to talk, before they would be given more difficult interviewing assignments.

There was never much close supervision or pressure in this room, since they were always well ahead of their production quota. Inasmuch as a portion of the personnel in the sample room was always changing, it could never be exhausted as a source of information. It was, too, a place where the interviewer could go for reassurance when he occasionally came across a balky respondent. One could even complain about an uncooperative man to the sample workers and, more often than not, they would be more critical of him than the wounded interviewer.

Perhaps our experience in the sample room can be generalized in certain respects: first, in studying a plant it seems desirable to set up a kind of "base of operations" within the plant. But this base should not be chosen in terms of the usual criteria for selecting an "office"; instead it should be selected in terms of its connections with the plant as a social system, and because of its social characteristics. Shops that are peripheral to the main production processes have much to recommend them for this role, because they are often "left alone" by supervisors.

At any rate, the base should not be in a strictly supervised area. Secondly, the base should, if possible, be a plant communications center for the advantages mentioned above.

In the mine, we had a second base of operations comparable to the sample room on the surface. This was the mine machine and repair shop. Like the sample room, it also served as a communication center, mediating in particular between surface operations and the mine face. It was a place which we would first come to and visit—as did everyone else— after we descended into the mine. Some of the interviewers soon became friendly enough with the shop personnel so that they could walk up to a conversation and the men would go on talking as before. This, incidentally, seems to be a useful rule-of-thumb method for gauging whether or not an interviewer is accepted by a group. After a while, we were able to take part in the discussions and horseplay that were always in progress.

We also had a forward base of operations in the mine at the face. We made special friends with the car-trimmers, the men who hammered the rock off the gypsum ore as it was being loaded onto the rail cars, because they were not continually on the move. Once rapport had been established, it was possible to sit around with the car-trimmer, and any of the miners who were not working, for long bull sessions. Occasionally, the car-trimmers would change jobs with the other men so that we could interview them. Like the sample workers, and the mine machinists, the car-trimmer also provided an anchor point from which we could work our way outward along the informal networks.

Further Aspects of the Research Process

As new persons were added to the team, and old ones left, some interesting experiences occurred. For one thing, all of the original members had been in the service, but some new ones had not. This became noteworthy in an unexpected way when one of the new non-veterans went down into the mine and was unable to conceal his embarrassment at the miners' profane language. Those of us who were veterans had apparently undergone "anticipatory socialization" for this experience in the service.

Again, at a later stage in the study, a young woman, Jo Ann Setel, was taken onto the field team. Everyone was concerned about how she might be received by the men in the plant. Actually, she got along wonderfully with the men, who in an effort to impress her, would often give her more revealing data than they might to a male interviewer. We did agree, however, that she would not go down into the mine. This was decided partly at the prompting of the surface workers, who prophesied terrible things if she were to come in contact with those licentious miners. We doubted this, but went along, not wishing to offend the surfacemen's sensibilities. For their part, the miners loudly "protested" our decision and made frequent demands to be interviewed by her. In retrospect, the writers are convinced that she would have gathered excellent interviews there, and in formal defense of the miners' honor, we wish to go on record with our conviction that she would have come to no harm in the mine.

The regular weekly meetings of the research team were probably one of the more distinctive features of our procedure and deserve further attention. Their role in promoting feelings of participation and solidarity, and thus motivating the team members, has already been mentioned. But their direct role in realizing the formal goals of the research needs greater clarification.

At a meeting, for example, a team member would comment that two of his respondents had praised the old plant manager, "Old Doug," in lyrical terms. Then someone else said he had heard the new plant manager, Peele, compared unfavorably to Doug. Another interviewer had picked up the comment that the new plant manager spent too much time in the plant. With each team member contributing his item to the group discussion, it was possible to detect a tentative, empirical uniformity, in this case, a generalization about the "Rebecca Myth." The main point here, of course, is that if the analysts had been working in isolation from each other, each would have had far less familiarity with other interviewers' protocols and would have been far slower to identify the similarity between seemingly disparate observations.

Once a significant area was detected by the group, provisional generalizations were advanced to link it with other observations, to suggest explanatory hypotheses, or to scan existent theory for interpretative hunches. Having identified a provisional empirical generalization, the group would then make a deliberate effort to check it in subsequent interviews. Similarly, the hypotheses which emerged in discussing a new empirical generalization also redirected the group's interviewing efforts. We then sought to gather data which could test the hypothesis.

To cite another illustration of the group processes as they affected research procedures: One person reported to the group that he had noticed new shacks being built near the assembly line for use as supervisors' offices, from which they could look out and watch the workers. Another person reminded the group that, until now, the supers had gotten along with unpretentious "holes in the wall" which were far removed from the line. Still another team member mentioned that he had noticed a new sign on the bulletin board saying that time clocks must now be punched in and out precisely at the proper times. Until then, a half-hour leeway had been allowed. Someone else contributed the observation that employees could no longer use Company equipment for home repairs or to help out neighboring farmers.

By themselves, none of these observations meant too much; but when reported together to the group they spelled out a pattern of increasing bureaucratization. Accepting this tentatively, we then sought new observations in other areas which we could use to check up on ourselves. We began to examine the relationships between the new plant manager and the supervisors, and found that they were increasingly governed by rules. This gave greater weight to our generalization concerning the increase in bureaucratization and, in turn, gave rise to hypotheses concerning the role of succession in the development of bureaucracy.

Throughout, there was also an intricate interplay between theorizing and data collection. For example, while we had, from the first, felt the need for several *types* of bureaucratic patterns, it was not until we had acquired concrete data on the safety regulations that we saw our way "clear" to developing our specific typology. All the interviewers had had intensive theoretical training and were able to contribute on this, as on other levels. At no time was anyone relegated to the role of a technical specialist. Indeed, at one time or another, everyone was engaged in all the research operations, however exalted or menial.

Though the team members were, with two exceptions, untrained undergraduates, they possessed compensatory experiences. For example, since the Lakeport area is a highly industrialized one, many of the team members had worked in factories to help pay their college expenses. Thus they knew about factories and workers from first hand experience, and this helped considerably. Moreover, though undergraduates, they were older and more mature than the usual run of students because they had been GI's. This common experience, incidentally, undoubtedly added to the group's solidarity.

Beyond this, and perhaps because of these experiences in the war, the team members possessed an impressive respect for individual human dignity. In fact, one of them felt quite guilty about "bureaucratically prying" into the privacy of the workers' lives. This is a real question to which there is no flip answer. We all argued the problem at length: What right *did* we have to intrude ourselves into others' lives? We could only say, finally, that we believed in our work and that we intended and hoped that it would help people; or, more properly, that it would provide them with knowledge so that they could help themselves in their human predicaments. We do not doubt for a moment that this concern for individuals and their welfare, a sensitivity that no formal education in research could ever hope to instill, struck a spark and helped us to gain acceptance from the workers.

BIBLIOGRAPHY

Note: The most thorough bibliography on bureaucracy is appended to Robert K. Merton et al., *Reader in Bureaucracy* (The Free Press). The items listed below are not intended as an exhaustive list of the sources on which I have drawn; instead they primarily consist of works which, in one or another way, have shaped the thinking that has gone into this study.

T. W. Adorno, E. Frankel-Brunswik, Daniel Levinson, R. Nevitt Sanford, in collaboration with B. Aron, M. H. Levinson, W. Morrow, *The Authoritarian Personality,* Harper and Bros., New York, 1950.

E. H. Anderson and G. T. Schwennig, *The Science of Production Organization,* John Wiley and Sons, New York, 1938.

A. Arakelian, *Industrial Management in the U.S.S.R.,* Tr. by E. L. Raymond, Public Affairs Press, Washington, D.C., 1950.

T. S. Ashton and J. Sykes, *The Coal Industry in the 18th Century,* Manchester University Press, Manchester, 1929.

Chester I. Barnard, *The Functions of the Executive,* Harvard University Press, Cambridge, 1938.

Chester I. Barnard, *Organization and Management,* Harvard Press, Cambridge, 1948.

Reinhard Bendix, "Bureaucracy: the Problem and its Setting," *American Sociological Review,* 1947, 12, pp. 493-507.

Robert A. Brady, *Business as a System of Power,* Columbia University Press, New York, 1943.

Goetz A. Briefs, *The Proletariat,* McGraw-Hill Book Co., New York, 1937.

Walter B. Cannon, *The Wisdom of the Body,* W. W. Norton, New York, 1932.

John Commons, *The Legal Foundations of Capitalism,* Macmillan Co., New York, 1932.

Charles H. Cooley, *Social Organization,* Chas. Scribners' Sons, New York, 1919.

John H. Crider, *The Bureaucrat,* Lippincott, New York, 1944.

Marshall Dimock and John Hyde, *Bureaucracy and Trusteeship in*

Large Corporations, Monograph #11, T.N.E.C., U.S. Government Printing Office, Washington, D.C., 1940.

Carl Dreyfuss, *Occupational Ideology of the Salaried Employee,* Vol. 1, Tr. by Eva Abramovitch, W.P.A. and Department of Social Sciences, Columbia University, New York, 1938.

Peter F. Drucker, *The Concept of the Corporation,* John Day Co., New York, 1946.

Emile Durkheim, *The Division of Labor in Society,* Tr. by George Simpson, The Free Press, Glencoe, Ill., 1947.

Frederick Engels, *Herr Eugen Dühring's Revolution in Science,* International Publishers, New York, 1929.

P. Sargent Florence, *Labour,* Hutchinson's University Library, New York, n.d.

Julian Franklin, "The Democratic Approach to Bureaucracy," *Readings in Culture, Personality and Society,* Columbia College, New York, n.d.

Georges Friedmann, *Problèmes Humaines Du Machinisme Industriel,* Gallimard, Paris, 1946.

Burleigh B. Gardner, *Human Relations In Industry,* Richard D. Irwin, Inc., Chicago, 1945.

Burleigh B. Gardner and William F. Whyte, "Methods for the Study of Human Relations in Industry," *American Sociological Review,* 1946, 14, pp. 512-519.

H. H. Gerth and C. Wright Mills (editors and translators), *From Max Weber: Essays in Sociology,* Oxford University Press, New York, 1946.

Carter Goodrich, *The Miner's Freedom,* Marshall Jones Co., Boston, 1925.

Robert A. Gordon, *Business Leadership in the Large Corporation,* Brookings Institute, Washington, D.C., 1945.

Alvin W. Gouldner, "The Attitudes of 'Progressive' Trade Union Leaders," *American Journal of Sociology,* 1947, 52, pp. 389-392.

Alvin W. Gouldner, "Discussion" of Moore's, "Industrial Sociology: Status and Prospects," *American Sociological Review,* 1948, 13, pp. 396-400.

Alvin W. Gouldner (editor), *Studies in Leadership,* Harper and Bros., New York, 1950.

Alvin W. Gouldner, "Red Tape as a Social Problem," in Robert K. Merton, et al. (editors), *Reader in Bureaucracy,* Free Press, Glencoe, Ill., 1952, pp. 410-418.

Allan Gruchy, *Modern Economic Thought,* Prentice-Hall, Inc., New York, 1947.

Frederick H. Harbison and Robert Dubin, *Patterns of Union-Management Relations,* Science Research Associates, Chicago, 1947.

Eduard Heimann, "On Strikes and Wages," *Social Research,* 1948, 15.

A. M. Henderson and Talcott Parsons (editors and translators), *Max Weber: The Theory of Social and Economic Organization,* Oxford University Press, New York, 1947.

William E. Henry, "The Business Executive: the Psychodynamics of a Social Role," *American Journal of Sociology,* 1949, 54, pp. 286-291.

E. T. Hiller, *The Strike,* University of Chicago Press, Chicago, 1928.

George Homans, *The Human Group,* Harcourt, Brace and Co., New York, 1950.

Schuyler D. Hoslett (editor), *Human Factors in Management,* Harper and Bros., New York, 1946.

Everett C. Hughes, "Queries Concerning Industry and Society Growing Out of Study of Ethnic Relations in Industry," *American Sociological Review,* 1949, 14, pp. 211-220.

Daniel Katz, *Morale and Motivation in Industry,* Survey Research Center, University of Michigan, Ann Arbor, Michigan, 1949 (mimeo).

Daniel Katz and Robert Kahn, "Human Organization and Worker Productivity," in L. Reed (editor), *Industrial Productivity,* Industrial Relations Research Association, Madison, Wisconsin, 1951, pp. 146-171.

J. Donald Kingsley, *Representative Bureaucracy,* Antioch Press, Yellow Springs, Ohio, 1944.

Oskar Lange and Fred M. Taylor, *On the Economic Theory of Socialism,* edited by Benjamin E. Lippincott, The University of Minnesota Press, Minneapolis, Minnesota, 1938.

Harold J. Laski, "Bureaucracy," *Encyclopedia of the Social Sciences.*

Harold J. Laski, *The Limitations of the Expert,* Fabian Tract #235, London, 1931.

Harold D. Lasswell, *Politics: Who Gets What, When, How,* McGraw-Hill Book Co., New York, 1936.

Alexander H. Leighton, *The Governing of Men,* Princeton University Press, Princeton, New Jersey, 1946.

Marion J. Levy, Jr., *The Family Revolution in Modern China*, Harvard University Press, Cambridge, Mass., 1949.

Kurt Lewin, *Resolving Social Conflicts*, Harper and Bros., New York, 1948.

Seymour M. Lipset, "Bureaucracy and Social Reform," *Research Studies, State College of Washington*, 1949, 17, pp. 11-17.

Seymour M. Lipset, *Agrarian Socialism*, University of California Press, Berkeley and Los Angeles, 1950.

Robert S. Lynd, *Knowledge for What?*, Princeton University Press, Princeton, New Jersey, 1939.

Robert S. Lynd and Helen M. Lynd, *Middletown in Transition*, Harcourt, Brace and Co., New York, 1939.

Nathan Maccoby, *Research Findings on Productivity, Supervision and Morale*, Survey Research Center, University of Michigan, March 11, 1949 (mimeo).

Norman F. Maier, *Frustration*, McGraw-Hill Book Co., New York, 1949.

Bronislaw Malinowski, *Magic, Science and Religion*, Free Press, Glencoe, Ill., 1948.

Floyd C. Mann, "Human Relations Training Through a Company Wide Study," Survey Research Center, University of Michigan, Ann Arbor, Michigan, 1950.

Herbert Marcuse, *Reason and Revolution*, Oxford University Press, New York, 1941.

Fritz M. Marx (editor), *Elements of Public Administration*, Prentice-Hall, Inc., New York, 1946.

Karl Marx, *Capital*, The Modern Library, New York, 1936.

Stanley B. Mathewson, *Restriction of Output Among Unorganized Workers*, The Viking Press, New York, 1931.

Elton Mayo and George Lombard, *Teamwork and Labor Turnover in the Aircraft Industry of Southern California*, Graduate School of Business Administration, Harvard University, Cambridge, Mass., 1944.

Robert K. Merton, "Bureaucratic Structure and Personality," *Social Forces*, 1940, 17, pp. 560-568.

Robert K. Merton, "The Role of the Intellectual in a Public Bureaucracy," *Social Forces*, 1945, 23, pp. 405-415.

Robert K. Merton, "Selected Problems of Field Work in a Planned Community," *American Sociological Review*, 1947, 12, pp. 304-312.

Robert K. Merton, "The Machine, the Worker, and the Engineer," *Science,* 1947, 105, pp. 79-84.

Robert K. Merton, *Social Theory and Social Structure,* Free Press, Glencoe, Ill., 1949.

Robert K. Merton, "Patterns of Influence: A Study of Interpersonal Influence and of Communications Behavior in a Local Community," in Paul F. Lazarsfeld and Frank N. Stanton, *Communications Research, 1948-1949,* Harper and Bros., New York, 1949, pp. 180-222.

Robert K. Merton and Paul F. Lazarsfeld (editors), *Continuities in Social Research: Studies in the Scope and Method of the American Soldier,* Free Press, Glencoe, Ill., 1950.

Robert Michels, *Political Parties,* Free Press, Glencoe, Ill., 1949.

John Stuart Mill, *Principles of Political Economy,* Longmans, Green, and Company, Ltd., London and New York, edition of 1926.

Delbert C. Miller and William C. Form, *Industrial Sociology,* Harper and Bros., New York, 1951.

C. Wright Mills, *The New Men of Power: America's Labor Leaders,* Harcourt, Brace and Co., New York, 1948.

C. Wright Mills, *White Collar: The American Middle Classes,* Oxford University Press, New York, 1951.

Wilbert E. Moore, *Industrial Relations and the Social Order,* Macmillan Co., New York, 1951 revised edition.

Wilbert E. Moore, "Industrial Sociology; Status and Prospects," *American Sociological Review,* 1948, 13, pp. 382-391.

Wilbert E. Moore, "Theoretical Aspects of Industrialization," *Social Research,* 1948, 15, pp. 277-303.

Wilbert E. Moore, *Industrialization and Labor: Social Aspects of Economic Development,* Cornell University Press, Ithaca, New York, 1951.

Richard C. Myers, "Myth and Status Systems in Industry," *Social Forces,* 1948, 26, pp. 331-337.

Franz Neumann, *Behemoth,* Oxford University Press, New York, 1944.

Franz Neumann, "Approaches to the Study of Political Power," *Political Science Quarterly,* 1950, 65, pp. 161-180.

E. William Noland and E. Wight Bakke, *Workers Wanted,* Harper and Bros., New York, 1949.

Charles H. Page, "Bureaucracy's Other Face," *Social Forces,* 1946, 25, pp. 88-94.

Talcott Parsons, "Capitalism in Recent German Literature: Sombart and Weber," *Journal of Political Economy*, 1928, 36, pp. 641-661.

Talcott Parsons, *The Structure of Social Action*, McGraw-Hill Book Co., New York, 1937.

Talcott Parsons, *Essays in Sociological Theory: Pure and Applied*, Free Press, Glencoe, Ill., 1949.

Donald C. Pelz, "Leadership Within a Hierarchical Organization," *Journal of Social Issues*, 1951, 7, pp. 49-55.

Karl Polanyi, *The Great Transformation*, Rinehart and Company, New York, 1944.

Leonard Reismann, "A Study of Role Conceptions in Bureaucracy," *Social Forces*, 1949, 27, pp. 305-310.

Lloyd C. Reynolds and Joseph Shister, *Job Horizons: A Study of Job Satisfaction*, Harper and Bros., New York, 1949.

F. L. W. Richardson and Charles R. Walker, *Human Relations in an Expanding Company*, Yale University Press, New Haven, Conn., 1948.

F. J. Roethlisberger and W. J. Dickson, with the collaboration of H. A. Wright, *Management and the Worker*, Harvard University Press, Cambridge, Mass., 1946.

Morris Rosenberg, "The Social Roots of Formalism," *Journal of Social Issues*, 1949, 5.

Morris Rosenberg and Seymour Bellin, "Value Patterns in the Trade Union Press," *International Journal of Opinion and Attitude Research*, 1949, 3, pp. 555-574.

Arthur M. Ross, *Trade Union Wage Policy*, University of California Press, Berkeley and Los Angeles, 1948.

Bertrand Russell, in collaboration with Dora Russell, *The Prospects of Industrial Civilizations*, The Century Co., New York, 1923.

Louis Schneider, *The Freudian Psychology and Veblen's Social Theory*, King's Crown Press, New York, 1948.

Philip Selznick, "An Approach to a Theory of Organization," *American Sociological Review*, 1943, 8, pp. 47-54.

Philip Selznick, "Foundations of the Theory of Organization," *American Sociological Review*, 1948, 13, pp. 25-35.

Philip Selznick, *TVA and the Grass Roots*, University of California, Berkeley and Los Angeles, 1949.

Nassau W. Senior, *Industrial Efficiency and Social Economy*, Henry Holt and Co., New York, edition of 1928.

Carroll Shartle, "Organization Structure," in Dennis Wayne (editor), *Current Trends in Industrial Psychology,* University of Pittsburgh Press.

Joseph Shister, "The Locus of Union Control in Collective Bargaining," *Quarterly Journal of Economics,* 1946, 60, pp. 78-112.

Herbert A. Simon, *Administrative Behavior,* Macmillan Co., New York, 1948.

Elliott Dunlop Smith, in collaboration with Richmond Carter Nyman, *Technology and Labor,* Yale University Press, New Haven, 1939.

David Spitz, *Patterns of Anti-Democratic Thought,* Macmillan Co., New York, 1949.

Survey Research Center, *Productivity, Supervision and Employee Morale, The Prudential Insurance Co. Study,* University of Michigan, Ann Arbor, 1948.

R. H. Tawney, *The Acquisitive Society,* Harcourt, Brace and Co., New York, 1920.

Ordway Tead, *The Art of Administration,* McGraw-Hill Book Co., New York, 1951.

E. L. Trist and K. Bamforth, "Some Social and Psychological Consequences of the Longwall Method of Coal Mining," *Human Relations,* 1951, 4, pp. 3-38.

Mary Van Kleeck, *Mines and Management,* Russell Sage Foundation, New York, 1934.

Thorstein Veblen, *The Engineers and the Price System,* B. W. Huebsch, Inc., New York, 1921.

Ludwig von Mises, *Bureaucracy,* Yale University Press, New Haven, 1944.

Charles R. Walker, *Steeltown,* Harper and Bros., New York, 1950.

W. Lloyd Warner, *The Social System of the Modern Factory: The Strike; A Social Analysis,* Yale University Press, New Haven, 1947.

Goodwin Watson (editor), "Problems of Bureaucracy," *Journal of Social Issues,* 1945, Vol. 1, No. 4.

Sidney and Beatrice Webb, *Industrial Democracy,* Longmans, Green and Co., Ltd., New York and London, 1926.

Alfred Weber, "Bureaucracy and Freedom," *Modern Review,* 1948, 2, pp. 176-186.

Leonard D. White, Charles H. Bland, Walter R. Sharp, Fritz M. Marx, *Civil Service Abroad,* McGraw-Hill Book Co., New York, 1935.

William F. Whyte (editor), *Industry and Society*, McGraw-Hill Book
  Co., New York, 1946.
William F. Whyte, *Human Relations in the Restaurant Industry*,
  McGraw-Hill Book Co., New York, 1948.

INDEX

Absenteeism, rules concerning, 141 *ff.*, 212 *ff.*
Albrecht, Milton C., 10

Barnouw, Victor, 10
Bendix, Reinhard, 92
Bidding system, 208 *ff.*; effects on middle management, 210; tension between seniority and ability in, 208-210
Blau, Peter, 16
Bureaucracy, barriers to, 146 *ff.*; charisma, traditionalism and, 222; defined, 19; efficiency of, 26, 205; functions of, manifest and latent, 24-27, 237 *ff.*; importance of internal differentiation within, 20-21, 26-27, 98-99, 240-242; Merton, Robert K., on, 19; mock, representative, and punishment-centered compared, 216-217; Parsons, Talcott, on, 22; pessimistic study of, 16, 26, 28, 237; punishment-centered, 10, 24, 207 *ff.*; representative, 24, 187 *ff.*, 196 *ff.*; resistance to, 235-237; succession and, 93 *ff.*; succession, rate of, and, 96-97; tensions in, 16, 218; Weber's theory of, tensions in, 19-24
Bureaucratic rules, 157 *ff.*, 237 *ff.*; apathy preserving function of, 174-176; close supervision and,

159-162, 176 *ff.*; explication function of, 162-164; leeway function of, 172-174; punishment-legitimating function of, 168-172; remote control function of, 166-168; screening function of, 165-166

Cantor, Nathaniel, 10
Cassirer, Ernst, 204
Close supervision, 87 *ff.*; and bureaucratic rules, 159-162, 176 *ff.*
Commons, John R., 98
Community organization, 34 *ff.*, decline of ruralism in, 42 *ff.*; effects on factory, 39 *ff.*
Consent, problem of, 223
Cooley, Charles H., 175
Curtis, Alberta, 84

Deviance, utilitarian conception of, 233; voluntaristic conception of, 233
DeVinney, Leland C., 161
Dickson, W. J., 74, 141
Dimock, Marshall, 15
Dubin, Robert, 167
DuMaurier, Daphne, 79

East, J. H., Jr., 114, 118
Expert, 224; reasons for subordination of, 226-227

FREE PRESS PAPERBACKS

A NEW SERIES OF PAPERBOUND BOOKS
IN THE SOCIAL AND NATURAL SCIENCES, PHILOSOPHY, AND THE HUMANITIES

These books, chosen for their intellectual importance and editorial excellence, are printed on good quality book paper, from the large and readable type of the cloth-bound edition, and are Smyth-sewn for enduring use. *Free Press Paperbacks* conform in every significant way to the high editorial and production standards maintained in the higher-priced, case-bound books published by *The Free Press of Glencoe.*

For information address:

THE FREE PRESS OF GLENCOE
A Division of the Macmillan Company, 60 Fifth Avenue, New York, N. Y. 10011